Agnes Smith

Through Cyprus

Agnes Smith

Through Cyprus

ISBN/EAN: 9783744756044

Printed in Europe, USA, Canada, Australia, Japan

Cover: Foto ©Andreas Hilbeck / pixelio.de

More available books at **www.hansebooks.com**

THROUGH CYPRUS

BY

AGNES SMITH,

AUTHOR OF 'GLIMPSES OF GREEK LIFE AND SCENERY,' ETC.

A ZAPTIEH.

Illustrated, with Map.

LONDON:
HURST AND BLACKETT, PUBLISHERS.
13, GREAT MARLBOROUGH STREET.
1887.

CONTENTS.

CHAPTER I.

LONDON TO SUEZ 1

The Start—Amenities of Travelling—Unpleasant Precedents—Very Miserable—At Lyons—Marseilles—Port Said—The Shaloof—Arrival at Suez—Expedition to 'Ain Mousa—'I am a Moslem.'

CHAPTER II.

IN CAIRO 19

Little Difficulties—Said's Trick—Taken for Moslem Ladies—Tel-el-Kebir—A Motley Crowd—Shepheard's Hotel—Climate of Cairo—I Try to Learn Colloquial Arabic—My Plan—Arab English—Arab Teachers —Wheat the Forbidden Fruit—Incivility of some English Travellers —A Mistake of Simplicity—Excessive Gaiety—Noble Exceptions.

CHAPTER III.

THE SIGHTS OF CAIRO 39

The Boulak Museum—Mummy of Rameses II.—The Tomb of the Caliphs—The Great Pyramid—Its Construction—View from the Top —Spurious Coins—The Sphinx—Description—The Mosque El Azhar —Conversations with 'Ulemas—The Kurân—The Great Hall or University—Moslem Students.

CHAPTER IV.

THE SIGHTS OF CAIRO (CONTINUED) 49

The American Mission—Evangelization its Work—Miss Whately's School—All Mohammedan Children—A Native Congregation—Most Picturesque—In Native Houses with Miss Thompson—Dining with

Coptic Families—Coptic Priests—A Coptic Family—A Coptic Marriage—The Coptic Cathedral—A Boys' School—Reflections.

CHAPTER V.

ALEXANDRIA TO BEYROUT 72

Miss Robinson's Soldiers' and Sailors' Homes—On Board the *La Seyne* —Fellow-passengers—Jaffa—Difficulty of Finding Servants for Cyprus—Tents or no Tents?—Risks of Travel in Cyprus—Roads in Cyprus—A Storm—Delay in Departure—Opportunity for Learning Language—A Roman Catholic Teacher—Beyrout Schools—Work of Americans—Mrs. Bowen Thompson—School of Society of Friends—Excursion to Nahr-el-Kelb.

CHAPTER VI.

BEYROUT TO CYPRUS 91

The 'Rio Grande'—Fellow-Passengers—Tripoli—Off Larnaca—The Custom House—Climate of Cyprus—The Tents—Origin of Name Cyprus—Mr. Hamilton Lang's Views—Mr. Watkins' Opinions on the Cypriots—Disturbed Slumbers—Our Cavalcade—George, the Dragoman—Peculiar Greek and More Peculiar English—Mangled Italian—George's Character—Salim—Constantine the Cook—A Confusion of Georges—Ibrahim the Arab.

CHAPTER VII.

CYPRUS DESCRIBED 104

Messaria—Mountainous in the West—Larnaca to Famagousta—The March—Village of Ormidia—Rain—A Perfect Little Oasis—Homœopathic Medicine—A Cypriote Church—A Service—Great Plain of Famagousta—First Sight of the Town—Varoschia—Famagousta—Torre del Moro—Fall of Famagousta—Bragadino's Fate—We Leave Famagousta.

CHAPTER VIII.

TRIKOMO TO KYTHEREA 124

Interview with a Priest—Dress of Cypriots—A Stroll into the Town—Britons or Greeks?—A Gathering—A Great Place for Birds—The Monastery of St. Andreas—Lefkoniko—Marathobouno—Locusts—Visitors—Improvements—Destruction of Locusts—Locust-trap.

CHAPTER IX.

KYTHEREA TO LEUCOSIA 141

In a Labyrinth of Hills—Perplexity—Trusting to a Boy-guide—The Convent of St. Chrysostom—Interior—History—First View of Leucosia—Besieged by a Crowd—Leucosia Improved under British Rule—A Greek Priest—Still Besieged—A Prison—Cathedral of St. Sophia—A Tragedy—A Priest Photographer.

CHAPTER X.

FROM LEUCOSIA TO LEFKA 156

The Turk, Mustapha—Nicosia, very Warm—The Dreaded Kofi—Lovely Landscapes—Bellapais Abbey—Kyrenia—Mr. Maurogordato—Crime in Cyprus—The Fort—Country Round Kyrenia Lovely—Along the Coast—Lapithus—Monastery of St. Pantalemoni—Encampment and Sunday Rest—The Bishop—Prospects of Union between Greek and Anglican Churches—The British Government and the Schools—At Morphou—An Archimandrite—Lefka—The Feast of St. George—Queen Victoria's Mistake—The Queen's Birthday.

CHAPTER XI.

FROM LEFKA TO KYKKO 177

A Case of Overloading—Deep Solitudes—A Pleasant Resting-place—A Testimony to British Rule and Improvement—Campos—Polite Reception—A Pleasant Road—Kykko—The Monastery—Reception there from Monks—Conversation with Them—Present of Wine—Monks come to Tea in the Tent—' Resurrection of the Virgin '—The Monks Chanting—A Scene of the Middle-Ages.

CHAPTER XII.

FROM KYKKO TO CHRYSOROGHIATISSA . . . 192

Bad Roads—Arabic for the Mules—Chrysoroghiatissa—The Monks' Welcome—Heavy Rains—Conversations with the Monks—Collapse of Tents—Lodgings in the Monastery—High Winds—The Village School—Advice to the Children—' Time is Money '—A Glimpse of Sunshine.

CHAPTER XIII.

FROM CHRYSOROGHIATISSA TO PAPHOS . . . 204

Baffo—Highly Picturesque—Paphos—Welcomed by Mr. Thompson—' Aphroditissa '—History of Neo-Paphos—Temple of Paphos—Hieroskipos—A Cave—De Cesnola's Views—Apples of Cyprus—Old Paphos—Legend of Cinyras—A Ruined Castle—'The Great Temple of Venus'—Claudian Quoted—Augustine Quoted—Virgil.

CHAPTER XIV.

FROM PAPHOS TO COLOSSI 228

The Cypriots and Cruelty to Animals—Pretty Village of Piscopi—A Storm—A Babel—Retreat from Tents—Still Unsheltered—Ruins of the City of Curium—Colossi—The Commandería Wine—De Cesnola's Discoveries.

CHAPTER XV.

LAST DAYS IN CYPRUS 240

'Canning Street'—Limasol—Many Invitations—Hot Winds—The Oldest City in Cyprus—The God Malika—Human Sacrifices—Heathen Miracle Plays—Vases—Sculptures—Pretty Hamlet of Zee—Visitors—Citi—Larnaca—The Royal Hotel—On Board the *Alphée*.

CHAPTER XVI.

GLEANINGS FROM THE HISTORY OF CYPRUS . . 255

First Notice of Cyprus—Divinities—Worship of Aphrodite—The Nine Kingdoms—Subject to Egypt—To Persia—The Cyprus Contingent for Invasion of Greece—Greek Influence—Evagoras—Abdemon's Plot—Sparta Supreme—Evagoras—Freedom Against Tyranny—Evagoras' Situation Becomes Desperate—Plots—Luxury—Menander's Satire on the Cypriots.

CHAPTER XVII.

HISTORY OF CYPRUS (CONTINUED) 285

Alexander—Cyprus a Persian Province—Cyprus and Alexander—His Gratitude—Part of Macedonian Empire—A Lapse of Years—A Province of Egypt—The Ptolemies—A Monster—Short Dream of Honourable Independence—Cato—Introduction of Christianity—Thirteen Bishoprics—Four Centuries of Peace—Rinaldo of Castile—The Crusades—Richard Cœur de Lion—Cyprus Sold to Knights-Templars—Guy de Lusignan—Saracen Ravages—Venetian Supremacy—Turkish Rule—British Occupation and Rule.

CONTENTS. ix

CHAPTER XVIII.

CONCLUSION 313

Capabilities of the Island—Products—Caroub-tree—The Olive—Wheat—Cotton—Wine—Grapes—Fruit—Copper—Henna—Salt—Products of Cyprus and Malta Compared—Character of Turks and Greeks—Desire of Greeks for Cyprus—Advantages of Speaking Greek—Greek Aspirations for Political Unity.

APPENDIX.

CLIMATE OF CYPRUS 341

LIST OF ILLUSTRATIONS.

OUR TRAVELLING PARTY (see p. 99)	*Frontispiece.*
A ZAPTIEH	*Vignette.*
CHURCH OF ST. SOPHIA, NICOSIA	To face p. 153.
RUINED MONASTERY OF BELLAPAIS .	,, 158.
COURTYARD OF MONASTERY AT KYKKO	,, 190.
MAP OF THE AUTHOR'S ROUTE .	*At end of Vol.*

Come travel ; soon thy friends will be replaced.
Come work ; and life's true sweetness thou shalt know.
Success and fame are never found in rest ;
But cares are. Leave thy native land, and go.
For water, that by standing waxeth foul,
Is sweet and good if once it 'gin to flow.
No eye of watcher will observe the moon,
Unless her wondrous changes she doth show ;
The hunter starts before the lion dies ;
The arrow hits not ere it leaves the bow ;
The world hath mines where gold is common dust ;
And climes where scented woods as fuel glow.
How rich the lore that some by travel seek !
How great the gains of some by travel grow !
From the Arabic.

THROUGH CYPRUS.

CHAPTER I.

LONDON TO SUEZ.

The Start—Amenities of Travelling—Unpleasant Precedents—Very Miserable—At Lyons—Marseilles—Port Said—The Shaloof—Arrival at Suez—Expedition to 'Ain Mousa—'I am a Moslem.'

EVER since the clever *coup* by which Lord Beaconsfield induced the British lion to place his foot upon Cyprus, an island which, from its position, might easily be made the key of the Levant, the public have been more or less anxious to know what our acquisition really is. Within eighteen months after the cession, several excellent books on the subject were published. It savours somewhat of presumption for anyone to venture upon ground trodden by an experienced observer like Sir Samuel Baker, a learned explorer like Franz von Löher, and a resident possessing the unequalled opportunities and the practical sense of Mr. Hamilton Lang. But several years have elapsed since their works saw the light; Cyprus has undergone a few changes, and it is just possible that the eyes of two lady travellers may have been able to discern something new and worth

B

telling, albeit they cannot pretend to vie in depth of research with Mr. Lang, nor in antiquarian knowledge with De Cesnola.

As our journey from London to Cyprus presented some remarkable features, we think we can best interest the reader by beginning our narrative with an account of it.

We started from home on Tuesday, January 11, with the intention of sleeping in Paris, and of continuing our journey the next night to Marseilles in a *coupé-fauteuils*, or a *coupé-lits*. This, however, would have debarred us from sleeping at Marseilles previous to embarking on the steamer of the Messageries Maritimes, and we adopted the suggestion of a lady whom we met in the train betwixt London and Dover, that we should continue our journey without sleeping in Paris. So, on arriving at the Paris station, we telegraphed to Marseilles to secure rooms, and drove to the Gare de Lyons, forgetting that *coupés* are not to be secured at a moment's notice. Unfortunately we arrived only a few minutes before the train started, and we did not know before we registered our luggage that there was no chance of a *coupé*.

We were asked to get into a first-class carriage in which six men were blowing clouds of tobacco-smoke from their pipes. However much one may tolerate cigars in the open air, the prospect of being shut up with such an abundance of tobacco perfume for the whole of a winter's night was not an inviting one. The conductor assured us that it was not a smoking-carriage, and that we had the right to make the gentlemen extinguish their pipes. We thought, however, that they would not be too pleasantly disposed towards us in consequence, so we insisted on being put somewhere else.

The train was quite full, and only two empty seats could be found anywhere. At the door of the carriage which contained these stood an English lady. The guard politely requested her to mount, as the train would start in two minutes. She gave a very silly laugh, and replied,

'Ma foi, je ne suis pas pressée, j'ai encore une demi-minute.'

The guard then desired us to enter without waiting for her convenience. Two French ladies were seated near the windows at the further end. Next them was a very stout Frenchman, and next him an English lady, who was keeping the empty seat near the window for the lady outside, her daughter. Opposite the young lady's seat was a young Englishman, and thus two vacant seats were left for us in the centre of the carriage.

Alas! we would have done better to have travelled with the smokers. Our entrance was the signal for all the passengers to rise at once, and declare that as they meant to pass the night there, they needed room to sleep, and that they would on no account allow us to intrude on their privacy. They tried to prevent our sitting down anywhere, or placing our rugs on the rack above. We tried to get out, but the conductor handed in all our small things, and shut the door. Then ensued a scene I shall never forget. The big, burly Frenchman seized my rug-case, which happened to contain nothing except Wahrmund's Arabic dictionary, I having carried the rug over my arm from the cab. He tried to pitch it out of the window, saying, 'Nous mettrons tout ça sur la voie.' The carriage was certainly full of small packages, but few of them were ours. My own share was a little black hand-bag and the almost empty rug-cover. Violet's packages were more numerous; she had a rug-cover similar to mine, well filled with a rug and a warm cloak, a little dressing-bag, and a small flat basket containing medicines. Our fellow-passengers had enormous packages of rugs, huge dressing-bags, and locked Gladstone bags or portmanteaus, each of which would have been sufficient luggage for a gentleman on a Swiss tour. Our rug-cases were, however, waterproof, and were furnished with straps in Mr. W. J. Adam's latest style, which possibly our fellow-passengers had not then seen, and which gave them an excuse for insisting that they ought to have been in the van. Nor would they allow that we had a right to the part of the rack immediately above the seats which we occupied.

When the French gentleman rose for the purpose of pitching my rug-cover out of the window, I rose also, and tried to remonstrate with him as quietly as I could, but I received a blow on the head from his arm, which knocked my hat off, and made me sit down quite helpless. He did not succeed in his purpose, the conductor being at the door, and the train moving very rapidly. Violet then appealed to the kindlier feelings of the English ladies, saying that I was not very strong. The elder lady replied that the Frenchman was an invalid, and required a seat on which to place his feet whilst travelling all night. For this statement, as she afterwards confessed, she drew entirely on her own imagination, not having had the honour of his acquaintance till that night.

The Frenchman sat down, as if tired with his efforts, and Violet pacified him by saying that she would have her rugs and her medicine-basket removed to the luggage-van, and registered on our arrival at Laroche.

Seldom have I felt so miserable in my life as at the prospect of spending the night in such unfriendly company. Their conduct to us was brutal, and I could almost have preferred being exposed to the bitterness of the cold, which covered the carriage windows with a sheet of ice, and induced our fellow-travellers to keep them closely shut. Before we reached Laroche, one of the English ladies discovered that Violet's medicine-basket could be turned into a footstool for herself, and that it would slip under the seat if she got tired of using it; so the decree went forth that it should remain. No sooner had the train stopped than Violet's bundle of rugs was handed to the conductor, with the request that he would register it. This he peremptorily refused to do, saying that the lady had a right to keep it beside her. Such a storm of words arose, however, at the bare suggestion that he was glad to take the package. Our fellow-travellers were all enveloped in their own wraps, and it seemed to me extremely cruel in them to deprive Violet of a similar comfort.

But what most irritated me was the tone of patronage with which the French gentleman said to the conductor, 'Nous avons concedé à ces dames d'entrer ici à condition qu'elles mettent dehors toutes leurs petites bagages.' As he had himself a ticket for one seat only, I failed to see what right he had to concede anything of the kind. No course was open to us, however, but silence and submission; neither of us feeling equal to the task of contradicting him.

When the train had again started, we pointed out to the English lady that they had all acted unjustly in not allowing us to speak to the guard about registering our own packages; every effort which we had made to do so having been frustrated by her interruptions and those of the Frenchman. She exclaimed indignantly that a large Gladstone bag ought also to have been removed.

'But it is not mine,' said Violet.

The young Englishman thereupon confessed that it was his, and the incident produced an agreeable diversion, for the English ladies immediately constituted themselves its protectors, and suggested that the things on the rack over our heads should be re-arranged, so as to allow of its being placed there. Whilst effecting this, the young man allowed a heavy bag to drop. It struck Violet on the chest, and caused her almost to faint.

We were very miserable, but the darkest cloud has its bright side, and there was one fact which gave me unspeakable satisfaction. It was this: that none of the party were my relatives. The morning would relieve us entirely from their presence. It seemed, too, as if they might afford us a little amusement, for we could not help noticing that a flirtation was going on between the young English lady and the gentleman, they often talked so confidentially; in fact, I more than suspected them of being a newly-married couple, and therefore framed a slight excuse in my own mind for their dislike to our presence. As the night wore on, however, the lady talked of her husband, and the gentleman of his wife. The reader, therefore, will not wonder if we found their conversation hardly so amusing as we had anticipated.

The guard made a point of presenting Violet's rugs at every station, and of demanding that she should take them. Her efforts to make him register them prevented her getting any of the nice hot coffee with which our fellow-passengers all regaled themselves. They had no compunction whatever in regard to this, although, in the high country about Dijon and Mâcon, it was intensely cold.

When the train reached Lyons about 8.20 a.m., I managed to get a bowl of coffee. I had to walk through deep snow when procuring this, and had some difficulty in finding the carriage. Our English fellow-travellers, who sat next the window, made no effort to direct me; I felt, indeed, as if they would have rejoiced had I been left behind.

Whilst Violet was speaking to the guard at one of these stations, a man suddenly shut the carriage door, and squeezed two of her fingers into it. This was, of course, accidental; but though one of her nails was plainly black, and the finger much swollen, the English young lady checked the gentleman's expression of sympathy by declaring that Violet was 'pretending it.' The nail came off about a month later, and several medical men who saw it said that it must have caused intense pain.

We felt somewhat strengthened by the bread and coffee we had enjoyed at Lyons, and were hardly so much disposed as we had formerly been to submit to being snubbed. The two English ladies remarked on our waterproof rug-covers, saying that these were ridiculous things to travel with. Their way of doing was much better and much cheaper; they bought a piece of American cloth and fastened it round their rugs with a strap, and had contrived to put a pillow and everything requisite for the night inside of this. They told us that they were much more experienced travellers than we were, and that we ought to take a lesson from them. We replied that they were only going to spend the winter in Mentone, whilst we intended to move about with horses and tents, a mode of transit which they had never tried; so that possibly a different kind of preparation from what they had made might be suitable for us.

Violet remarked to me that she thought of speaking to the station-master at Marseilles about the treatment we had received.

'You need not do so,' I replied, 'for I mean to write to the *Times* about it.'

The English ladies from that moment began a series of small coaxings, which became more effusive as daylight advanced. Perhaps conscience whispered that they had acted unjustly to us: perhaps they were really afraid of their conduct being made public, but they were changed as if by magic. They took the deepest interest in the smallest article belonging to us, and the mother declared that she had not understood that the Frenchman wished to pitch our things out of the window. This was strange, for he expressed his intention in very good English, as well as in French. The French people seemed much perplexed at the unaccountable friendship which had apparently sprung up between us.

I did not write to the *Times*, and I have since regretted this, as public attention was just then forcibly drawn to the subject of the safety and comfort of railway-passengers. Two nights afterwards Monsieur Barrême, Prefect of the Eure, was murdered in a train between Paris and Cherbourg. We came safely out of our disagreeable adventure, but it indicates a real danger to which travellers are exposed, and which is intensified as the means of transit between one country and another become more and more rapid. On the line betwixt Paris and Marseilles the trains are always as full as they can possibly be, because the government levies a tax on every railway-carriage which leaves the Paris stations, and the station-masters decline to put on an extra carriage till every seat is occupied. Many people who appear quite amiable in ordinary society, often get unreasonably cross when travelling at night; many, too, consider that there is an unwritten law which gives to the first occupant of a railway-carriage the right to treat later arrivals as intruders. Suppose that some irritable traveller uses violence to another, what is the aggrieved party to do? In our case we were two against six, who made common cause against us, and none of whom would, in the event of an action for damages, have represented the facts exactly as they happened.

On reaching Marseilles we were too tired to complain to the railway authorities; moreover, we did not wish to do anything which would have made us lose the steamboat on the day following. Our fellow-travellers were carried away with express speed, and, except in the case of the two English ladies, we knew not whither. It seems to us that the day is not far distant when some kind of international police will have to be instituted for the especial protection of travellers.

Our haste to reach Marseilles did not profit us. The weather was so stormy that we were advised not to take the Thursday boat to Alexandria, but to wait till Sunday for the 'great China boat,' which would convey us to Port Said or to Suez. We therefore embarked on board the *Saghalien*, bound for the Indian seas. The passengers were a motley company, consisting of Englishmen, Frenchmen, Dutchmen, Chinese, Malays, Japanese, and Javanese. There were also a few Burmese, chief of whom was Theebaw's late ambassador to Paris, going home after his master's deposition, and Mr. Cope Whitehouse, an American archæologist full of projects for the improvement of the Fayoum by the re-filling of Lake Mœris, and of the delta by the drainage of Lakes Menzaleh and Mareotis.

We stopped for a few hours at Port Said, and then entered the canal, which at first is fringed by the salt-water expanse of Lake Menzaleh. The golden hues of sunset were reflected in this wondrous mirror; then came the moonlight, casting its glory over the sandy desert, and glittering in the canal close to our cabin window. The banks were continually being washed down by the rush of water caused by the steamers, the protection of stones and stakes availing little. A few months of neglect, such as Turkish governors well know how to apply, would be sufficient to destroy much of M. de Lesseps' laborious work.

We remained stationary during the night. In the morning we had desert views on both sides, a plain sprinkled with sand-hills stretching far as the eye could reach. We passed an arm of the salt-water lake, whose surface was almost covered by flocks of white birds; then a hamlet named Kantara, consisting of a hut shaded by palm-trees on one bank, and the rudiments of a wooden village on the other. Near the hut was a large placard, similar to those at railway stations, with the inscription, 'Siphon.' The word Kantara being nowhere visible, I not unnaturally took 'Siphon' to be the name of the place. Some of our fellow-passengers, who were amused at this, tried to make me believe that the next place was named 'Magasin.' 'Siphon' referred to the supply of sweet drinking water.

We stopped between very high sand-banks to let another steamer pass. A gentleman, bound for Singapore, told us that this was the spot where a dredger fell in and stuck fast in June of last year, stopping all the traffic for eleven days. The dredger had not been securely fastened, and the wash of a passing steamboat loosened one of its ropes as it swung into the stream. Just then a second vessel struck it, causing it to sink. Our informant had the misfortune to be in one of the steamers which were detained. The difficulty was got over only by a fresh channel being made for the water of the canal, which now takes a curve at this spot. The banks are everywhere very precarious. The best way of holding them together would be by planting grass or some desert shrub; but it is very difficult to make anything grow in the absence of sweet water.

Some of our Swiss fellow-passengers were resident in Japan. They said that it is an exceedingly beautiful country, and that Miss Bird's descriptions of it are accurate; but they thought she might have seen all she did without going through so many privations.

We anchored for the night in the Bitter Lakes. Early in the morning we steamed through the Shaloof, a part of the canal which is cut in the rock, and caught sight of the rocky cliffs above Suez, a white town standing in a wide sandy plain, at the foot of hills which show no vestige of verdure. The colouring of the sea in the gulf was something extraordinary. It was a brilliant green with a strip of purplish blue nearer us, and a fringe of white on the barren shore just below the bare cliffs, over which many purple shadows were flitting. I had seen these effects of colour in pictures of Eastern subjects, but never before in reality. At eleven o'clock we steamed out of the canal, and then came leave-takings and exchanges of cards. We got down a steep ladder into a tiny steamer, no larger than an ordinary fishing-boat, which was rocking about on the waves, and offered us shelter from the glaring heat in the shape of a tiny cabin.

Suez stands at the head of a long, shallow gulf, whose waters are hardly more than four feet deep; rendering it impossible for sea-going vessels to come near the town. We secured our rooms at the Hotel de Suez, and then went to find our boxes at the custom-house, where, as the officer could not speak English, I tried Arabic, and found that he understood me. But, much to my disappointment, I could not make out a word that the common natives said to each other. Some of them struggled and fought for the honour of carrying our boxes, and were hard to satisfy in the matter of bakhsheesh.

We made inquiries at once about the best way of accomplishing an excursion to 'Ain Mousa, those brackish wells where the Israelites are supposed to have raised their song of triumph after crossing the Red Sea. A friendly old German colonel, who sat next us at the *table-d'hôte*, tried to dissuade us from the attempt by saying that the wind might be against us in a sailing boat, that we might be detained for hours on the return journey, and get a dip in the water; also that 'Ain Mousa was not worth seeing. Violet believed him, and we resolved to give up the excursion. We, however, engaged a dragoman to remain with us during our stay in Egypt, and protect us from the attacks of rough men and boys desirous of carrying our luggage. His name was Said Mohammed; he had excellent testimonials, and was a Moslem. Mr. Sutherland, the manager of the hotel, told us that, in the event of our being dissatisfied, he had the power of making Said refund any money of which he might cheat us. This was, happily, unnecessary, as Said proved himself quite honest and exact in his accounts.

Next morning, when we descended to breakfast, the old colonel told us that the wind was remarkably favourable for 'Ain Mousa, so we hurriedly determined to go.

We engaged two boats, one for ourselves, the other for our donkeys. It was a lovely morning; there were clouds in the sky, but they did not seem to threaten rain. Our boat was a deep one, with a big sail. Two men in white and blue shirts propelled it by running along the ledge of it from bow to stern and pushing their oars against the ground, singing a rhymed chant. Said steered and talked Arabic to me, promising that he would make me speak fluently in a fortnight. I had great difficulty in understanding him until I suddenly discovered that there exists a great difference in pronunciation between the Egyptian and the Syrian dialects, that the consonant *g*, especially, became in Said's mouth hard, like *g* in give, whereas I had been taught to pronounce it like a *j*. Having found this clue I hoped that I should understand the natives better; and I saw that Said purposed arrogating to himself the credit of my being his pupil. He professed to like the English, for they were much better than the inhabitants of Egypt, who were mostly ' nâs bâtil,' rubbish !

Violet protested that no human being could be exactly rubbish, and she inquired what religion Said professed.

'I am a Moslem,' he answered, ' but I read the New Testament in English. I read some of it every morning. The Kurân and the Bible are both good,

for they both came down from heaven, only Jesus
Christ he better than Mohammed, because he was
the Son of God.'

Having said this, *in English*, Said asked me in
Arabic if I knew the Fatha, and, on my replying in
the affirmative, proceeded devoutly to repeat it,
ostensibly for my benefit, but doubtless to impress
the two boatmen with an idea of his own orthodoxy.
I perceived that he keeps two strings to his bow; he
is a kind of Christian when speaking or reading
English, and a Moslem when speaking or thinking
in Arabic. He was evidently shutting his eyes to
the fact that the Kurân expressly denies the possibility of Jesus Christ being the Son of God.*

We soon reached the canal, and, after touching
once or twice on sandbanks, landed exactly at the
same time as a party of gentlemen who had started
an hour before us. We all mounted on donkeys,
and the gentlemen soon got far ahead of us; for I
checked the impetuosity of the donkey-drivers by
quoting an Arabic proverb which states that 'haste
is from Satan, and leisure from the Merciful One.'
We passed over a wide expanse of hard, stony sand,
and over little hillocks where nothing grew except
a few tiny clumps of a low, thorny shrub. The
Arabs were much pleased at finding I could talk to
them; only they said that my language was 'kallam
Bagdad,' speech of Bagdad, and not of Egypt; the
latter being in their eyes, and in those of Said, the
standard of everything classical and correct. One
of them tried a little Greek, another Italian, their
accent in both being pure, but their stock of words

* Im Sûrat-el-Ikhlâs.

meagre. There was something delicious in the extreme dryness of the air, with the pure, sapphire sky above, and the cloud-shadows which flitted over the distant hills before us; beyond which hills is the road to Sinai. After a ride of two hours we came in sight of 'Ain Mousa, an oasis of palm-trees, consisting of three or four gardens enclosed by low walls. We took lunch under a shed close to the chief fountain, which looked like a reservoir of stagnant green water with something bubbling up inside of it.

We then partook of coffee in tiny cups, and wandered under the leafy palms amid patches of wheat, lupins, and potatoes. We visited two other gardens, each containing a spring, and tried to speak with an old, grey-haired Bedawee woman, a perfect picture of neglect and misery. The proprietor of the garden was quite shocked when Violet asked if she were his wife, and I if she were his mother. 'She is a Bedawee and I an Arab,' he indignantly exclaimed. We were not very clear as to what is the difference. It is, perhaps, more in habits of life than in race. Said tried his best to persuade us into undertaking the journey to Sinai. We told him that we might try it another year, and that I wished to ascertain if I were fit for it by riding on a camel.

One was accordingly led up, and I got on to the part of its back on which Arab women generally sit, and held on to the two sticks which formed its rudiment of a saddle.

I kept my balance without difficulty whilst it rose from its knees, and, when it began to walk, I found its motion very pleasant, easier, indeed, than that of a horse or a donkey. I would have ridden on it down to the canal, a distance of five miles, had not the clouds suddenly broken into a heavy shower of rain and hail. It was a curious sensation to feel the strong wind of the desert in our faces, with the consciousness that we were getting thoroughly wet, and that miles of sand lay betwixt us and shelter. The camel was led by a Bedawee, clad in a robe that had once been white; Said was walking by my side, and, as Violet had got far before me on her donkey, I saw that it would be imprudent to continue on such a slow-paced animal, in the face of an advancing storm; and, by so doing, to get separated from Violet. The camel growled horribly when it was made to kneel. I leaned back as well as I could, and got off quite easily. I then mounted my donkey, and galloped after Violet. We had no waterproofs, so we soon got very wet, and were well pelted with hailstones.

We at length perceived that the storm was passing over us on to the sea, shrouding Gebal el Attaka, the mountains on the African side of the gulf, in clouds, and deepening the brilliant blue of the water which lay between these two continents. We had a good view of the traditional spot where the Israelites crossed, and we thought that the theory held by some of our fellow-travellers—which accounts for their passage by the ebb and flow of the tide—is a perfectly untenable one. The tides are, no doubt, greater in the Red Sea than in the Mediterranean. Still, a tide which could leave the bed of such a gulf uncovered, even for a few minutes, would be as miraculous as the facts narrated in Exodus.

c

The sky gradually cleared, and nothing could exceed the delicious lightness and transparency of the air. The wind was a little cold, and we galloped fast, till it dried our damp clothes.

On reaching the canal, the stalwart Arabs lifted us into our boat, and we found that we had more difficulty in returning than in going, the wind being against us. The two boatmen ran up and down the ledge, propelling the boat with their oars and singing a chant, of which I made out:

'Hûa âmâli sidi, hûa âmâli sidi habibi, banât 'arab.'*

This, I suppose, referred to the Almighty, for I frequently caught the word 'Allâhi.' I should like to know why it is that Moslems bring their religion, imperfect as it is, into their daily life so much more than Christians do. This was the more strongly impressed upon us as we noticed a man in another boat saying his prayers, and prostrating himself under difficulties, he being alone, and having to contend with wind and wave. I wondered also if the Arab word habibi (my beloved,) may not be the origin of our word baby? No sounds are so likely to be transmitted and retained as those of endearment from a mother's lips.†

We ran aground several times, and signalled in vain for a little passing steam-tug to tow us. But at length our sail caught the wind, and we glided up to the pier at Suez.

* 'He is my hope, my Lord, He is my hope, my Lord, my beloved, daughters of the Arabs.'
† Dr Ogilvie, in the 'Imperial Dictionary,' gives the derivation of 'babe' from the Syriac and Arabic, but connects it with the root 'babah,' from which we have our 'papa,' the Germans their 'Bube,' and the Americans their 'pappoos.'

CHAPTER II.

IN CAIRO.

Little Difficulties—Said's Trick—Taken for Moslem Ladies—Tel-el-Kebir—A Motley Crowd—Shepheard's Hotel—Climate of Cairo—I Try to Learn Colloquial Arabic—My Plan—Arab English—Arab Teachers—Wheat the Forbidden Fruit—Incivility of some English Travellers—A Mistake of Simplicity—Excessive Gaiety—Noble Exceptions.

NEXT day we went by rail to Cairo. There was a scene of confusion at the station, although it was evidently under European management. We had been forewarned that we should find the journey very dusty, also that the carriages would be over-crowded. We instructed Said to secure for us, if possible, a compartment where we should be alone; but we were hardly prepared for the way in which he obeyed our orders.

We two were placed in a first-class carriage, seated for eight. Our small packages were laid in the empty places, quite in the orthodox manner. But we were surprised to see that Said had also put in two large leather bags, with brown waterproof covers (which were very useful in the cabin of a steamboat, but which we always considered luggage to be registered when we went by rail).

'You have made a mistake, Said,' we said. 'These bags ought to have gone with our heavy things.'

'No, no,' replied Said. 'Why should you pay so much for over-weight? They are better here.'

'But they fill up the space at the door,' we urged. 'You may try to keep other passengers out of this compartment, but, if anyone should insist on entering, he will have a right to complain of these things, and you will get us into difficulties.'

'Now, don't be cross with me,' said Said. 'No one will object, for no one else shall come into this carriage.'

'How can you be sure of that? There is a great crowd of travellers.'

'Leave that to me. I tell you it's my business, and I understand my business better than you do.'

'Said, you *must* take away these things.'

Said, however, pretended to be deaf, and said, 'Anti ghadbânat' ('Thou art cross to me') in such a coaxing way that I was obliged to laugh. We could see other European ladies and gentlemen going about distractedly in search of seats, and had a conviction that every carriage, excepting ours, was as full as it could hold. Each time that we stopped at a station, Said appeared at the door, his presence alone seeming to deter anyone from entering.

We felt far from comfortable, however, as we dreaded a repetition of the scene we had had betwixt Paris and Marseilles, and we knew that the presence of these great bags would effectually debar us from having the right on our side. When we stopped at Ismaïla, there was a rush of fresh passengers.

Yes! They were making for our carriage. Said

planted himself before the door, and shouted, in a voice of authority, 'Hareem!'

The effect was magical, but on the first comers only. There really was too little room in the train, and some adventurous spirits wished the guard to let them have a look at us.

Then Said got excited. He flung up his arms, shouting, 'Hareem, hareem, hare-ee-ee-m!' till every-one was fain to beat a retreat. The illusion as to our being Moslem ladies was kept up, not only by the blinds being drawn down, but by my looking out of the window once or twice with a silk hand-kerchief on my head.

We felt that Said's trick was in no way justifiable, but, as we had not suggested it, we were highly amused, and took the benefit.

We passed Nefiche, where the first shots were fired in the conflict with Arabi, and concerning which I recollect writing:

'"Our loss has been slight," was the message that flew
With the flash of the light o'er the billowy blue;
Two wounded, whom patience and love may restore,
Two dead, who shall follow our banners no more.

'"Our loss has been slight." It is manhood's proud grace,
With the mark of his Maker on form and on face,
'Tis the half of two lives when for labour most fit,
'Tis the gleam of two lamps that can ne'er be re-lit.

'In a far Highland valley two mothers must weep
For those in the ditch of Rameses who sleep;
Two brides must be widowed, two homes must be bare,
And vain to all seeming the pleadings of prayer.

'Oh, bold be the warriors our rights who defend!
And wise be the chiefs whom to battle we send!
But ne'er let them say, when they rest from the fight,
"The cost was as nothing, our loss has been slight."'

Alas! these were only the first drops of that river

of blood which Britain has since poured out upon the deserts of Egypt!

We got a glimpse of the fort at Tel-el-Kebîr, and we found that we had formed an accurate idea of its position from reading the newspaper descriptions. All French people and some Americans with whom we have conversed insist that Lord Wolseley won the victory by means of 'La cavallerie de St. George,' meaning the colonial sovereigns which bear the impress of St. George and the dragon. Said, on the other hand, informed Violet that 'four thousand English officers were killed at Tel-el-Kebîr.' This statement, outrageous as it is, shows that the Egyptians do not think the battle was easily won.

The railway offered us nothing but desert views until we reached the valley of the Nile. Then the country became beautiful, for the young green crops were pleasantly dotted with mud villages, all shaded with feathery palm-trees and enlivened by the leanest of kine and smallest, but liveliest of hens. Nowhere does one see the ribs of all kinds of animals more clearly defined than in Egypt.

There was of course a motley crowd at the Cairo station. A man was laying a courbash, or native whip, rather heavily on the shoulders of the people outside of it. I suppose they had no business to be there; but one hardly likes to see such a proceeding in a city which is under British protection. It is the symbol of authority, and its use is perhaps as much needed as was the application of Ulysses' sceptre.

We went to Shepheard's Hotel, where Mr. Sutherland's telegram had secured us the nicest possible bed-room, looking out directly on the verandah. The old square, formerly so dusty, is now covered with handsome houses, but we missed the picturesqueness of the crowd who used to assemble in front of the hotel, and the amusing chaffering of the donkey-boys with their would-be employers or victims.

The donkeys are now relegated to a side street, English ladies having decreed that a ride on them is somewhat *infra dig*. There are still travellers, and residents too, who steal round the corners, so that the *grande monde* may not see them in the act of mounting. Otherwise, the appearance of Cairo is much improved since our visit to it in 1869. The streets are in better order, and the animals, though by no means well-used, do not present so revolting a spectacle of mute suffering. There is now a beautiful public garden, containing a miniature lake, pretty grottoes, trees, and plants of luxurious growth. Here the Khedive's band plays every afternoon, and here one can always find a welcome refuge from heat and dust. The climate was, however, colder than we had anticipated. We stayed from January 25 till March 15, and during that time there were few days in which a little rain did not fall either during the night or in the early morning. The Suez Canal is said to have brought more moisture into the air.

The climate, too, is variable. I believe that the changes of temperature during the twenty-four hours of a spring day will be found more numerous in Cairo than in England.

The sanitary arrangements of the city are radically bad. For some weeks in winter the water supplied to private houses was so offensive that one lady of our acquaintance could not summon courage to approach the ewer in her bed-room after it had been filled. Not only did this water filter through a cemetery, but a large sewer was discovered flowing into the chief conduit.

One Sunday afternoon some time in April, while the Khamsîn winds were blowing, the water supply of Cairo ceased altogether, causing great alarm. The man in charge of the Nile Barrage had allowed the river above the Barrage to sink to a lower level than the mouth of the conduit.

But that is not all. Cairo is declared by the *Egyptian Gazette* to stand on a 'heaving mass of rolling sewage.' An English general, having taken the lease of a house, and being determined to purify it, had no less than eighty tons of this material removed from around its basement, and in this were the bodies of several infants, and one body of a full-grown man. Many instances of a similar kind might be cited. The Esbekieh quarter, before it was built upon, was a marsh, some of whose malarious vapours may still possibly find their way to the surface.

Cairo, in short, could not be put into a healthy condition without an expenditure of at least half-a-million sterling.

All Eastern cities are, I strongly suspect, in much the same state. The natives, being to the manner born, do not feel it so much as Europeans, yet they too pay the penalty in a high rate of infant mortality, in cholera and in plague, whenever the atmospheric equilibrium is much disturbed. The true remedy in the case of very ancient cities like Teheran, Damascus, and Cairo would be to remove them to another site. This, we may safely assume, will not be done by the present generation. Yet Providence sometimes does for man what he will not do for himself, and we who know of these things must feel as if Nineveh and Babylon have been destroyed quite as much in mercy as in judgment.

Enteric fever was, of course, prevalent. We could describe many sad instances of its ravages, but to do so would be to make our pages too melancholy. It spared neither the young, the strong, the wealthy, nor the highly placed.

We arrived, as I have stated, in January. We did not care to make the Nile trip, having done so years before in a dahabeah from Boolak to Wady Halfah. We did not wish to spoil our romantic memories of the river by going in one of Cook's steamers, which were, moreover, so overcrowded that the best of them, having berths for fourteen, brought twenty-four first-class passengers down from Luxor, with what results as regards comfort and cleanliness may be imagined. It was far too early to start for Cyprus, so I employed my time in trying to gain a colloquial knowledge of Arabic, a language whose grammar I had studied with some diligence, and which I hoped would prove useful to us in our future wanderings.

My plan was this. Rising early, an hour before Violet did, I took a walk, accompanied by Said, in the Esbekieh gardens, conversing with him as I did so. I then went to a school for native girls, and, as

Miss Whately's was somewhat distant, I chose that of the American Mission, within a few yards of the hotel. I sat with the pupils in their classes for arithmetic, spelling, grammar, Bible history, and astronomy, taking my turn in reading and answering questions, and making myself a source of much amusement to the girls. I talked also with a professional teacher for an hour and a half, telling anecdotes and listening to them by turns. In the afternoon I learnt a little writing and read a book on astronomy with an intelligent girl from the Fayoum, she reading and I repeating every sentence after her with the view of acquiring a correct pronunciation.

I, of course, in the space of seven weeks, got to know all the school-girls, and to estimate their mental powers pretty accurately. I found no difference whatever between them and the generality of English girls—yes, even of those girls who were once my own school-fellows. Many of them were boarders in the house of Miss Thompson, the head teacher, and were being trained to habits of cleanliness and order. Some of them were learning French, music, and painting, whilst all had daily instruction in English and needle-work.

The Arabs pride themselves not a little on the ease with which they acquire our language, as compared with our slowness in comprehending theirs. But, as I pointed out to some of them, their advantages are quite exceptional. In the American schools, and doubtless also in Miss Whately's, the pupils get a lesson in English every day, and are made to speak it all day, even when learning other things. In the American one they have the advantage of hearing it from the lips of two ladies whose mother tongue it is, and who put their whole hearts into the effort to make their pupils understand it. For these advantages they pay a very small sum, and some receive their instruction gratis. This continues with them for many years of childhood and youth.

An Englishman, on the other hand, who wants to learn Arabic, and who is not residing at a university, has the initial difficulty of finding a teacher. If he prefers a native, on account of the pronunciation, he will find most of the Arabs who come to this country quite ignorant of their own grammar. If he seek instruction from an English university professor, he may no doubt acquire a thorough knowledge of the language from a literary point of view, but will have no facility in speaking it. And it may perhaps not be convenient for him to change his place of residence.

I myself was exceptionally fortunate in studying under Mr. Habîb A. Salmoné, of University College, who is a learned man and a native; but I had sometimes to be content with a lesson once a fortnight, or once in three weeks, owing to the pressure on his time. Practice in conversation was thus out of the question, and when I tried to supply the want by getting native teachers who knew no European language to converse with me when in the country, they were so afraid of saying anything I might not like, that I actually had four of them, and had acquired considerable fluency in talking before I found out that qâf is pronounced differently from kâf, or the first hâ from the second hâ. Need I say that the teacher who drilled me in these things, Mr. George El Hage, of Beyrout, was esteemed by me more than his predecessors.

'If you Moslems,' I said to Said, 'will send missionaries and teachers to England to teach us the Kurân, and to teach us Arabic, you will see that we shall learn your language quite as easily as you do ours.'

'We cannot do that,' replied Said. 'You and the Americans are rich, that is why you can do these things.'

'Not at all,' I replied. 'If you will only believe me, it is not the rich people who send you the missionaries, either in England or in America. It is people of all classes, who love the Gospel, and want you to know and love it too. You are always telling me that the Kurân is the " mother of books, the property of the world." If you loved it as much as we love the Gospel, you would have sent us missionaries years ago.'

Said made no answer, and I did not tell him, as I might have done, that while there are English places of worship all over Europe, Africa, and Asia, there is not a single mosque in England, nor, I suspect, in France, and this notwithstanding the numbers of Moslems, rich and poor, who visit our shores.

I had often curious discussions with him. One day we spoke of the fall of Adam, and Said insisted that the forbidden fruit was wheat. I replied that we in England generally believed that it was an apple, although the Towrah gives us only the indefinite word 'fruit.'

'It was not an apple,' persisted Said, 'it was

wheat. Since then Allah has decreed that man shall live principally on wheat, and that he shall wander in search of it; and he does not always find it where he seeks it, and so he has to go all round the globe and never rests.'

I laughed. 'You think that the love of travel was sent to us as the punishment of sin,' I said. 'Then we English must be much worse than other people. But you know, Said, that we don't all travel in search of bread; some of us do so to gain knowledge.'

'What sort of knowledge can you gain?'

'Well, you know there are remains of antiquity in other countries, a sight of which enables us to understand better the history of our forefathers. Besides, in Italy, for example, there are works of art, statues, and paintings which are finer than anything we see at home.'

'But that is a sin!' exclaimed Said. 'God has forbidden us to make a likeness of anything!'

There was no use in arguing the point. I contented myself with explaining that we understand the second commandment to refer only to the use of images in worship, a use which tends to lower the worshipper's conception of God. The Moslems are decidedly in the right on this point, but we may feel sure that the Almighty, who has endowed man with imitative and creative faculties, never intended to forbid their rational use.

Said informed me that the Mohammedans pray every day, and the Christians only upon one day in the week, viz., Sundays.

I of course informed him that he was in error,

his mistake arising from the fact that we Christians obey our Lord's command, 'But thou, when thou prayest, enter into thy closet, and when thou hast shut the door,' etc. I confessed at the same time that many of us err in concealing our religion, while the impulse of the Moslems is to make it as public as possible.

'Does the Kurân teach you,' asked Violet, 'to be kind to animals?'

'No,' replied Said, 'it says nothing about it.'

'Then Mohammed was very careless,' said Violet, 'for he might have seen how much his countrymen need the lesson.'

I was surprised with one idea of Said's. I happened to hear one Sunday, in the American mission church, a native preacher discourse from the text, 'A prophet shall the Lord God raise up unto you of your brethren, like unto me.' On Monday morning, by way of practising my Arabic, I gave Said a sketch of this sermon, stating, of course, that Moses referred to our Lord Jesus Christ.

'No, he did not,' said Said. 'He meant our Lord Mohammed.'

I was still more astonished to find that he considered our Lord's promise of the Comforter to refer to the Arabian prophet. I was told that many Arabs believe the word 'paraclete' to belong to their own tongue, and get quite angry if you tell them it is Greek.

On another point Said was very obstinate. Cherishing an intense hatred to the Copts, he would never allow that they were Egyptians. In vain did we point out that the name of the country and the name of the people are from the same root, ' Copt ' being the ' gypt' of the Greek word Αἴγυπτος, and that these people, being the true descendants of the people of Pharaoh, have as good a right to dwell in the country as their conquerors, the Arabs. Said always ended the discussion by saying,

' Well, they may be Egyptians, but they are not Moslems.'

It happened that the dragoman who in 1869 accompanied us over the Holy Land, was a Copt. We inquired about him during the first days of our sojourn in Cairo, and were told that he was dead. Some weeks afterwards a Coptic gentleman told us that this was a mistake, so we had the pleasure of meeting again and of conversing with Armanûs Tadrûs.

'We had a fearful time of it,' he said, 'during Arabi's insurrection. If the British troops were to leave the country, we should most of us be massacred. But now all the heart is gone out of the Moslems, their spirit is quite crushed.'

We asked him what he thought of the expedition to Khartoum.

' I know the Soudan well,' he replied, ' for I have often been there. Once I was there as private dragoman to Baker Pasha. The people are black, and the country is black too. Lord Wolseley thought he could conquer it all at once. Nobody ever did that before. Mahomet Ali got possession of it gradually. When he had beaten one black tribe he made it help him to fight against another black tribe till he had got it all.'

The American missionaries are of opinion that

our government had no course open to it but that of quelling Arabi's insurrection. The French residents, who are so fiercely jealous of us, would none of them be here now were it not for the English. At the same time we cannot wonder at merchants and tradesmen feeling sore at the losses they have sustained owing to the stoppage of trade with the Soudan, a trade which our government has surely tried the impossible in attempting to restore. They have more reason when they complain of the insecure prospect which lies before them. Yet people who leave their own country to seek for higher profits in Mohammedan ones, must be prepared to take the risks of living under bad and unstable governments.

No visitor to Cairo, however, can shut his eyes to the fact that our countrymen have, as a rule, failed to earn the love either of Europeans or of natives. Some would go so far as to say that they have earned hatred, and there is no use in our altogether disguising the fact.

This is doubly sad in view of our influence as a Christian nation. With the Moslems it may spring from religious bigotry, with the French from sheer envy. But let us look a little deeper, and try to find out if any of our countrymen give cause for it.

The world, I suppose, believes in an Englishman's love of justice, and far be it from us to suspect him of any sort of direct oppression or dishonesty. We have sterling qualities which merit esteem. Why, then, do people not always rejoice at being under British rule?

We think that we have found it out through

observing the conduct of two families who sat opposite to us at the *table d'hôte* of 'Shepheard's.' We knew their names, and, from what we overheard of their conversation, we gathered that some of their intimate friends had been the companions of our childhood. Yet, during seven weeks, for three hours daily, these people faced us, and never once said good-morning, nor acknowledged our presence by a civil bow. We had, of course, no introduction to them, and we could attribute their conduct to nothing personal on our part, seeing that they regarded all who occupied the seats next to us with the same indifference; and some of these even asked to have their seats moved in consequence.

Now it is precisely here that the etiquette of our insular manners differs widely from that of every other civilized nation. Many of us there are who have been led by our own good sense and our intercourse with foreigners to adopt the more natural and the more human code, but there are still many who imagine that they are impressing others with a sense of their own high position in society by conduct which sometimes amounts to downright rudeness. We have noticed that these often belong to the minor gentry of our country, to a class which can lay no claim to high birth, but which is always hanging on, so to speak, to the coat-tails of the aristocracy, and endeavouring to pass for what they are not. We have never seen it practised by those whose position as leaders of society is well assured; these are, on the contrary, distinguished for their urbanity; but we have

D

met with it in the case of people who, as we afterwards discovered, were leading very obscure lives at home. Sometimes this class of people display haughtiness of the passive kind. They gaze on the unintroduced world with a simple stony, British stare, until their faces settle into an expression of inanity, which is not pleasant to behold. Others (these are chiefly ladies) talk to the people they do know in a loud tone, completely ignoring the presence of anyone else in the room.

The mischief which such conduct causes does not consist merely in the feelings of a few individuals being hurt. No, for it engenders in those who practise it a habit of mind which incapacitates them from understanding the nature of their fellow-creatures, except within a limited circle; and is it not just possible that this may be at the root of much of our troubles in Ireland? The peasantry of that country have certainly been misguided; they, in their dense ignorance, have lent a willing ear to the unscrupulous agitator; but would they for so many centuries have persisted in looking upon their landlords as an alien race, had members of the upper classes invariably spoken to them as men should speak to their fellow-men? I have seen the bad effects of such conduct often. I have heard an English officer's wife speak contemptuously of the Arabs whilst being waited on by Arab servants; yes, even of the private soldiers whom her husband was commanding. I have heard a young Englishman, sitting at a Trouville *table-d'hôte* amongst French gentlemen not unacquainted with our language, complacently inform his sister that there was no society anywhere on the Continent fit for an Englishman to associate with.

My dear readers, and especially my dear sisters, do not misunderstand me. It is not expected that you shall make intimate friends with the strangers whom you may chance to meet in a public hotel, nor even that you should converse much with them. Each one of us, I hope, maintains her right to decide who shall and who shall not share the hospitalities of her home; and for her preference of some to others she is not bound to give a reason. But you should recollect that civility goes a long way, and it costs little; also that nothing so offends and irritates your fellow-creatures as the idea that they are being despised, or, what is worse, patronised by those who have no shadow of a right to do either. Perhaps it never occurs to you that the estimate put upon you by others *may* be very different from that which you put upon yourselves. Foreigners are not in the least impressed by your acquaintance with, nor even by your relationship to, people of title; for it is simply astounding how little one nation prizes the nobilities of another nation. It is much more likely, indeed, that they will attribute your habit of keeping yourselves aloof to a deficiency of intellect, or of education; and, if they observe that you pursue this course towards your fellow-countrymen, they will use it as a handle to make fun of the English.

Once, in my simplicity, I thought that the mission of Great Britain was to civilize the world; that, wherever her flag floated, it would be the symbol not only of all that is just, but of all that is pure and of good report. I have not yet got rid of the notion that we are, on the whole—that is, we who dwell at home in these isles—a more moral and a more sensible people than—let us say our Gallic neighbours. But my two months of observation in Cairo have shaken my faith in this. Our civil servants and our officers who reside there have surely undertaken a serious task. They are responsible not only for the good government of Egypt, but also for the well-being of our brave soldiers in the Soudan.

How comes it then that so much of their time is given up to frivolity? No one could be surprised at a few balls or other entertainments taking place in the season, but such a constant round of dissipation as they indulge in, involving as it does the continual turning of night into day, must make the most conscientious of men sometimes unfit for his work. Lady Baring did not postpone her ball on the night when the news of Gordon's death arrived. It was thought that her doing so would have had a bad effect on the natives. I ask what effect can this fiddling and playing over the loss of Khartoum have had? Many old-fashioned people at home will think that it was hardly a time to give balls, whilst the fate of the heroic Gordon hung upon a thread, possibly even on the nerve and activity of a man who was engaged in waltzing. For we poor, human creatures are so constituted that we find a difficulty in attending to two things at once.

I know not how it was in the spring of 1885. But I know that in 1886, to quote one of the newspapers, 'Society has seldom been so gay as now. It can hardly get back from its picnics and lawn-tennis matches to be in time for its operas and its balls.' Now the people who kept up this sort of thing were—the male part of them—being paid by the people at home for serious work. Ladies, of course, have much unoccupied time on their hands, but we cannot help thinking that, had they taken their pleasure more moderately, we should have seen fewer deathly-pale faces, and heard of fewer whose debilitated frames fell victims to the ravages of typhoid fever.

A few of our countrymen found other ways of employing themselves. One (I regret that I have forgotten her name) kept a room in her house open in the evenings, for the benefit of private soldiers, affording them a pleasant change from the monotony of barrack life, and partly supplying the want which is so admirably met in Alexandria by Miss Robinson's excellent 'Soldiers' and Sailors' Institute.' Another, Mrs. General Watson, not only set herself to learn Arabic, but spent a morning every week in imparting instruction in Scripture knowledge and in water-colour drawing to some of the girls in the American mission-school. It seems to me that other ladies might have found ways of occupying themselves profitably, when we consider the number of invalided soldiers who were being brought down the Nile, and the lack of comforts experienced by the healthy ones who were at the outposts.

This brings me to another question. We were told in Cairo that the commissariat was lamentably defective; that our soldiers, beyond the first and second cataract, had to subsist on salt meat and hard biscuit, without even tinned vegetables; and that they were required to sleep on the bare sand, a thing which never hurts the natives, but which no European can do with impunity; and this although palm frames, costing a franc each, might easily have been sent to them. Several officers, however, to whom we mentioned the subject, laughed, saying,

'Do you think that soldiers in front of the enemy can expect to be treated as if they were in a dahabeah or a first-class hotel?'

We happened, whilst travelling from Alexandria to Beyrout, to meet an intelligent young Persian who had been as far as Dongola in the capacity of contractor to our troops, and we took the opportunity of asking his opinion on the subject.

'No doubt,' he replied, 'the men up there have suffered very great hardships, but those who complain about it should take into account that the trouble and cost of conveying anything to them was simply enormous. Why, what could we do? If we tried to convey things by land, the camels died. If we tried it by the river—well, you have seen what the second cataract is. For every tin of biscuits that was got safely up, ten at least were sunk in the bottom of the river, and everything else in like proportion. Palm frames would have been an additional impediment during a march. In my opinion, European troops should not have been sent to that region at all.'

CHAPTER III.

THE SIGHTS OF CAIRO.

The Boulak Museum—Mummy of Rameses II.—The Tomb of the Caliphs—The Great Pyramid—Its Construction—View from the Top—Spurious Coins—The Sphinx—Description—The Mosque El Azhar—Conversations with 'Ulemas—The Kurân—The Great Hall or University—Moslem Students.

WE had examined the sights of Cairo well on our former visit, so all we cared to do was to refresh our memories by an occasional peep at some of them.

We always took a drive in the afternoons either across the Nile to a spot where some of our countrymen were generally engaged in the spirited game of polo, or to the gardens of one of the Khedive's palaces. Here the most splendid Paris furniture is eclipsed by wardrobes and cabinets from the workshop of Parvis, the artist who has brought Italian taste to the work of reproducing the old Arabic designs.

Twice we visited the Boulak museum, a place whose treasures are unique and extraordinary. It is no light thing to gaze on the mummy of Rameses II., whose features have become so familiar to us from numerous colossal statues, and whom Egyptologists identify with the Pharaoh of Exodus. One of his obelisks stands in the Place de la Concorde, of Paris, and he is, in truth, the most prominent figure of ancient Egyptian history. Yet how cold would our interest in him be were it not for the fact that his daughter drew Moses out of the river? The mummy which lies near him is probably hers. About that of Sethi, his father, there can be no doubt, for every royal mummy-case bore the cartouche of its occupant. Few there are who would not envy the feelings of Brugsch Pasha when he stepped into the subterranean chamber at Dayr el Baharî, and, though half swooning at the puff of air which had been stagnant for three thousand years, succeeded in reading, by the dim light of candles, those historical names which must have thrilled him with an intense awe.

The mummy has since been unbandaged, revealing the monarch's very features. The low, narrow forehead, the thick eyebrows, the eyes probably small, the hooked, Bourbon nose, the prominent cheekbones, the round ears standing far out from the head, the strong, massive jaw, and the thick lips, form a physiognomy which corresponds well with the character of the Pharaoh who made the lives of the children of Israel bitter with hard service. Our minds grow weary in trying to realize the changes that have passed over Egypt and over the world from the hour when the body was swathed in its linen wrappers, till that in which these were unwound from it. Then, Moses was a fugitive in the land of Midian; now, his fame has not only eclipsed that of Rameses, but his teachings have been the living seed out of which the world's best civilization and the world's best hope of future progress have sprung. Rameses failed to perpetuate himself in the heart of humanity because his works, stupendous as they are, only dazzled men's eyes. Moses appealed to something deeper, and therefore Time, which destroys the memory of others, can never fail to bring new realms under his influence.

The Arab museum, near Bâb el Futûh, is noteworthy, though perhaps of less consuming interest. It contains some exquisite old wood-work, and many curious lamps, mostly removed thither from mosques. We asked the custodians why these things could not have been left in their original places.

'Because they would have been stolen,' they replied.

'By Moslems,' we asked, 'or by strangers?'

The men laughed, and did not answer.

In one of the rooms stood a huge glass water-pot with a paper tied round its neck containing about a dozen lines of description, neatly written in Arabic. Violet asked me to read it to her. I explained that I should require some time to decipher it, as it was not printed, and I was not accustomed to Arabic handwriting. She then asked Said if he could read it.

'Yes,' was the reply.

'Can these two men read it?'

'Yes, certainly.'

'Then read it to me, Said.'

Said began: 'This came from the Mosque of El Azhar' ('Wasal min Masgid El Azhar').

'Will you show me where these words are?' said I.

This, however, was beyond the power of Said or anyone else to do, simply because the words were not there. I felt convinced that, had I not been present, all the three men would have pretended to read it fluently.

We also visited the tombs of the Caliphs, those exquisite specimens of Moslem architecture. No words of mine could give the reader an idea of them half so good as he can get from a fair photograph, so it is well that I say little about them.

I was determined to climb the Great Pyramid, because not having done so on our former visit to Egypt, I have so often been obliged to answer 'No' when asked whether or not I had performed that feat.

We left Cairo shortly before ten o'clock, and reached the pyramids in less than two hours. They have been a puzzle and a wonder to each successive generation, and we instinctively feel their deep, mysterious meaning without at all subscribing to Professor Piazzi Smyth's theory that they were intended as a revelation of the will of God as to measurements. The fact of a large ancient cemetery being quite close to them is a point strongly in favour of the theory that they were designed for royal sepulchres; nor can we forget that the ancient Egyptians buried their dead on this side of the Nile. Violet did not wish to go to the top, and the guides object to the company of dragomans, so it was arranged that I should go with the help of three men and a handsome sheikh. On starting with them I recited the Arabic proverb, 'Haste is from Satan, and leisure from the Merciful One.'

Each tier of the pyramid forms a step, which is much too high for any lady to attempt unaided. Two of the Arabs assisted me by holding my hands, another gave me a little push. They were very gentle and considerate; all the more so when I addressed them in their own tongue. We sat down and had a little talk every three minutes, but they were more anxious to know all about my family connections and the reason of my being in Egypt than to give me any information. There are forty Bedâwy whose only employment is to conduct travellers up the pyramid. They form a sort of guild, under two sheikhs, and charge two shillings a head, expecting bakhsheesh. This they begged that they might receive from my own hand, and not from the dragoman's.

We had a splendid view from the top, the green fields on the Cairo side forming an inpressive contrast to the barrenness of the illimitable desert. I question, however, whether I was really repaid for the trouble of climbing. I believe that the view from the Mokattam hills behind the citadel of Cairo, a spot easily accessible, is quite as fine.

My four guides each pulled out a handful of spurious-looking coins and little images, urging me to buy before beginning the descent. I firmly declined to do so; but I hardly felt at leisure to enjoy the view, and, as Cairo and its green plain were fast getting shrouded in a rising mist, I thought it well not to linger. I stopped at the entrance of the pyramid to contemplate the very curious triangle above it, but I did not attempt to enter, being so overcome with fatigue that for the first time in my life I needed assistance to walk along the sandy pathway to the house, where Violet and another lady awaited me.

We rode to the Sphinx on donkeys, which possessed the peculiarity of each requiring the services of three men to keep itself and its rider from falling. In vain we protested against the useless escort. The Sphinx herself, with her worn and battered negro face, was not more deaf than were our conductors. The breast of the Sphinx was visible, having lately been cleared of sand, and showed a cartouche of hieroglyphics. Troops of women and children were carrying the sand away in baskets. We saw a temple built of Assouan granite and floored with alabaster. Its stones displayed no figures nor inscriptions of any kind, although some of them were eighteen feet long and of very great thickness. I could not make one of the nine Arabs who accompanied us tell us its name; they said it was simply 'El Kaniset' (the church).

There was a dreadful struggle for bakhsheesh after we got into the carriage, the two sheikhs doing nothing to restrain their followers. We were glad to be whirled away from the yelling, gesticulating crowd.

Said hardly approved of my constant visits to the American mission-school. There, he said, I should get only the learning of the Copts. The learning of the Arabs was much above it, and its chief seat was at the Mosque el Azhar.

'But can I hear a sermon there?' I asked.

'Certainly. The Sheikh el Islam preaches there every Friday. They will only be too delighted to see you, if you want to learn anything of our religion.'

'Are you sure they will not be angry at the idea of a Frank lady listening to a Moslem sermon?'

'No, they won't. But I must get an order for you, and I'll guarantee you a good place.'

We drove through the narrowest of streets, close to the bazaars, and exactly at twelve o'clock presented our teshkari at the entrance of the Mosque el Azhar. An 'Alîm, standing in the doorway, declared that we must remain outside until the sermon and the prayer were over.

'But it is for a lady who understands Arabic,' urged Said.

The 'Alîm hesitated, and consulted with one of his colleagues. He then said that they would willingly make an exception in our favour if it only depended on themselves, but that some of the people would not understand it, and would get very angry.

I addressed him in coaxing tones, and he invited us into the room of another 'Alîm, a very learned man, who lived within the gate. Its window was exactly opposite the door of the mosque, so that we had a good opportunity of seeing the crowd of worshippers, all men, who streamed in and out. We amused ourselves with watching the operations of the barbers, who were washing and shaving heads just beneath the window of the room in a style that was more picturesque than pretty. A young man came in and announced himself as the son of the learned 'Alîm who owned the house. He was interested in knowing where I had learnt Arabic. We found that he knew a little French, so he had some conversation with Violet. His father and another 'Alîm appeared. Finding that I understood their speech much better than that of the ordinary Egyptians, I told them that I had read the Kurân twice, and, to prove that I was making no false pretences, I ventured to repeat the Fatha. I tried to do this with proper solemnity, seeing that I was in the very stronghold of Moslem faith and fanaticism. I had hardly got to the third sentence, however, when, to my great surprise, both men began to laugh, and, the more I repeated, the more did their merriment increase. I was greatly relieved, for I had feared that they might be offended at my presumption. Said laughed too, and of course my own gravity broke down, so that I was unable to give them the beginning of the second Sûrat, as I had intended. Violet quieted us all by asking if what I was saying was intended for a prayer, or was addressed to the Almighty? I saw that I could not go on without causing further irreverence.

The two 'Ulema excused themselves, as they had to go into the mosque for prayer. Said asked permission to go and perform his devotions with them, so we were left for half-an-hour with the 'Alîm's son, and with another youth, who wore European dress, and who, after talking to me for some time in grammatical Arabic, suddenly told me in English that he was a Christian. The two 'Ulema returned with prayer-books, out of which they made me read until I complained that the small type hurt my eyes. They sent to a book-shop for another copy, which I bought for three francs, and in the meantime Said returned, looking quite dazed, and muttering the end of his prayer in a way intelligible only to himself. For a few minutes he did not seem to be quite conscious of his surroundings.

Violet had in the meantime been talking to the

'Alîm's son about the advantages of women, especially of mothers, being well-educated. The 'Alim himself, a stately man in a black turban, escorted us out into a large open court, where hundreds of turbaned, barefooted students were reclining or squatting on the ground, singly or in groups, some reading the Kurân, others studying from written papers. We passed into the great hall of the university, where other groups were similarly employed, but, as it was Friday, no lessons were being given. It was very strange to feel that we were at the very hearth of Islâm, with no one of our own faith near us. We arranged with the 'Alim that I should return on Saturday of the following week, for the purpose of hearing some of the lessons.

This I did, in company with another lady. We found the open court filled with groups of boys, and the central hall with grown men, all squatting round their respective teachers. The students were listening with eager attention, the boys swinging their bodies backward and forward, and the masters directing them to keep time in doing so. Our old acquaintance, the 'Alim, led us to a group where a lesson was being given by a man in a green turban. It was about either the inheritance or the marriage of daughters, but the reverberation of so many voices from the roof prevented my hearing well. Our learned friend offered to escort us to a place where we should hear a quieter lesson. It was in a little side mosque; but the lesson was unfortunately just finished when we arrived. So he took us back to the large hall, and we stood behind an old man in a huge turban who sat on a kind of wooden throne, and whose pupils ranged in age from seventy to twenty. I leaned against a pillar to hear him. All the stray youths in the place gathered round, more anxious to watch me than to listen to the professor. The old fellow became conscious of some one behind him, and, looking up, started on seeing a lady's face. I said, 'Nahârkum sa 'id,'* with a smile which made everyone laugh. Then I tried to listen, sorely disturbed by the strangeness of the scene, the beauty of the wooden lattice-work in the windows, and the twinkling eyes of the swarthy youths who stood around. I could only catch a phrase here and there, without the connecting words which would have enabled me to make sense of it. Could I have squatted on the ground at my ease in front of the professor, I should soon have got accustomed to his voice.

My friend the 'Alîm suggested that I might come there every day. But this would have involved getting a daily teskari, costing five shillings, besides the distribution of at least five shillings in bakhsheesh, and some remuneration to the teachers who might give me the opportunity of hearing them. So I concluded that the money would go further if spent on private instruction.

I am told that the students at El Azhar devote at least ten years to studying nothing but the Kurân and grammar. They do so after an antiquated method, trusting more to the memory than to books. Both subjects are of course thoroughly learned, but the time expended on them excludes all possibility of modern knowledge entering into the curriculum.

* 'May your day be blessed.'

49

CHAPTER IV.

THE SIGHTS OF CAIRO (CONTINUED).

The American Mission—Evangelization its Work—Miss Whately's School—All Mohammedan Children—A Native Congregation—Most Picturesque—In Native Houses with Miss Thompson—Dining with Coptic Families—Coptic Priests—A Coptic Family—A Coptic Marriage—The Coptic Cathedral—A Boys' School—Reflections.

I FOUND a more congenial sphere in the precincts of the American mission. Having spent four hours daily for nearly two months in the girls' school, and attended the Arabic services on Sundays, I am able to form something of an estimate as to the amount of good it is doing.

America leads the van in the cause of evangelical religion, and of European education throughout all the dominions of the Sultan. England comes second to her, but though she can boast of Mrs. Mott's (formerly Mrs. Bowen Thompson's) excellent schools in Beyrout, and of Miss Whately's in Cairo, there is no doubt that our cousins from the Far West have done more than we, and done it in the systematical, practical, thorough way which alone can insure permanent success. Robert College, on the shores of the Bosphorus, and the college at Râs Beyrout in Syria, now represent a power in the

E

land. Not only are numbers of young Turks and Arabs being introduced into the vast storehouses of Western learning, not only is the veil of prejudice which had hidden from their sight the accumulated treasures of the ages being torn away, but the missionaries themselves have become masters in the art of speaking and preaching about the unsearchable riches of Christ to the common people, in a tongue which presents peculiar difficulties to a European. English Oriental scholars have confessed to us with sorrow, not unmixed with chagrin, that the missionaries of the Church Missionary Society have hardly yet solved the problem of what kind of language they shall use in the pulpit, whether the pure grammatical Arabic of the Kurân, which might be understood, but would sound unfamiliar, or one of the vulgar dialects, unpleasant to an educated ear, and hardly befitting the solemnity of the subject. The only clergymen of the Church Missionary Society who have as yet acquired any fluency in preaching Arabic are none of them English by birth. I was told of one reverend gentleman, a thorough scholar, whose sermons are regarded by the natives with the greatest possible respect and admiration, although not one of his hearers ever dreams of understanding a word of them.

The American missionaries in Cairo have no college, as they devote themselves more especially to the work of evangelization. They have three schools, one in the street called 'Street of the Two Schools' (Hârat el Madrassataîn), close to Shepheard's Hotel, on the ground floor beneath the church, and the dwelling-houses of the pastors. This school has four hundred and sixty boys, and three hundred and twenty girls, thirty-five of whom are boarders. The boarders pay from twenty to fifty francs a month, the average being forty francs; and for this they receive a training quite equal to that of well-to-do tradesmen's daughters in England or Scotland. Day scholars pay five piastres, about a shilling a month, five francs extra for English, and five francs for French. Their numbers are recruited chiefly from Coptic families, though there are a few Mohammedans amongst them. All receive instruction in the Scriptures, and are not pressed to change their faith.

There is also a school near Boulak, with two hundred girls and sixty boys. That at Abd Ed Din numbers four hundred girls, all Mohammedans, no boys.

Miss Whately has three hundred boys and two hundred girls in her school. They are all the children of Mohammedans, and no direct attempt is made to proselytize them, only all are obliged to study the sacred Scriptures. Miss Whately gets all the waifs and strays, liberated slave girls and children from the Soudan. We saw two little creatures who had just been brought. They were supposed to be Gallas, though no one knew a word of the language they spoke. It was pitiful to watch the dull, sad little faces, unrelieved by a spark of intelligent interest while the other children sang an Arabic hymn.

Great attention is given to the study of English, and Miss Whately's school has supplied many interpreters to the British army. No wonder all these schools are popular, for they offer, to the boys at least, a direct method of advancement in life.

Yet it would be a mistake to suppose that they do not feed the Christian church. Miss Whately's converts attend the ministrations of the Rev. Dr. Klein, of the Church Missionary Society, and the growth of the American church is not only unmistakeable, but marvellous when we take into account how unsuitable their rigid Presbyterianism appears to be to the fervid, imaginative nature of Orientals. The Shorter Catechism, with its clear and comprehensive system of doctrine, and its preference of the idea of election over that of free grace, is carefully taught, yet the congregation grows and multiplies, fed by the attachment of the young people who have passed through the schools. The place where they met for worship in 1869 would be much too strait for them now. Not only so, but in that year the late Dr. Hogg had just settled at Asiout, where the rudiments of a church had been formed. This year he died, leaving a flourishing congregation the result of his sole labours, followed to the grave by the Moslem governor of the city, and sincerely mourned for by hundreds of natives.

The training college at Asiout was begun in 1870. The mission schools there number this year about eight hundred pupils. As a result, more than forty self-sustaining village schools have been established in Upper Egypt, and new life has been infused into many Coptic schools. What is the secret of this success?

I know what it is, for I worshipped with the native congregation. It is something that no apostolic succession can ensure, something that the most orthodox, I might say the most scriptural, form of church government may fail to compass. It is because the men who occupy the pulpit have a simple reliance on the power of the Divine Spirit, a single purpose in view: to make known the love of God in Christ Jesus to perishing men.

The native congregation is an interesting sight. I became accustomed to it, but my first view of it impressed me deeply. The church is curtained down the centre, so as to leave one side of it, one staircase, and one entrance from the street quite to the fair sex. I could not of course see the men, but there were seventy women present on that occasion, with only some half-a-dozen bonnets amongst them. The sermon was conducted by Mr. Harvey, who preached from Acts ii. 47, 'The Lord added to the church daily such as should be saved.'

It was noteworthy that they sang only the psalms of David, which adapt themselves readily to Arabic measures. They eschew hymns. At Beyrout the preference is for the latter, some of Moody and Sankey's strains being apparently favourites. The congregation was, indeed, different from any with whom I had before worshipped. I had plenty of leisure to observe them, for no sooner was the service over than they began salaaming to each other, chattering, and exchanging kisses in a way which made me at once comprehend how strangely appropriate to the East is the Apostle Paul's injunction in 1 Corinthians, xvi. 20, and how many things must be modified to suit a society where both sexes meet each other freely.

No assembly could possibly be more picturesque. The forms of nearly all the worshippers were graceful; some displayed black faces under white veils, some brown ones under blue, and some white ones under scarlet, whilst everywhere rich ornaments of gold and silver lay upon bronze necks and bosoms. It was difficult for me to pass through them, the more so as each of the missionaries' wives and the lady teachers stood at the end of their pews shaking the hands of some and receiving the kisses of others on their own. The oftener I went there, the more I came in for part of the first ceremony and the more diligence I had to use to escape undergoing the latter.

On the following Sunday, I counted forty-five school girls and eighty-five grown women. The male part of the congregation is always the more numerous. I understand that it generally numbers two hundred and fifty.

In the evening, I attended a service in English, held in the same building. The greater part of the audience belonged to the Black Watch; and I felt that it was a privilege to have worshipped on the same day, under the same roof, with conquerors and conquered.

Miss Thompson, the head teacher in the girls' school, took me to a native women's prayer meeting, which she herself conducted in a private house. Twelve women were present. She gave them two short, simple expositions of scripture, and then engaged in prayer. Her example was followed by two young women, one of whom (married two years ago) was very pretty, and tastefully dressed.

My knowledge of the language enabled me to comprehend fully all that passed. I was deeply interested by the thought that those women who attended on the ministrations of our Lord and of His Apostles probably looked and spoke very much like these.

When they had finished, I took courage, and told them that it gave me great pleasure to see them meet for such a purpose; that our Lord has promised to be in the midst of even two or three who meet in His name, and that I felt sure they would get a blessing, seeing that they had asked for it.

Miss Thompson took me into some other native houses. I was much impressed by their punctiliousness in the matter of salutations and polite expressions of welcome. Those Europeans who despise the Arabs as a nation of savages, are perhaps not aware that the poorest, dirtiest, and least clothed amongst them has his code of manners, which he never neglects, and which savours not a little of the courtly. When you enter their houses, they say, 'Tafaddal' ('Do us the favour'); and as you descend a stair in going away, you are followed by repeated exclamations of 'Anistînâ' ('You have been good company to us'), 'Sharaftînâ' ('You have honoured us').

I once partook of the Lord's Supper with the native congregation. I seated myself, as usual, in the front pew, for the purpose of hearing well, and found myself next to two young girls in white 'yashmaks,' who were about to be admitted to the membership of the church—*more Presbyteriano*. Before the distribution of the elements, the American ladies, pastors' wives, and school teachers came and seated themselves round a table in front of me, the congregation of Oriental women being in the pews behind. I was the only European, the only representative of the old country present, and it struck myself and others as singular that I should have placed myself exactly betwixt the children of the East and those children of the Far West who have brought back to them the Word of Life. It made me realize vividly how all nations may become one family in a common Saviour; and I trust that it was an earnest of the time when African, American, and European shall all be gathered round His throne.

Twice I dined with Coptic families. On both occasions the guests sat round the table, and ate with their fingers, round cakes of native bread doing duty for plates. The cookery in both houses was rather better than it generally is in first-class hotels, albeit the soup was flavoured with ginger, and the roast turkey stuffed with pistachio nuts and raisins. After the repast water was poured over our hands from a massive silver ewer, and we dried them with richly embroidered towels. On both occasions one member of the family did not sit down with the guests, but assisted the servants in waiting. The custom is evidently unchanged since the day when 'Martha served, but Lazarus was one of those who sat at meat with Jesus.'

One of the families who entertained us was beginning to adopt European manners, and all its members, with one exception, dined with us. In the house of the other, we only saw the ladies. These usually partake of what their husbands and sons leave, but the order was reversed on the occasion of their receiving us.

One of our hosts tried to persuade me that I was following a wrong method in learning Arabic.

'There is no use in studying the grammar,' he said. 'Ours is a tongue that can never be acquired from books. The Egyptian pronunciation is superior to that of any other country. We put a "sh" after many of our words, and this gives our speech a peculiar delicacy, which the Syrians have not.'

Had I followed the contradictory advice I received on this subject, I should have changed my teachers every week. A lady long resident in the country, who speaks Arabic fluently, told me that she never catches a new word from anyone's lips, unless she has already seen it in print; and I knew the 'sh' to be a vulgarity which educated Egyptians would like to drop.

The Copts have two strong claims on our interest. First, as their name (a shortened form of Αἰγύπτιοι Egyptians) implies, they are supposed to be descendants of the original inhabitants of the country, of the race which has left behind it such wonderful memorials of its religion, its art, and its civilization; the race which reared the pyramids, wrote the hieroglyphics, and embalmed the mummies. Secondly, they are without doubt the descendants of the early Christians of Egypt; their church is a relic of the one founded by St. Mark, or more probably by St. Peter, Babylon being the old Roman name of Cairo.

The name of the Copts first occurs in literature about the middle of the seventh century. They early seceded from the Church of Greece, or Byzantium, and were therefore treated as heretics. So bitter was the enmity thus engendered, and so heavy the oppression under which the Copts groaned, that they gladly welcomed the Moslem invaders, and brought on their own necks a yoke which has crushed all the intellectual life out of them. Still they excel in the industrial arts. Many competent judges are of opinion, although the point is far from being fully elucidated, that what we call Saracenic art is altogether a product of Coptic skill. Coptic masons built the splendid mosque, and reared the graceful minaret; Coptic artists carved the exquisite wooden screen, and laid the marble mosaics; Coptic weavers gave us all the rich fabrics which we are wont to attribute to their masters. They did everything, in fact, except write Arabic poetry and illuminate the Kurân.

Be that as it may, there is no denying that the best jewellers and other artisans now in Cairo are Copts; that as merchants they are more prosperous, and as secretaries more capable, than their Moslem fellow-citizens.

The Coptic Church does not differ much from the Greek in its tenets. It does not hold the doctrine of transubstantiation, its chapels, even those ancient ones which are hewn in the rock, and which date from the time of Helena, have no stone *altar*, only a communion *table*. The Copts consider that an altar would be out of place where there is no sacrifice.

'We gave up the altar,' they say, 'when we left the religion of our pagan ancestors.'

Their priests must be at least thirty-three years old when ordained. They are not allowed to marry, though they may keep a wife whom they have married previously; but, if she dies, they must not take a second wife. Pictures are used in the churches, but graven images are strictly forbidden.

One afternoon we called on a Coptic family, and one of the younger members told me he was going to a wedding. They were not people with whom he was intimate, he had only been invited by the bridegroom, who, like himself, was a clerk in the employment of the railway company. As oriental houses are on such occasions open to all comers, he good-naturedly proposed that I should accompany him.

Said was perfectly horrified that I should think of going to such a common wedding. But the manners of the lower middle classes are far more interesting to a foreigner than those of the higher ones. So at half-past five my young friend took me into a very narrow street, made still narrower by the windows projecting from the first floor. It is called Sûq-el-Kebîr, because it was formerly the best street in Cairo. We stopped at a house from which a number of ropes were stretched to the windows of the house opposite, all hung with little red and white flags and coloured lanterns. A band of musicians sat before the door, making a great clatter with their voices and their instruments, chiefly cymbals. We passed through two rooms, or open courts, on the ground floor, where many men sat smoking, and where two enormous glass chandeliers hung suspended from the windows of the top floor by common ropes. Mr. S—— led me up a stone staircase, and directed me to peep into an inner room, forbidden to him, where a bride squatted, dressed in pink, with her female friends round her. She had a glitter of silver spangles on her breast, and over her face was a short thick white veil embroidered with gold, the whole being almost concealed by a silk yashmak. On the very top of her head was a wreath, or diadem of crystals.

Mr. S—— then took me into the inner room, which was prepared for the ceremony. Sofas and chairs were placed against the walls, four arm-chairs being at the further end. In the centre was a small table, on which lay a Bible in a splendidly chased silver case, bearing an inscription in the Coptic tongue.* At the four corners of the table were four silver candlesticks, or rather taper-sticks, in the form of Maltese crosses.

The company were still below, and cymbals were clashing, whilst women and boys made such a noise of singing, or rather caterwauling, that we could hardly hear each other speak.

Mr. S——- advised me to sit on the corner of a sofa close to an open window which looked on to the court. I saw the reason of this; for a crowd of men and boys came streaming in. Each of the latter carried something tied in a coloured handkerchief. They undid these bundles, and pulled out what I at first supposed to be dirty linen. I was mistaken,

* The Coptic language is supposed to be identical with the ancient Egyptian. It has furnished the key to the hieroglyphics.

for they were white tunics, embroidered some with silver spangles, some with coloured wools, some showing large Maltese crosses, and some pictures of saints. These were the choir-boys. They next brought out embroidered sashes, which they threw across their little shoulders, and richly ornamented caps, which they placed on the top of their tarbooshes. Next came three priests, wearing black turbans. The one who was to officiate put on a vestment like a long apron, reaching from his throat to his feet, embroidered or painted with two long rows of pictured saints. They sang together the Lord's Prayer in a monotonous chant; then the boys went out, and returned leading the two bridegrooms, who, we were told, were uncle and nephew. Each was enveloped in a parti-coloured robe, worn over his European dress. They were placed in two of the arm-chairs, and the two brothers of the bride began fanning them with fans. Some more psalms were chanted, first in Coptic, then in Arabic; then the boys went out again and returned, followed by the two brothers, leading the two brides. The faces of the ladies were completely hidden by the short, gold-embroidered veils which fell a little below the chin. When each had been deposited in an arm-chair next to her betrothed, the boys sang a hymn, which must have resembled that sung in the Greek marriage service, for I caught the Arabic words,

'Christ is risen, is risen from the dead.'

The priest then asked the fathers of the two bridegrooms and the two brides,

'Do you consent to your children's marriage, and

can you say that there is mutual love and trust between them?'

The four fathers answered, 'Yes.' This was simply ridiculous, for we all knew that the two youths had never seen their brides' faces, nor would they do so until the company had gone. But they looked just as happy as bridegrooms are wont to do in Europe.

The officiating priest then read a portion of the New Testament, and a psalm in Coptic, one of the choristers reading them in Arabic after him. This they did with railway speed, without a trace of reverence. I could hardly have believed that human lips could have achieved such a triumph of celerity. Coptic is no longer a spoken language. I doubt if many of the priests understand a word of what they read. As to the Arabic, the only words of it which I caught showed me that they were reading the latter part of the fifth chapter of Ephesians just as they do in England and in Greece, also that the exhortation to the bridegroom and the bride finished word for word exactly like the marriage service of the Church of England. This was satisfactory, but the rapidity with which the whole was performed made me quite understand why the Coptic Church is spoken of as a dead one. I could not help wishing that some young curates in our own land who seem to have studied the art of reading quickly could have listened and taken warning. There was so much noise and chattering throughout the ceremony that the priest had often to stop and call out 'Uskût' ('Hush!') to the boys, 'Uskûti' to the girls.

Rings were now put on the fingers of brides and bridegrooms, and small gold diadems on their heads. Last of all a handsome embroidered napkin was thrown over the heads of each couple, their hands placed in each other's by the priests, and their faces laid against each other's in a most curious fashion. The boys, whilst singing, opened their mouths well, but the sound emitted was like the monotonous drawl of Turkish and Greek priests. Their ivory teeth gleamed from under their chocolate skins, but it was sad to observe the utter absence of intelligence in their fine black eyes. Incense had been freely swung at us, and the room was now full of all sorts of odours; the open window giving me a fresh dose of cold.

The brides now retired to another apartment, where the crowd of women made it impossible for me to approach them. The bridegrooms made haste to take off their gay robes, and I noticed that they wore white kid gloves.

We shook hands with them, saluting them in the most complimentary Arabic phrases we could think of, then descended the stairs, followed by a clatter of cymbals and a Babel of voices indescribable. Of course we had been asked to stay for supper; but I thought that this would be too great a risk for my health.

As we returned to the hotel, Mr. S—— explained that the marriage took place in the house of the elder bridegroom. Only invited guests were expected to go upstairs, and the one condition of welcome to the lower rooms was that a man have on a wedding-garment.

Mr. S—— told me that the style of singing I had just heard is supposed by some people to be identical with that of the old Hebrews. It may be so, but I cannot help thinking that Miriam must have struck her timbrel to a livelier strain.

The Copts have the custom of standing during the reading of the Gospel and during the prayers. They sit whilst singing. Kneeling at prayers is unknown, as they say that standing was the custom of the early church. I was somewhat surprised to find this point of resemblance between this ancient community and the Church of my native land. Nor is it the only one. Marriages are in Scotland celebrated in the house, and I have known old-fashioned people who think, like the Evangelical Copts, that hymns are an unwarranted innovation.

One day during Lent, I went to the Coptic cathedral, at the time when morning prayers were being read in a small room near the sacristy. Said accompanied me to the door, but would not enter. About fifty men were present, and, as there was a latticed wooden screen at the further end of the room, I suspected the presence of women behind it. A man accosted me, and I asked him to give me a chair, explaining that I was a stranger, who had never seen Coptic worship. He brought one from the sacristy, and directed me to sit, so as not to intrude on the space which is considered sacred. When praying the men prostrated themselves, touching the ground with their heads exactly like Moslems. I could not help thinking that this hardly agreed with what Mr. S—— had told me. But man is an imitative animal, so it is probably an innovation.

The service was all chanted in Arabic. I understood only the portions of the Gospel which were read. They were from the first chapter of St. Mark, about the preaching of John the Baptist. St. Mark is the patron saint of the Copts. Sometimes a priest came round and swung incense in our faces, sometimes a man approached the priests, and, kneeling, kissed their hands.

I sat there for about half-an-hour, then went out and found Said. A boy in the street asked if I would like to see the school. As I replied in the affirmative, he went in and brought the chief master. I addressed him in Arabic, and explained that being a foreigner, and understanding something of that language, I was curious to see what his boys were learning. He conducted me, without Said, into a large school-room, where I found myself in presence of some thirty boys from fourteen to twenty years of age.

Some of them read to me in Arabic from a history of Egypt in mediæval times. They spoke with great distinctness, being much better trained in this respect than the girls in the American school. But this is owing entirely to the difference of sex, the girls being early impressed with the idea that it is a breach of propriety for a woman to let her voice be heard above a whisper.

Another master came in who spoke a little English, and asked if I would like to hear what progress the elder pupils had made in that language. An English book was then brought. It contained

F

short histories of the various European countries. Four boys read from it. They had acquired a pretty good pronunciation; but they have not the advantage of conversation in English, as their master spoke only Arabic to them. The substance of what they read to me was to the effect that the Christian religion is much superior to the Moslem.

'You may travel all over Asia,' it said, 'and you will find whole countries in which there is not a single temple in which the true God is worshipped. European cities, on the contrary, are full of churches, schools, museums, hospitals, and charities of all kinds.

'Stop a moment,' said the master, speaking partly in Arabic, partly in English, 'can any one of you give me a proof why the Christian religion is better than the Moslem?'

'I'll tell you when I come to the end of this,' said the boy, who was reading.

I considered this disobedience, but the master was perfectly contented. 'Taîb taîb,' he said, and the boy continued,

'How important it is to be a real Christian!'

'Now can you give me a proof?' said the master. There was silence.

'Then *I* will give you one. You know the Christian religion commands us to be temperate. A Christian must have only one wife, whereas a Moslem may have many. And a Christian must fast during Lent, he must eat no flesh, nor fish, nor eggs, nor butter, nor milk. Now, is it not much better for you to be Christians than Moslems?'

It happened that I had eaten an egg that very

morning, so I was by no means inclined to subscribe to the master's definition. The boys all said, 'Eiwa' (' yes,') and the master 'Khalas,' which means 'It is finished,' making a gesture as if he considered the lesson over. But I determined to try to put a fresh idea into their young heads.

'There is something I wish to say,' I said. 'Will you let me tell you what I think a proof of the excellence of our religion?'

'Certainly,' replied both the masters. The boys seemed eager to hear what I had to say. They were evidently amused and pleased at hearing a foreigner speak Arabic.

'You know,' I said, 'that Mohammed tried to conquer the world by the sword, but our Saviour conquered it by love. He said, "Love your enemies." Now is that not a proof?'

'Eiwa, eiwa,' they said, quite delighted.

'I want to tell you,' I continued, ' what I think a real Christian is. You know that in our churches in Europe there are some things different from what you have in your church. But there is one thing in which all our churches agree, and it is that to be a real Christian we must love the Lord Jesus Christ, who is the Son of God, and our Saviour, and we must love the New Testament, the *Angeel*, because it is His Word.'

Masters and pupils seemed highly gratified. One of the former, indeed, repeated my words with a few variations of his own after I had finished.

I said a little more about the value of a good education. I told them that it was possible for them to earn a great deal of money, and then lose it, but that what they acquired in school would never be lost, it was a property which they could carry with them wherever they went. I then made the customary salutations, and the boys all stood up respectfully as I left the room, followed by the two masters. On reaching the outer hall I paused to ask a few questions.

'How many boys have you in the school?'

'Three hundred,' they replied.

'And how many girls?'

'Two hundred.'

'Do you teach the girls the same lessons as the boys?'

'No; the boys learn English and French, and the girls only Arabic. Foreign languages are not much use to a girl. The boys can earn their bread by knowing them. And we only teach the girls simple things.'

'I quite agree with you about languages,' I replied. 'I don't see why the girls need anything beyond their own tongue. But our girls in England have the same lessons that the boys have. We find it much the better plan.'

'But we don't want our girls to know too much,' exclaimed one of the masters. 'We don't want to change the customs (sunnat) of our fathers. We love our church, and we have our old customs, and we don't want to change anything.'

'That does not surprise me,' I said. 'But if it *was* the custom of your fathers to keep their women shut up behind a curtain, and teach them as little as possible, they got that custom from the Moslems, for it is not in the Gospel. St. Paul said that women were to keep silence in the churches: but he never said they were not to learn anything.'

The two men's faces were getting graver as I spoke. They had been pleased, nay, delighted, when I spoke to the boys about our Saviour's love, and I was really grieved at finding a point on which we differed so widely. They looked far from satisfied when I bade them farewell. My first care on returning to the hotel was to find an Arabic Old Testament, and commit to memory the passage in which we are told how the Lord God said, 'It is not good that the man should be alone; I will make him an helpmeet *like unto him.*' I thought the passage would be a good one to quote to Mohammedans as well as to Copts, and the *mu 'in nazîrahi* of the Arabic version seemed to me much more emphatic than do the words of our Revised Version. This is noteworthy, seeing that Arabic is the sister tongue of Hebrew.

I told my friends of the American mission about my visit to the Coptic school.

'The boys get a fair education there,' they said. 'When we first came the Copts had few schools, now they have good ones all over the country, and they are always trying to improve them, in the hope of keeping the children from coming to us. They call us "ravening wolves." But we rejoice in their progress, for we feel that we have been indirectly the cause of this good.'

I related the story of my visit to a gentleman long resident in the country. He was very much amused with it.

'Do you not know,' he said, 'that the education of

women is a burning question with the Copts. They are very sore about it, for European influence bears hard upon them, and they are beginning to feel that they cannot keep their women in such great subjection much longer. It is really a question of expense. At present the wife is a servant. She does all the household work, and stays in the kitchen, whilst her husband apes the European. If she were better educated, he would have to hire a servant, and let his wife sit at table with him. He would have to spend as much on dress and luxuries for her as he does for himself. So they want to keep off the evil day as long as possible.'

'A young Coptic gentleman, an acquaintance of ours, is in great perplexity on this subject. He really thinks he will have to go to England to get a wife, for marry an Egyptian he cannot. He would rather have the company of his dog than that of a Coptic woman. And he has picked up a little dog from the street, and trained it to be both intelligent and affectionate.'

I suggested that this young man would have a difficulty in getting an English lady. No one would care to become a subject of the Khedive by marrying a Copt, and, if the young man were to get naturalized as a British subject, he would be like an exotic in his own country.

We may see from this that all efforts to improve the education of foreign races must, if they are to be really effective, aim at the elevation of both sexes, *pari passu*.

I was told of a case where the conditions are reversed. It was that of a school in Syria, I think in

Nazareth, where husbands cannot be found for the girls. They are trained to European habits of cleanliness, and to English notions of propriety. Were one of them to wed one of her own countrymen, she would be simply miserable, and this even if he were the kindest of spouses.

CHAPTER V.

ALEXANDRIA TO BEYROUT.

Miss Robinson's Soldiers' and Sailors' Homes—On Board the *La Seyne*—Fellow-passengers—Jaffa—Difficulty of Finding Servants for Cyprus—Tents or no Tents?—Risks of Travel in Cyprus—Roads in Cyprus—A Storm—Delay in Departure—Opportunity for Learning Language—A Roman Catholic Teacher—Beyrout Schools—Work of Americans—Mrs. Bowen Thompson—School of Society of Friends—Excursion to Nahr-el-Kelb.

WE thought, when at Cairo, that it might be possible to engage a dragoman there who had been in Cyprus. A fatal objection to Said was that he knew no Greek. Though the natives of these countries have a *lingua franca* which serves them for all practical purposes, we felt that our journey would be more profitable under the guidance of one who was in thorough sympathy, religious and linguistic, with the people.

Our consul, to whom we applied for advice, had no other resource than to recommend our applying to Cook's agent. The proprietor of one of the restaurants in the Ezbekiah garden had spent some years in Larnaca. His wife tried to dissuade us from going there. She said that we could not spend more than a week in the place without catching fever; that there was no decent hotel, and no food fit for a European. She had lost her health there.

We suspected, however, that the bad quality of the food and of the wine might have resulted rather from a temporary ebb in the family purse than from a lack of fruitfulness in the ground, so we took her husband's opinion also. He said that Larnaca was certainly not attractive, but that Cyprus was fairly healthy, especially in the mountain districts. The island, moreover, has great attractions for the antiquarian, and the accommodation in the houses is not bad. Neither he nor anyone else could tell us whether or not we should take tents. The advice given by Mr. Hamilton Lang and by Sir Samuel Baker is decidedly against their use in a climate where the dews are so heavy.

We at length resolved to defer providing ourselves with a dragoman until we should reach Beyrout.

Said accompanied us to Alexandria. The principal streets of this city were blocked with building materials, heaps of stones, open drains, cart-loads and piles of sand much blown about by the wind. Handsome houses are being erected, most of them having shops on the ground-floor, and the noise of hammer and chisel prevails. One side of the great square is still in ruins—not a trace remains of the hotels and shops which we knew on our former visit; the other side is partly rebuilt, the handsome style of its houses and shops showing that there is no drying-up in the perennial stream of wealth which always flows through the place. The Alexandrian forts will, however, long retain traces of the bombardment, many human remains being still found in the battered walls.

Opinions vary as to how far our Government was

justified in this action of our fleet. It was certainly the beginning of our armed interference in the affairs of the country, and perhaps Arabi's rebellion, which was a danger to Christendom, could not have been checked without it. But what foreigners urge, and what always brings the blush to an English cheek, is this: why did our guns open fire before Admiral Seymour knew that he had a force ready to land for the preservation of order? Why was the refuse of society left free to set the city on fire? If neither our admiral nor our government were to blame, is there not a defect in our system either of naval training or of management? It certainly strikes us as remarkable that the axiom: 'Never bombard unless you are prepared to land troops,' should be spoken of as one of the commonplaces of military knowledge, and yet that our people should have been completely oblivious of it.

Brighter thoughts were suggested by a visit to Miss Robinson's admirable 'Soldiers' and Sailors' Institute.' Politicians may come and go, but one feels on its very threshold that the heart of a people whose daughters design and manage such a scheme, is sound. It consists of a handsome house, with a commodious iron hall attached to it. The hall is full of chairs and little tables, books and book-cases.

It was early morning when we entered, but a man was busy arranging things at a tea and coffee bar. A young lady, who had helped to manage the place during the winter, showed us the billiard-table and the pretty little garden, also the hall used for lectures and entertainments, which had just been supplied with a new piano, and where ladies and gentlemen, many of them being officers and their relatives, have the opportunity of employing their talents for the instruction and amusement of the men. There are smaller rooms where secular classes are held during the week, with Scripture ones on Sundays; others are fitted up with bunks, &c., where men on leave may pass the night. Connected with the place, but approached by a separate entrance, is a luxuriously-furnished gentlemen's club, with a library; and two small parlours, as the beginning of a ladies' club.

Said was perfectly amazed that such provision should be made for common soldiers. He was unable to answer the question, 'Why do you Egyptians not do the same for your own people?' Beer is permitted on the premises, but no wine nor strong drink. All British soldiers and sailors have the right of entry without payment, but of course each defrays the cost of the victuals he orders.

Said's only sister lives at Alexandria. She is the wife of a Pasha, who was for many years Governor of Suez, and still enjoys a pension from the Khedive. We were invited to pay them a visit. Their house is a pretty villa, situated in a garden. Said's sister is very fine-looking, and is now the only wife. She sometimes walks abroad, attended by her servants, or drives in a carriage, but is never allowed to walk or sit in the garden. In the vestibule of the house, eight mollahs sat on the floor, reciting a portion of the Kurân. The Pasha pays them to do so for several hours a day, and this is considered a meritorious act on his part, though it is not in the least necessary that he should listen to them.

We left Alexandria on March 14th in *La Seyne*, of the Messageries Maritimes. Her captain was a clever, agreeable man, who, having few passengers, did his best to persuade us into altering our plans, by going on straight to Larnaca, and there securing both tents and dragoman. He and an intelligent French priest from the Lebanon reiterated the opinion, which we had heard from the lips of several of their fellow-countrymen, that Cyprus is not worth seeing; that the English have done nothing for it; that it is full of fever, and that we should be completely disappointed.

The air was at Jaffa filled with the scent of orange-flowers, which the captain positively asserted he has sometimes detected when at a distance of twenty miles from the shore. The sea was somewhat rough, and a large party of Cook's, who had travelled with us from Port Said, were disembarked with difficulty in the little boats. A number of wild-looking Arabs stood on the gangway, hustling the passengers down, and flinging about their packages in a way that baffles description. They had a fight about one package, a bundle of rugs. They struck and kicked each other; they knocked one man's teeth out, and one of them, seizing his adversary by the chin, pressed back his head till I thought he would be strangled. Two Roman Catholic priests, residents in Syria, sat calmly looking on in the boat which was rocking beneath, whilst the captain, steward, and sailors looked on from above, amused, but apparently unconcerned. I, supposing that I was about to witness a murder, got rather excited, and begged one person after

another to interfere. Two Arab merchants, travelling in the first-class, to whom I applied, said,
'Thou needst not fear; a dog never gets strangled.'
The captain said: 'Oh, I believe it's all for bakhsheesh. It happens every time we stop at Jaffa. That fellow will claim that he has defended some gentleman's property at the risk of his life.'

This may be quite true; but I submit that a scene so alarming ought not to be permitted on the gangway of a well-ordered French passenger boat.

The Beyrout boatmen behaved better, possibly because they belong to a town which is, for the most part, Christian. The landlord of the 'Hôtel d'Orient' (to whom we had telegraphed) came, with a boat, to take us ashore; and the only difficulty we had was at the Custom House. Our boxes were opened on the quay, or rather on the dusty street, in the midst of a motley crowd, who made remarks about everything. It was very annoying to see the hands of an Arab official thrust deep down amongst our well-packed dresses. Much amusement was caused by his exploration of my writing-satchel. He got hold of the ink-bottle, and was evidently unable to read the three letters descriptive of its contents, which were inscribed on it. In vain did I tell him, and so did the crowd, that it was 'hibr.' I knew that a touch of the spring with his clumsy finger would inevitably result in the bespattering of his face. Fortunately, however, he did not succeed in discovering the spring.

We got a beautiful room, with windows on two sides, commanding a fine view of the bay and the lofty mountains of the Lebanon, some crowned with snow, and others dotted with villages. The glossy green of the gardens, relieved by the yellow of the orange and the lemon and the bright red of the pomegranate, the broad streets, better kept than those of most Eastern towns, and the delicious freshness of the sea breeze, made us at first think Beyrout one of the most delightful of residences. We were soon told, however, of intolerable summer heats, from which the wealthier Europeans take refuge in the mountains; and of a still more serious matter, the insufficiency of the tide to carry off the sewage flowing into the sea.

Soon after our arrival, a dragoman presented himself. He had excellent testimonials, but none of these were of later date than 1879. This did not quite satisfy us, as we like to know how a man conducted himself during his last engagement. Moreover, he had never been in Cyprus, nor did he know a word of Greek. And there was too much swagger about him to please us.

The British consul, Mr. Eldridge, had been for some time incapacitated from attending to his duties. His place was filled, *pro tem.*, by a young man whose experience could not be equal to his chief's, but who knew enough of the country to say that it would be extremely difficult to find a dragoman who had already been in Cyprus; that Arab servants would be necessary, if we wished to travel with tents, but that few of these understood Greek.

The Belgian consul, who frequently came to the hotel, told us that we had been badly advised to think of travelling in Cyprus. 'There was not a tree,' he said, 'on the whole island; and we would find that we had had enough of it in a fortnight. It was extremely unhealthy, and the English had done nothing for it.'

We went to the only bookseller's in the town for the purpose of securing the works of De Cesnola, or of Sir Samuel Baker. Neither were to be heard of anywhere in the neighbourhood; but we purchased the small volume of De La Mas Latrie. The bulk of this book is a history of the reign of the Lusignan family, to whom our own sovereign, King Richard I., once sold the island. It is, therefore, less interesting to us than to the author's fellow-countrymen; but we were delighted to find in its pages, not only enthusiastic descriptions of beautiful scenery, but a very favourable account of the climate.

We asked the opinion of a Church of England missionary, whose duties involve travelling over Asia Minor for a great part of the year. He smiled at our apprehensions.

'Spring is not the season for fever,' he said, 'and you are not the people to take it. In places which are considered unhealthy, attacks occur when the waters get low in autumn or late summer. If you once take intermittent fever you can never quite get rid of it, but are always liable to its recurrence. This my wife and I know to our cost. It comes on you when the body is exhausted by a long ride or other great exertion, and you have not a good meal ready for you in the evening. No one who travels about with a cook need fear it.

There were, happily, two families in the hotel who

could give us almost all the information we sought. There was a Mr. and a Mrs. Thornton, who had themselves travelled over Cyprus, with tents, for two months in autumn, shortly after the cession of the island. They were now preparing for an expedition to some place in the south of the Holy Land. There was also a Miss Ripley, who had done the same thing, and was now about to start on an adventurous trip with a lady companion across the country to Bagdad.

All these had travelled with tents, and seemed to be unaware of any danger attending their use. Mr. Thornton was especially indignant at the notion that the English have done nothing for Cyprus.

'Why, they have made excellent roads over a great part of it,' he said, 'roads, I mean, that are good enough for a carriole, though not for a large carriage. You should just see the road the soldiers who were encamped on Mount Troados made from there to Limasol the very first year we had it.'

All three agreed that there was no danger of fever, not even at Famagousta. All three travelled without a dragoman: Mr. Thornton because he has been often in the East, and is a good Arabic scholar, and Miss Ripley because she has found a native 'contractor' who does the duties of one without being tied down to a written agreement.

We ourselves thought it would be a good plan, seeing that I could talk Greek, to engage a travelling servant, paying him wages and availing ourselves of his help in making bargains with others, while defraying our daily expenses.

There was, however, a difficulty in procuring

tents, as all the owners of them were at this season journeying through the Holy Land, and making more profit as dragomans than they would do by hiring them out.

The only tents we could hear of belonged to Mr. Joseph Mezher, landlord of the Hôtel d'Orient, who had formerly been a dragoman himself. Mr. Mezher did not approve of our plan. He thought it would prove very expensive, as everyone would try to impose on us, and give us a great deal of worry.

'I have good tents,' he said; 'but I cannot hire them out to a man whom I do not know personally. You, Miss Violet, proposed the other day to take George Wakîm, the commissionaire of the hotel, as travelling-servant. I can recommend him confidently as a dragoman, and I will guarantee that you shall have everything first-class.'

We fixed Monday, April 5th, as the date of our departure. In a few days, however, the mountains of Lebanon became shrouded in mist, and heavy rains set in. The nights were bitterly cold, and the prospect of sleeping in tents did not seem inviting.

The Thorntons left in spite of the weather. Miss Ripley postponed her departure for three days, sharing the general opinion, that these were the regular spring rains which had come rather late this season, but which, once over, would recur only for a few hours at a time until November. As the opportunity of going to Cyprus came only once a fortnight, it was necessary that we should be decided. Violet wished to postpone the date of our sailing. She feared lest we might be detained in some lonely place by storms, and as we had suffered much from floods and mud last year in Thessaly, she had a vivid recollection of what we might have to endure. I, on the contrary, was anxious to lose no further time, and represented that this was April, a month generally propitious to travellers, whereas our unlucky Thessalian expedition occurred in March. We at length agreed to consult Mr. Stuart, manager of the Imperial Ottoman Bank, who had spent many years in Nicosia.

This gentleman gave it as his decided opinion that we should wait. Fine weather might follow the 5th of April, and the eastern part of Cyprus might be very agreeable. But, supposing the weather there to be anything like what it was at Beyrout, the mountain paths in the Troados, or western part, would not dry in a day, and were very difficult to traverse when muddy.

Mr. Stuart quite approved of our taking tents, and sketched a route which he thought we might follow. He also gave us the names of some excellent muleteers, who live at Athieno (sometimes called the muleteer village), half way betwixt Larnaca and Leucosia, working backwards and forwards between the two towns.

Miss Ripley told us that she had found the roads in Cyprus generally good, and that doubtless they had improved under British rule. One road, however, that between Lefka and Kykko, was the worst she had ever seen. It ran over a wild mountain pass, and was so narrow that there was no room for a man to walk by the side of your horse to assist you should it make a false step and slip over the edge of the precipice. She had trembled to think what might have been the result had anyone happened to meet her who was going the other way. The distance between the two places is given in Murray as three hours, *i.e.*, nine miles. Miss Ripley said she believed it was so, as, to the best of her recollection, she had done it in a short day.

I therefore promised Violet that we should try to avoid this road, and seek to discover some other route across the western part of the island.

Mr. Mezher had taken tickets for us in the Austrian Lloyd boat for April 5, and gave up the cabin very unwillingly when he found that we had decided on waiting. I too regretted this when the weather became brilliant.

So we retired to rest on Saturday, April 3. About midnight the wind rose, lashing the sea into huge, roaring billows. There were four windows in our room, none of which was securely fastened, and my bed was placed against one of them. All of them overlooked the sea, and the outer shutters, being loose, rattled and struck the walls. My bed seemed to get several knocks, and we congratulated ourselves that we were not about to start for Larnaca.

The sea was a glorious sight next morning. The wind howled furiously over a wilderness of tossing billows. All who intended to sail next day were groaning, and we looked forward to an invasion of people who had been unable to land at Jaffa. Five steamboat companies are wont to make their vessels arrive at Beyrout on a Monday morning—the Austrian Lloyd, the French Messageries, the Russian, the Khedivial, Papayanni's, and probably others.

We walked in the afternoon to Râs Beyrout, past

the American College, as far as the lighthouse. To our extreme surprise, we found that the sea on the southern side of the cape was less rough, and we could observe exactly where the commotion began.

The storm abated towards evening. Next morning it was so calm, and the air so warm, that even Violet began to regret our decision.

Looking out at 7.15, we saw six huge steamers sail in together. But it soon began to rain, and heavy clouds gathered on the mountains. One result of the steamboat arrangements is that the Beyrout hotels, after being nearly empty towards the end of the week, get overcrowded on Mondays. Howard's party, twenty-two in number, and Stanger's, almost equally large, were waiting to go, and the new arrivals could not get apartments until they should be off. There were four immense tables at luncheon-time, and all were congratulating themselves on the calm sea.

But, alas! no sooner did we rise than the sea began to rise too. We spent the afternoon on the balcony witnessing a most exciting scene. The waves were as high as could be, and the only place where boats could safely leave the shore was a sandy creek fringed with rocks in front of the hotel. The only approach to this from the embanked roadway was down a steep wall, against which was planted the roughest of ladders, and down this one lady after another descended, a man behind holding down her skirts. A white horse got loose, and began kicking amongst the crowd; it was at last cleverly caught by George, our future dragoman. The ladies were carried, each by two men, from the shore into the little boats. As these, one by one, set off on the raging sea, the people in the hotel who had not yet left were in a state bordering on distraction, wishing that they had either gone on board an hour earlier, or that they had not got Gaze's* tickets, and were at liberty to wait for better weather. Every moment the sea was getting worse. We took a short walk, and were half-blinded by the sand and gravel blowing in our faces.

As each boat went and returned, it was lost to view in the trough of each succeeding wave, and we spent the afternoon praying fervently for the safety of the travellers, and of the brave boatmen. The Arabs on shore cheered lustily whenever a boat came riding into the creek on the top of a great billow. I know that I should not have risked my life by embarking had I been so unfortunate as to hold a ticket even from Beyrout to Marseilles.

One boat, containing two gentlemen, was overturned when close to a steamer. They were, however, fished out by the Arabs, and all got away without further accident.

We had now another fortnight to spend at Beyrout. I profited by the opportunity to get another Arabic teacher, the master of a boys' school, who knew no European language, and was therefore ready to converse in his own. He was a most painstaking man, and was, as I have already mentioned, the first of my native instructors who did his best to give me a correct pronunciation. I had

* Gaze contracts with Howard to take his tourists through the Holy Land. I believe these were all, in 1886, well-satisfied with his arrangements.

not till then realised the difficulty of Arabic gutturals, and it seemed passing strange that I should have been allowed to study Dr. Wright's grammar and to read the Kurân carefully twice before being made aware that such gutturals existed. When I consider that languages are taught to boys in England more by the eye than the ear, and that Orientals are so lethargic, I feel less disposed than I used to be to share Captain Burton's astonishment at so few of our British officers speaking it.

This delightful tongue, besides the *h* of him, and the *ch* of the Scotch *loch* (usually written *kh*), has at least four guttural sounds which have no equivalent in a European tongue. To pronounce one of these (the *'ain*) I was directed to imagine myself choking like a naughty child when it cries, and to think at the same time of a raven's croak. Another (the *ghain*) is the sound emitted by a newly-born baby camel. It comes from the soft palate, and to pronounce it you must imagine that you are gargling, or rather that you wish to be sea-sick. Another (the *h* of *ahsan*) is soft to the ear, but requires the full force of one's lungs for its formation. It comes from the top of the windpipe, and cannot be comprehended unless heard. I felt exhausted after practising it. The fourth is the *q* in *Qurân*. It is produced by a jerk in the soft palate, or by trying to say *k* without moving the tongue.

Mr. Thornton thought that I had gone to work in a very difficult way, by trying to acquire the spoken dialects of Egypt and Syria. As he lays great stress on purity of style, he has himself no wish to speak with the common Arabs. I, on the other hand, value the knowledge of a foreign tongue chiefly for the opportunities it gives me of intercourse with the natives. I find a peculiar charm in exchanging ideas with people whose thoughts run in a groove widely different from my own.

My Beyrout teacher was a Roman Catholic. Whatever he taught his boys, I am sure they would know well, but I was astonished to learn that he had no map in his school except a small one of France, for the benefit of those who were learning French from an assistant-master. I judged him to be a sincere Christian, but his knowledge of geography and other subjects was woefully circumscribed. When I described to him our trip to the North Cape and our view of the midnight sun, I believe he thought it was a tale from some European version of the Thousand and One Nights.

Very interesting to us were the Beyrout schools. Foremost of them is the Syrian Protestant College, founded by American missionaries, whose aim is to give a thorough literary, scientific, medical, and pharmaceutical education, with a correct knowledge of English and Arabic. Students are charged from eleven to twenty-three pounds for board, with about four pounds ten shillings for tuition fees in the preparatory and collegiate departments, and nine pounds in the medical. The building is a very handsome one, occupying by far the finest and healthiest position in the neighbourhood, and standing in several acres of garden. It has nineteen professors. Since its opening in 1866 it counts two hundred and thirty-three graduates, and four hundred and seventeen other students who have taken a partial course of study. We were told that pupils of the Jesuits' school sometimes finish in it. The language of the college is, as far as possible, English, all the examinations being held in that tongue.

I at first doubted the wisdom of this arrangement. It seemed to me hardly necessary, seeing that Arabic is so rich and flexible, so perfectly capable of expressing all modern ideas; seeing also that the American professors have translated into it so many scientific works. It seemed to me that they were neglecting a valuable means of ennobling and improving an ancient tongue, and thereby encouraging the scattering of fresh ideas amongst the masses. I was told, however, that a perfect knowledge of scientific English opens to the Eastern student the whole treasure-house of European knowledge, and enables him to appreciate at once every fresh addition to it.

We certainly ought to thank the Americans for an indirect result of their labours. By insisting on the use of English they are doing much to increase the power of British influence in the Levant. It is unreasonable, but nevertheless it is the fact, that a man's sympathies go most with the nation whose language he understands.

But we ourselves are not behind in good works. An English lady, Mrs. Bowen Thompson, just after the massacres of 1860, founded an excellent training-school for girls, to which are affiliated more than thirty day-schools in various parts of the town.

The training-school is a handsome house in a fine garden, situated high above the sea, and commanding lovely views. It has fifty-three boarders, and thirty-six day-boarders, who all take part in the house work and the laundry. The rooms are large, airy, and well-lighted. The infants are taught on the Kindergarten system. They sang some of their little Arabic songs, and went through a play exercise representing a hen and her chickens. In the garden was a gymnastic apparatus, which proved the public opinion of Beyrout to be more advanced than that of Egypt. My young friends in the Cairo school dare not have used such a thing. I noticed also that, though the two sexes sit separate in church during the Arabic service, there was no curtain to hide them from each other.

Mrs. Bowen Thompson died a few years ago. Her place has been ably filled by her sister, Mrs. Mott, who, in view of her now feeble health, has lately conveyed the management and titles of the property to a board of trustees.

We had only one regret, after seeing this admirably planned and admirably managed institution. It was this, that schools of a similar kind, where domestic economy and mental culture are both attended to, are not more common in England, and that the money of our countrymen should be spent in giving Syrian girls a training beyond the reach of English girls of the same class.

These schools have the great advantage of being managed, not by a committee, but by a philanthropic and practical lady, who need fear no interference with her plans from outsiders.

The Society of Friends has also an hospital, training homes for boys and for girls, and a dispensary at

Brumana, a beautiful and healthy spot on Mount Lebanon. They have day-schools in eight of the villages. This mission was begun about ten years ago, and their staff of workers, though small, must form an invaluable supplement to the more imposing missions from America and from England.

The people of Beyrout are indeed to be envied. All the great nations of Europe, and America likewise, vie with each other for the honour of teaching them. The Jesuits have a large school, of course under French influence; the Kaiserswerth deaconesses have a seminary for young ladies; and Italy, too, has her educational representatives. The Arabs can thus learn several languages at first-hand. We can only hope that they appreciate their privileges.

We did not think of visiting Damascus, partly because we had done so on our first visit to Palestine, and partly because it would have involved two fatiguing days in the diligence, or else a journey with tents, which it was hardly worth while to take for so short a time. We contented ourselves with an excursion to Nahr-el-Kelb, the Dog River, so called either because a rock in the sea near its mouth has a striking resemblance to a dog with a fine, black tail, or because the idol of a dog or a wolf was once worshipped there. Near it are some figures and inscriptions on the rocks, so obliterated as to be hardly worth seeing, but possessing great historical interest as being memorials of the Egyptian Rameses II., and of the Assyrian Sennacherib.

CHAPTER VI.

BEYROUT TO CYPRUS.

The 'Rio Grande'—Fellow-Passengers—Tripoli—Off Larnaca—The Custom House—Climate of Cyprus—The Tents—Origin of Name Cyprus—Mr. Hamilton Lang's Views—Mr. Watkins' Opinions on the Cypriotes—Disturbed Slumbers—Our Cavalcade—George, the Dragoman—Peculiar Greek and More Peculiar English—Mangled Italian—George's Character—Salim—Constantine the Cook—A Confusion of Georges—Ibrahim the Arab.

WE left Beyrout on April 17, in the steamship *Rio Grande* of the Messageries Maritimes. This involved a two days' voyage to Larnaca, but the Austrian Lloyd's boat was appropriated by two parties of Cook's, numbering ninety in all, and there had been no possibility of securing a cabin for us. The *Rio Grande* had not many passengers, owing, probably, to the fact that the Messageries Company never give reductions in their fares, and are thus shunned by the great tourist agents. Our waiter, cook, and Arab muleteer, with the tents and luggage, went in the Austrian boat, so as to arrive a day before us.

Our only notable fellow-passsenger was a young Persian, who had been contractor to our troops in Afghanistan and in the Soudan. He is a British subject, but, as his parents and the rest of his family still live in Persia, he has not lost his nationality, and we were anxious to know his opinion about affairs in the East. He considered that the Soudan campaign cannot be called unsuccessful, because it effectually checked the wave of Moslem fanaticism which otherwise would have broken over Egypt and Turkey. At the same time our Government have acted wisely in withdrawing our troops from Dongola. Those who clamour for an advance on that place have no idea how enormously a few more rocks in the river multiply difficulties of transport, and entail untold hardships on our poor, brave soldiers. These stand the climate badly, but they bear everything without a grumble; their devotion to duty being surpassed only by that of the Sisters who come out to nurse them. No doubt, the people of Dongola, who have supplied our troops with provisions, will suffer by their absence, but then it was a question of the life or death of our men, whose presence up the Nile was a fearful drain on our army, and tied our hands as regards Russian intrigue in Afghanistan.

It is nonsense to say that the arrival of Stewart a few days sooner would have saved Gordon, for the Mahdi had Khartoum in his power for months before it fell, and used it as a decoy-duck for the British troops.

'What do you think of Afghanistan?' we asked.

'Your Government does wisely,' he replied, 'in helping the Afghans to arm against Russia. But you can never quite count on the Afghans, they are bad people. You can count, however, on the loyalty of all classes in India. The Indians know, of course, that your rule over them is founded on might; but they know also that Russia would treat them very much worse. Your great strength lies in the fact that you deal equal justice to all. We Persians prefer living in India to living in our own country. Where else could we enjoy such freedom?'

'And what do you think of Lord Ripon's policy?'

'He was perfectly in the right, notwithstanding the outcry that was made against him. He gave the power of trying Englishmen only to a few native magistrates, one of whose qualifications for office is, that they have been educated in England. There are districts in which a solitary English planter lives, and such an one has been known to kick and abuse his native servants, and there is no means of punishing him unless he can be brought before a native magistrate. Besides, a native judge will deal far more gently with an Englishman than with one of his own people, having a natural wish to stand well with the ruling race; and there is so much newspaper criticism that a case of injustice would be known at once all over the country. Lord Dufferin has just wisely continued Lord Ripon's policy, without making any noise about it.'

We landed at Tripoli, and spent a day amongst its orange gardens. It is picturesquely situated at the foot of Mount Lebanon, but is not such a good port as Beyrout, steamboats having to anchor very far out, and the landing being dangerous for little boats in rough weather. We walked to the upper town, and had the pleasure of seeing a place that still remains thoroughly Oriental, not a European face to be seen in it, and not a European word to be heard.

We were off Larnaca by six a.m. Violet had her

luggage ready strapped, the captain having told her that the sea there always got too rough for landing comfortably after half-past eight. I was not so active, nor could *pratique* be got in a moment; so it was eight before we found ourselves in the little boat which our waiter Salim had brought for us. We had to row some distance to the shore. There is a new asphalted street all the length of the beach, and a long wooden quay, built at a cost of one thousand pounds, with two sets of rails, for the conveyance of goods on wheeled cars. Larnaca is a small, straggling town of white, flat-roofed houses, enlivened by a few palm-trees and two slender minarets. The hills around it are white, with very scanty verdure, and this gives strangers, on their first arrival, very false ideas about the scenery of the island.

We went first into the Custom House, where the chief officer, a Maltese, was very civil, and said that we need not open our boxes, if we would sign a document to the effect that they contained nothing contraband. But he could not find a declaration paper, some one having mislaid a key. So we sat for about half-an-hour watching his proceedings, whilst he examined everything in the boxes of some Arabs. One of these was an old Bedawee, who had just come from Tarâblûs (Tripoli). A painter would have become famous could he have caught the pathetic expression that came over this man's face when his gun was taken from him, and a receipt written out for it. It was deposited in a cupboard, to be returned to him when he should leave the island. He seemed hardly able to grasp the idea of a state of things where a man can be safe and respected without his weapons. Boxes of women's clothing were next opened, and the Maltese took away many oranges and lemons that were hidden amongst their folds.

'We must be very strict in not allowing fruit to enter,' he remarked to us. 'It would hurt the island greatly.'

We thought he meant from a commercial point of view. We have since learnt that the islanders fear the introduction of tree disease from Egypt or Turkey. The same officer had pitched into the sea on the previous day a quantity of oranges, lemons, and tomatoes which had been brought for us from Beyrout.

'How do you like Cyprus?' we asked him.

'Very much,' he replied. 'This is a far finer climate than Malta. No one would ever take fever here, if they would only use a little reasonable care.'

The key could not be found, so we came away without signing the declaration. George promised to send for it in the evening, but I believe he forgot to do so. Our saddles had already been placed on two mules, and, as it was very hot, we were glad to mount, and ride to a little grassy hill above the town, where our tents had been pitched.

These were three in number, a dining one of fourteen cords, a sleeping one of twelve, and a small kitchen one. I wished to have our beds moved into the largest tent, but was told that it was older, and not quite so good as the other; we therefore agreed to let matters stand as they were.

The tents were all white on the outside, but were

beautifully ornamented within by a design in dark-blue, red, and yellow. This, of course, added nothing to our real comfort, but it made an impression on strangers of great luxury and magnificence. The ground beneath was quite concealed by thick Turkey carpets. Our own iron bedsteads, thin cork mattresses and waterproof valances, with blankets, pillows, and blue counterpanes, all fitting into a pair of brown waterproof valises, were exactly the same as we had had in Greece.

The weather was very sultry, so we spent the day in resting, and in arranging for the morrow's journey. Having made the acquaintance of two muleteers who had sympathetic faces, and spoke very intelligible Greek, I went into the town in the cool of the afternoon.

Larnaca occupies the site of the ancient Citium, or Chittim, which was a Phœnician colony. Its name is unpleasant to classical scholars, for it signifies 'a coffin,' though in very early times λάρναξ was simply a chest where household stuffs might be kept.* Some have suggested that the lugubrious title arose from the prevalence of fever; but the number of ancient tombs in and around the town are quite sufficient to account for it. More than half the town, Mr. Hamilton Lang tells us, stands upon the cemetery of Citium, and a marsh occupies the site of the former enclosed harbour, the sea having retired considerably from this part of the coast. This explains why the once-famous seaport is now only an open roadstead.

We learn something about the origin of that sea-

* Iliad xviii. 413.

port from the Book of Genesis. One of the sons of Japheth was Javan, who is supposed to be the progenitor of the Ionian Greeks. Javan's four sons were named Elishah, Tarshish, Kittim, and Dodanim;* and Josephus tells us that Chethimus, or Kittim, possessed the Island of Chethima, which is now called Cyprus, and from this all islands and maritime places were called Chethim by the Hebrews.†

Mr. Hamilton Lang supposes that the expression 'Ships from the coast of Chittim,' of Numbers xxiv. 24, arose from the fact that all ships sailing towards Syria, made Cyprus their last station. If this be so, the phrase, 'Ships of Tarshish,' may have had a similar origin, and the application of the prophecy, 'And the ships of Tarshish first,' of Isaiah lx. 9, to our own country, may have no solid foundation. It is curious, however, that Tartessus should have been near the Straits of Gibraltar.

Citium was the birthplace of Zeno the Stoic, and of Apollonius the physician. Larnaca, which occupies its site, is still the most important commercial place in the island, and the residence of the foreign consuls. These dwell mostly in the street called 'Marina,' which faces the sea. The rest of the town consists of low Oriental houses, built of unbaked brick, generally white-washed, and surrounded by gardens, with hedges of prickly pear.

We soon made the acquaintance of Mr. Cobham, the Commissioner, and of Mr. Watkins, who has succeeded Mr. Hamilton Lang in the management of the Imperial Ottoman Bank. Both gentlemen

* Genesis x. 4. 1 Chronicles i. 7. † Josephus i. vi, 1.

were cordial in their offers of help; and Mr. Watkins kindly took our heavy luggage into his premises until we should have completed our tour.

I asked Mr. Watkins if he thought that the Cypriots are contented under British rule.

'Undoubtedly,' he replied. 'Before the cession they never could call their lives their own. It is only a few hot heads who wish for annexation to Greece. One thing is certain, the island will never go back to Turkey. The great curse of the population is the bad feeling between Moslem and Christian.'

Several ladies whom I met in Mr. Watkins' drawing-room had resided long in Cyprus, and assured me that we were in no danger of taking fever, and, that if we did take it, it would not do us much harm.

On returning to the tents, I found Violet superintending the saddling of some mules which had been recommended for our use. We rode a short distance on one of them, then took a stroll, and saw a gorgeous sunset, the sky being all ablaze with a burning red, against which the clouds looked inky black.

Our slumbers were disturbed by the cry of a hyæna, the croaking of myriad frogs, the ringing of church bells, and striking of the Larnaca clocks.

We rose at five a.m., and, as no one was stirring, opened one of our tent doors whilst we dressed, and, looking across a deep-blue sea, saw the Eastern horizon all aflame at the approach of the sun. We did not manage to start until half-past seven, there being much discussion betwixt Salim and the

Cypriot muleteers about the fitting of loads, their
difficulties being much aggravated by their total
ignorance of each other's language. We kept out
of the squabble, the baggage-mules being no business
of ours; but we could see that there were two
objects of contention. One was a wooden box containing the cook's utensils, the other was Mr.
Mezher's very large canteen. We had stated, on
first seeing this article at Beyrout, that we feared it
might prove too heavy for a mule, and had desired
that it should be lightened as far as possible by the
abstraction from it of all articles not absolutely
necessary for the comfort of two people, the box
itself having been evidently constructed for ten.
We ought really to have objected to its size; but
its owner had been so long accustomed to Eastern
travel that we deferred to his superior judgment.
Salîm was evidently taking the entire command of
the muleteers; he spoke to them in Arabic, never
looking to see if they understood him. George only
interposed occasionally to interpret for him. Whilst
we waited, the postmaster came to ask if he should
forward our letters to Nicosia.

And now I must introduce my readers to our
strangely assorted cavalcade, which consisted of two
ladies, an Arab dragoman, an Arab waiter, a cook,
one Arab muleteer, and five Cypriots, each of whom
owned three mules, so that we had fifteen beasts at
starting.

George, the dragoman, had never before acted in
that capacity, nor indeed had he ever earned more
than five shillings a day. But all who knew him
in Beyrout concurred in thinking him most trust-

worthy. Nothing could exceed his anxiety to oblige us, and he was, moreover, a born polyglot. Not that I think he knew his own language thoroughly; some of the Beyrout waiters, indeed, made fun of him for telling me ungrammatical expressions; but when the hotel suffered from a plethora of guests, and he took part in waiting, I was astonished at the readiness with which he addressed people in Arabic, English, French, German, and Italian alternately. Whilst at Beyrout I conversed with him only in Arabic, and really did not know what he could do in other tongues. In Cyprus I was at first surprised and delighted with the fluency he displayed in speaking to the natives; he seemed to have seized on the peculiarities of the Greek language, and was never at a moment's loss for a word. But when I came to talk Greek with him myself—the presence of Cypriots sometimes necessitating this—if my hair could have stood on end, it assuredly would have done so at his total disregard of etymology and grammar. Here are specimens. To a native, ἔχεις καμμία παιδί. To a schoolmaster, when offering a cigar, φυμάρεις καπνόν. Should any professor of Greek in this country wish to supply his pupils with plentiful examples of what to avoid, or to ascertain their skill in the detection of errors, he could not do better than employ George.

His English I seldom heard; but Violet said it left something to be desired. Once he tried to talk Italian to us, with the result that we understood the beginning and the end of his sentences, but never the middle, which was doubtless borrowed from some other language; perhaps from Turkish, which he understood also. His ears must have been uncommonly sharp, as they were his sole aids in acquiring knowledge. We were not aware till the last day of our stay in Cyprus,—when he was obliged to put a cross over the stamp of the receipt which we asked in return for the money we had paid him,—that he had never been at school, and could neither read nor write.

Such men are not uncommon in the East. They have a natural cleverness, which might have developed into something valuable had they received a regular education. They impose on foreigners, on Englishmen especially, by their wonderful versatility in languages, their knowledge of which extends only to the use of the commonest words, and a skill in the art of twisting any word into French, English, or Hellenic forms. Abundant opportunity for the study of this science may be had in Cyprus.

George's disposition may be called a supple one. His chief defect was a lack of personal dignity, which made it difficult for him to ensure the obedience of those whom he employed. Salim supplied the want admirably; but then Salim did not accompany us on our rides, and was himself nominally under George's authority.

Salim was a tall, powerful, energetic man, who would have made a splendid dragoman, could he have spoken English or French. His acquaintance with these tongues extended to knowing the names of a few table articles, which names, however, he never could recognise when he heard them; so that my services as interpreter betwixt Violet and him were in daily requisition. He was a good waiter, and took the charge of pitching the tents, etc.

Constantine, the cook, was an Arab, but spoke Greek with a pure accent, and, I think, belonged to the orthodox church; George Wakîm and Salîm being what is known in Syria as Greek Catholic— *i.e.*, owning allegiance to the Pope, but having services in Arabic. Constantine was an adept at his business, a devotee in religion, and strongly tinctured with superstition. He suffered from a weakness of the eyes, and wore blue spectacles.

Two of our muleteers were named George. This was inconvenient, but England's patron saint was also theirs, it being supposed that he killed the dragon in this part of the world, possibly on the banks of the Nahr Beyrout. By way of distinction, we resolved to call the Arab dragoman George, and to reserve the Greek name Georgî, or Georgie, for the two Cypriots, distinguishing them as Georgie I. and Georgie II.

Georgie I. acted as our guide. He was a short, soft-spoken, soft-mannered man, with a bronzed face and an easy disposition. His chief fault was a desire to take liberties with his Arab namesake, to pose as dragoman whenever he could, and to consider every divergence from his opinion as a mark of barbarous ignorance. He spoke a Greek that was on the whole pretty correct, the Greek of Cyprus, in short, purified through intercourse with strangers. I noticed that he would say, Θέλοντος Θεός, where an Athenian would have said, Θεοῦ Θέλοντος.

The other muleteers were named Paraskevás, Zannetes, Georgie II., and Aristides. The last-named was the most picturesque in his dress, and the most obliging in disposition.

Ibrahîm, the Arab, had been taken for the sake of the tents. The Cypriots dubbed him ὁ ξένος, because the poor fellow could not talk to them. He was a good-natured, patient man, who wore a skirt of striped cotton, and whose bare feet seemed never to see soap. But he had the art of getting on under difficulties.

CHAPTER VII.

CYPRUS DESCRIBED.

Messaria—Mountainous in the West—Larnaca to Famagousta—The March—Village of Ormidia—Rain—A Perfect Little Oasis—Homœopathic Medicine—A Cypriote Church—A Service—Great Plain of Famagousta—First Sight of the Town—Varoschia—Famagousta—Torre del Moro—Fall of Famagousta—Bragadino's Fate—We Leave Famagousta.

IF my readers will glance at the map, they will see that Cyprus consists of two perfectly distinct regions. The eastern half of the island consists chiefly of a large plain, whose monotony is broken by few trees. To the north of this plain, along the coast, is a range of picturesque mountains, some of which rise to a height of three thousand three hundred and forty feet, and which stretches far into the sea at its eastern end, terminating in the promontory of Cape St. Andreas. The southern slopes of these hills, when viewed from the plain, appear to be as barren as do the slopes of Helicon from Orchomenos, but a nearer inspection reveals a wealth of verdure in the shape of lentisks and juniper. The northern side, overlooking the sea, is, on the contrary, richly wooded, and abounds in streamlets.

The large plain is named the Messaria. It has a soil which may surpass that of Egypt in point of fertility; but, as the harvests are gathered in May, it remains subject for four months to a consuming drought, and soon takes on the appearance of a parched and dreary wilderness, relieved by a few oases in the shape of villages, a few only of which nestle in the verdure of mulberry-gardens, others being as grey and bare as the soil from whence the unbaked brick of their houses is taken. The plain stretches from the gulf of Arta on the west to the marshes near Famagousta on the east. Nicosia or Leucosia, the capital, stands on it, and it is traversed by several good roads, the work of the English government. This plain is, by its situation, exposed to the same heat as Syria, but this is made more intense by the chain of mountains stretching from east to west, which catches every ray of the sun, and throws them back into the valleys.

The western half of Cyprus differs from this as Switzerland does from Prussia. It is a mass of lofty mountains, traversed by magnificent passes, and partially clothed with forests. The highest of these mountains, the Oros Troados, or Olympus, is six thousand five hundred and ninety feet high, and retains the snow on its summit for the greater part of the year. Here the climate is cool and bracing. Foreign residents and well-to-do Cypriots naturally come here for their summer quarters, living in tents during July and August. Here, too, are *sanatoria* for British soldiers, worn-out with the heat and the hardships of Egyptian or Indian warfare.

We arranged to traverse the eastern half of the island first. Had it been autumn we should have done exactly the opposite.

Murray was the chief counsellor for our routes.

Violet left the arrangement of these, with the choice of resting-places, entirely to me, as I could talk to the muleteers, and George knew nothing about the matter.

How far should we ride the first day? Murray gave the distance from Larnaca to Famagousta as eight hours. Mr. Stuart, the Beyrout banker, said he could do it easily in three, and that we, riding slowly with mules, ought to do it in five. Georgie, however, was quite positive that it would take seven; and insisted that we should stop half-way at a village named Ormidia. Our English friends at Larnaca laughed at the idea of Ormidia being considered a day's journey. It was difficult to decide who was right, but it was best not to fatigue ourselves too much at first, so we decided for Ormidia.

Georgie the muleteer rode in front on a white horse, whose age he could not specify. Violet and I followed on mules, and George brought up the rear.

We at first followed an excellent road near the shore, made with gravel from the beach. It led us for two hours over pasture-ground, diversified by a large marsh and two small ones; then over some low, chalky hills, where sheep were feeding, and where anemones, primroses, and other wild flowers nestled amongst the thyme. Here and there was a patch of splendid wheat or barley, or a bit of ground being ploughed with oxen and a primitive plough.

In three hours and a quarter we came in sight of the village of Ormidia, and decided to take our luncheon before entering it, so as to be free from spectators. The ground was something like that on

Mount Hymettus; it had, perhaps, fewer lentisks, but a far greater variety of blooming shrubs and brilliant wild flowers. Violet was just remarking on the ignorance of the many Frenchmen who have assured us that Cyprus is not worth seeing, and Georgie was knocking a few clusters of white-shelled snails off the bushes in preparation for his own poor Lenten supper, and the Arab George spreading out the contents of his luncheon bags, when the clouds, which had till now lent us their grateful shade, broke into rain. We hastened to gather up our belongings, and walked to the village.

Ormidia is a perfect little oasis of orange and lemon gardens. Its low houses are built of stone or of sun-burnt brick, and are without chimneys, the smoke issuing from under the roofs. We found a lovely field, bright with poppies, where we resolved that the tents should be pitched, and then looked about for a shady place to take our lunch. I chose a garden, planted with some small orange and pomegranate trees, about which little channels for irrigation had been dug in the clay. Here George spread our carpet, but, on Violet's coming down to it, she discovered that it was close to a great hive of bees. We moved a little further on, still keeping under the pomegranates, for the sun had become intensely hot. A stately, grey-haired woman brought us out two dirty cane chairs from her cottage, and we ate amidst alternate sunshine and rain. Then George told us that our tents had arrived and were already pitched not in the place where we wished them, but in another almost as good, though overlooked by a few of the houses.

We rested till the afternoon. Then a woman from the house above presented herself, carrying a baby, which she said had got τὰς θέρμας, meaning the fever. Violet gave it some homœopathic medicine; and the woman invited us to accompany her to the village church after sunset, this being the eve of Good Friday.

I went with her, after dinner, she carrying the sick baby, with its head uncovered. It was pitch dark, and we picked our steps along a narrow foot-track by the help of a Chinese lamp, which George carried. Sometimes we encountered cows, sometimes a black pig ran grunting past us. The little church is built of stone. On entering, we found it filled with humble worshippers, the men and boys being all in front, and the women behind. I, however, was directed into a side-stall, with a moveable seat. There was a large, heavily-gilt screen, on which were depicted the Twelve Apostles, and beneath them a row of scenes from our Saviour's life. In the gilt doorway stood a grey-haired, grey-bearded old priest, intoning in a very nasal voice passages of the Gospel. I distinguished the familiar,

‘'Ορθὴ σοφία νὰ ἀκούσωμεν τοῦ ἁγίου Εὐαγγελίου,'*

('Father, save me from this hour,' 'They all forsook Him, and fled,' etc.) A wooden cross stood a few yards in front of the screen, with a very rude picture of the crucified Saviour painted on it. Each man, as he entered, bowed and crossed himself in front of this, touched the ground with his head, and kissed the picture's breast. There was also a candle-stick, with a huge candle in the

* Right wisdom that we listen to the Holy Gospel.

centre, and a number of little tapers round it, all of which were blown out and re-lit at certain passages. I waited for nearly an hour; then slipped out, followed by George and the muleteer Aristides, who carried a lantern. Fearing that our reputation as being Christians might suffer from my not having stayed till the end, as well as from our not very meagre dinner, I repeated to Aristides all the verses which I had heard droned out by the priest. George, having asked my permission, told him that I meant to present a wax candle to the church.

We were ready to start next morning at seven, but had to wait half-an-hour for Georgie and the mules. George asked us if we would eat meat to dinner, and we explained that fasting was an ordinance of his church, but not of ours. I hoped the muleteers would be a little less lazy after Easter, and that they would try to make the length of a day's journey something more than three and a half hours. We purposed to reach Famagousta by mid-day, and, after visiting its churches, to ride on to the monastery of St. Barnabas, which 'Murray' said was two hours further, but which Georgie was positive we could reach in one hour. As all his ideas of the distances between other places are about twice as long as 'Murray's,' I was rather charmed with this singular exception.

Crossing the brow of a low hill, we entered the great plain of Famagousta by a track extremely good for horses and mules, but hardly good enough for carriages. Georgie said that there was another carriage road, but that it was an hour longer than this one, as it passed by many villages. We could see the white hills near Larnaca behind us, and on our left the rugged chain of mountains which bounds the plain to the north. They looked very barren in the distance, but are far from being so when you approach them. Our way was monotonous. There was not a cloud in the sky, but a fresh breeze blowing from the sea made the heat bearable. The plain is singularly destitute of inhabitants, and even of sheep. We saw only one village, Angouri, one or two solitary mosque-like churches with cupolas, and a building which we mistook for a barn, but which is, nevertheless, the monastery of Hagia Maria. Occasionally there was a poor crop, and occasionally a very fine one of wheat or lentils. Most of the plain was, however, covered with thin clumps of thyme or juniper dotted amongst the thinnest of grass, and enlivened by gay anemones. Hardly a living thing was to be seen. I asked Georgie repeatedly why so much land is allowed to lie waste.

'We Cypriots are few,' he answered. 'To till it would cost more in the way of implements than we should ever get out of it.'

The plain became more and more desolate as we approached Famagousta. The first sight of this famous town startled us. It was like a ghost from the dead Past appearing to tell us how powerful were the knightly rulers of the island; and yet how much more powerful were the Moslems who shattered their magnificent walls.

The sight of these walls was a revelation. Nothing that we had read, or that anyone had said to us, had in the least prepared us for seeing so interesting a relic of the Middle Ages.

An erroneous tradition derives the name of this town from Fama Augusta, and attributes its foundation to Augustus, after the fall of Antony and Cleopatra. The truth is that it occupies the site of the ancient Ammochostis, which means 'a sand heap.' The Greeks of the Middle Ages pronounced this Ammochoustos,* just as they turned the name Trikōpai (three oars) into Trikoupes. This degenerated into Famagousta.

Varoschia, its modern and Christian suburb, stands on the shore a mile to the south. Before entering the town, we rested and refreshed ourselves at a spot where stood some few poor huts and a garden. The latter was owned by a priest, who kindly welcomed us to take shelter from the heat amongst his well-watered pomegranates. We sat beneath a spreading fig-tree, and, as there was no sward to spread our things on, the good father lent us four cane chairs, we inwardly wondering at our own impudence in feasting there on Good Friday.

We had some conversation with the priest, whose eyes sparkled as he said,

'We are free now, for we are under the English.'

He was a Cypriot, but I found that his sympathies were entirely with Greece in the unfortunate diplomatic struggle which Monsieur Deliyannis was then carrying on with the Great Powers of Europe. He insisted that our government had ill-treated Greece, by not giving her a little more territory

* ου in modern Greek has the sound of *oo*, as in French.

in accordance with the promises of the Berlin Treaty. It was impossible to make him see that we could not well give what is not ours.

Famagousta, appearing in the distance, had startled us, rising as it does from the edge of a desolate, lifeless plain. Our wonder was not lessened as we rode along a bridge over the broad, ancient moat, filled with green turf and enclosed by walls seventeen feet thick, founded on the solid rock; much of which, indeed, is comprised in their structure. We passed under a vaulted gateway, and along broad streets flanked on either side by solidly-built, decayed stone houses. Some of these have been repaired, and the upper windows furnished with Cairene latticed woodwork for the seclusion of the harem. We paused in astonishment before the beautiful, ruined Gothic façade of the mosque of Hagia Sofia.

This was once a Christian church, and is supposed to have been built by the Venetians, though the style of architecture points, in the opinion of some experts, to the work of English artists. The interior has round, Norman pillars and pointed arches, just passing into the Decorated style. The old Gothic windows have been filled in with Arab lattice-work, which has a very picturesque and curious effect. Many swallows flew freely about.

We asked several people in vain to direct us to the bomb-proof magazines, and at last a Turko-Cypriot soldier, who spoke Greek, offered to accompany us. We were amazed at the exceeding strength and solidity of the fortifications. George compared them with the walls of Baalbeck, but we pointed out to him that no possible resemblance could exist, seeing that this represents the ideas of the thirteenth or fourteenth century, whilst the origin of that is lost in pre-historic mists. In his mind, and that of his Cypriot namesake, mediæval ruins are more interesting than Grecian or Phœnician, whilst both alike yield in value to the last tumbledown house of a few years ago.

Famagousta would, I think, still stand a siege, even were the might of modern ordnance to come against it. I have not been able to ascertain the date of its walls, but they probably belong to the same epoch as the church of Hagia Sofia. One infers this from the existence of a roof with a rosette in its centre, and two Gothic arches springing from it, exactly similar to one that occurs in the church.

A round tower near Famagousta is called Torre del Moro, and was once the residence of a certain Cristoforo Moro, a Venetian lieutenant of Cyprus, who has been identified with Shakespeare's Othello.

Nothing that we know of the history of Famagousta, however, so well became it as its fall. After the heroic Bragadino had six times hurled back his infuriated Moslem assailants, whose trenches and batteries were of a size never before witnessed, he was at length obliged by his starving soldiers and by the populace to surrender. Mustapha, the Turkish general, agreed that the garrison should retain their arms, that those who wished to leave the island should be conveyed to Crete in Turkish ships, and that those who wished to remain should be unmolested in the exercise of their religion and the disposal of their property.

Trusting to this solemn compact, on August 5, 1571, Bragadino rode out. Mustapha received him with insults, ordered his nose and ears to be cut off, and three hundred of his soldiers to be slaughtered. For days the city ran with their blood. Bragadino himself was compelled to work on the new entrenchments, and at length, worn out with toil, humiliation, and hunger, he was flayed alive, the upper part of his body being completely stripped before he expired. His skin, stuffed with hay, was tied to the mast of Mustapha's ship, and carried to Constantinople, where it was exposed to the view of the Christian prisoners, until, twenty-five years later, it was purchased by his relatives, and buried with due honour in the church of St. John and St. Paul, at Venice. Fourteen months after the fall of Famagousta, the power of the Turks received its first serious check in the waters of Lepanto.

What would Bragadino have said could he have foreseen that three hundred years later the Christian Powers of Europe would be in league to retard the natural decay of Turkey, and to perpetuate its rule over Christian races?

We left Famagousta at five p.m. under a broiling sun. Willingly would we have lingered to explore the harbour and the Moor's Tower; but, as our tents had gone by a shorter route to St. Barnabas, there was no help for it. We had arranged this part of our route badly; we ought to have given the whole afternoon to Famagousta, and gone next day to Trikomo, passing by the Cyclopean wall which is all that remains of Salamis, the *ambiguam Salamina futuram*, which, as Horace tells us,

Apollo promised to Teucer after he had fled from his father and his native land, and to which a better fortune at length bore him and his companions, leaving to all future emigrants the motto, 'Nil desperandum.'

Our haste was partly caused by a promise which we had made to our friends that we would avoid sleeping at Famagousta, which has an evil reputation for fever. In spring, however, there is really no danger, and we saw that in future we must trust entirely to our own judgment, and relinquish the hope of getting any advice from our Cypriot muleteers. There are Greek peasants who feel a glow of pride as they point out to foreigners the remnants of their ancestors' greatness; the Cypriot passes such things every day of his life without bestowing on them a glance.

We travelled along a good road over a plain so monotonous as to force from us the remark that the very desert is prettier. Our mules were much teased by the swarms of gnats which hovered over the scanty herbage. I was curious to see whether Georgie would really improve upon Murray by taking us to St. Barnabas in an hour. He at length left the high-road in order to cross the plain by a mule track. Very soon we came to a bit of black mud, through which a stream flowed lazily. The stream did not seem deep, and Violet was prepared to follow Georgie across as his old white horse stepped in. But, just as he ought to have landed, down sank the animal, plunging and struggling in the filthy bog. Georgie sprang off, with the help of the long pole which he always carried, and after helping his own beast out, not without difficulty, called to Violet's mule to come on.

The animal was accustomed to obey him, and to follow wherever the white horse might lead. Violet had, therefore, to pull hard in order to keep herself out of a very uninviting bath. She turned away, and insisted on dismounting, being, in truth, much frightened, and said that she would rather go back to Famagousta than cross at such a place. It was provoking, too, to see that those of our bags and rug-cases which had been slung across Georgie's saddle, and which we took a pride in keeping clean, were in a state too dirty to contemplate with patience.

I dismounted also, and offered to take Violet across on foot, at a narrower place. But, alas! the green banks on either side were treacherous, and I began sinking when I tried to approach it. We were in no little perplexity, for the monastery appeared to be more than an hour's ride distant, and the sky was reddening with the hues of sunset. To cross this stream was impossible, and yet—were we to sleep on an unhealthy marsh, or find our way in in the dark back to Famagousta?

All the wealth of George's vocabulary was now expended in scolding. This, however, had little effect on the good-natured, imperturbable Georgie, who could not understand why he should be expected to make his horse re-cross. We insisted that he should do so, however, and tried to make him understand that it was one thing for him to risk sinking in the mud, seeing that he could roll off so easily, and quite another thing for a lady with her long clean skirts and her side-saddle. To him the accident meant only a little annoyance and extra trouble in cleaning things, to one of us it might mean a broken limb. I doubt if our reasoning carried any sort of conviction to him; but it had the effect of making him say that we might cross by the bridge.

'And why did you not tell us there was a bridge?' demanded George, indignantly.

'Because it is a much longer road,' replied Georgie.

'Don't waste time, then,' said I. 'Take us to the bridge immediately.'

After some delay, owing to Violet's mule having taken the opportunity of running about loose, we remounted, and retraced our steps to the high-road. The marshes formed by the river Pedios, formerly called the Cyprian Nile, have been well bridged over since the advent of the English. Georgie had disdained to avail himself of the new way, and had sought a more direct cut across the bogs.

After we had ridden for some distance, we had again to leave the road, and make our way towards the monastery without the help of any path for the space of about a mile. We could dimly see that our tents were pitched under its walls; but the sun had completely set, and we had no idea of what sort of ground we were treading on. Every moment we expected to meet with holes, or with new bogs. Our hearts sank somewhat too, when we realized what sort of spot had been chosen for our night quarters. The monastery itself looked like a huge domed church, it being all that remains of a once wealthy foundation. It was the one solitary beacon in a wide stretch of treeless, houseless plain; for though there was a village a mile away it was too poor and insignificant to be discernible. The whole place had a forsaken look, not a shred of cultivation anywhere, the weeds grew rank up to the walls; so rank, indeed, that it would not have been easy to get through them on foot. And this was in the plain of Famagousta, whose *malaria* has won for it so evil a reputation. We thought that perhaps it might be better for us to sleep in the monastery.

A solitary monk, or rather priest, stood ready to welcome us. We asked if he would take us in, and he replied that he would do so willingly, only it would be necessary to sweep out one of the upper rooms, as he quite failed to remember when they had been inhabited. On dismounting, we found that some of the tall, flowering weeds had been mown down for our tents, and that while the dining-tent and the kitchen one were tolerably free from them, they clustered thickly round our sleeping-tent. George disliked the idea of our going into the monastery, and suggested that worse things than weeds might be found within its walls. Salim said that he had never seen such a camping-ground, that he had been fairly puzzled what to do when he arrived, for round and round not a clear spot was to be seen.

Violet was so fatigued and discouraged that she did not at first care to dine, and everyone was in a bad humour; the cook much disappointed that his labours were not more appreciated, George and I scolding Georgie for not having had the sense to

tell us that this was not a place for tents. At length
we decided that we would risk sleeping outside the
walls; a dozen hands worked eagerly to tear and cut
away some of the luxuriant herbage; we got a cup
of tea, and Violet was persuaded not to go to bed
fasting. It was after ten p.m. when we dined; then
I dropped asleep, thinking that this was something
like the Roman Campagna, and fully expecting to
awake shivering. The only thing that disturbed us
was the voice of a hyæna, and we rose at half-past
four in time to see the sun rising out of the blue
waters of the Bay of Salamis. I was surprised and
delighted to find myself wonderfully well.

Our first care was to greet the priest, and tell
him that we wished to see the interior of the church,
as we understood that it had been built in honour
of St. Barnabas, whose body, with an autograph
copy of the Gospel of St. Matthew, was found in
this spot in A.D. 473, in virtue of which discovery
the Church of Cyprus has ever since been auto-
cephalos, or self-governing, owing only a nominal
allegiance to the patriarch of Constantinople, robing
her archbishop in purple, and allowing him to sign
his name in red, like an emperor.

The priest, who is now the solitary inhabitant,
and who is, I think, married, took us into the building, which is evidently the fragment of a much
larger one, and consists of a nave and apse, with
arched roofs and little windows filled up with Arab
woodwork. There is a very fine old carved wooden
pulpit, a painting on wood of St. Barnabas, and a
beautiful, tall, fluted monolith pillar supposed to
have been part of the church built here by the

Emperor Zeno, and cannonaded to pieces by the Turks. Behind the church are the ruins of the monastery. The priest told us that he had read the service during the night at two o'clock, with the help of a boy to give the responses.

'Did many come to hear you?' we asked.

'Very few.'

'Why are there not more monks?'

'Because we are very poor. The monastery owns nothing.'

The priest wore a piece of crape drapery on his high black cap, so that he may have had some degree of rank; but his black eyes sparkled when we gave him a few francs. Our cook profited by the opportunity meanwhile, and went about kissing each of the pictures in turn, and asking about their history. George said it was delightful to see a man so devout, but Violet thought he was taking too great liberties with his saints.

After emerging from the flowering weeds, we found a good path on the other side of the monastery, which in three hours brought us to Trikomo, a considerable town of unburnt brick houses, dotted with a few white ones (which latter are the property of Englishmen), and situated at the foot of the northern range of mountains. Passing a huge white farm-house, belonging to General S——, we sat down under an olive-tree in a newly-reaped corn-field, near a garden of pomegranates. As we partook of lunch, I began debating whether or not I should carry out my scheme of visiting Cantara that afternoon.

We had chosen Trikomo as the place of our

Sunday rest, partly because it had good water, and partly because Violet hoped that we might meet with some English people, who could tell us about the way, and that possibly we might find a better guide than Georgie. It devolved on me to plan our route so as to complete the tour of the island in thirty days, and make sure of returning to Larnaca in time for sailing homewards to Marseilles with the French steamer on May 19. Knowing that Violet disliked rough paths, it occurred to me that I might save a day by making the excursion to Cantara without her that afternoon.

The plan seemed feasible, seeing that Murray gives the distance between St. Barnabas and Cantara as five hours, and that we had done three in coming to Trikomo. Georgie dissented energetically, declaring that Cantara was at the top of the hill, in a spot all but inaccessible to laden mules; that it would take four hours to go there, and four to return. We agreed that the best way would be to ask some of the Trikomo people.

We had not been seated many minutes before a man in European clothing came towards us. Violet was delighted; she was tired of hearing only Greek, with no variation except George's bad English and Salim's Arabic. The man turned out to be the Italian steward of General S——, who was then away from home. We asked him how many hours it was to Cantara.

'Two,' he at once replied.

I was, of course, triumphant. The remains of Aphrodite's temple, marking the spot where she had first stepped ashore, were, he said, quite close to the village. He promised to send a trustworthy guide about three o'clock, who would conduct me there. I did not quite believe in the connection of Cantara with Aphrodite, seeing that the Island of Cythera claims to be near her birthplace; and so, with more show of reason, does Paphos in the south-west corner of Cyprus. But no doubt there has been an altar to her on these heights, and I knew that the view would more than repay me for the labour of climbing them.

So, when our tents had been pitched in a neighbouring field, I took my mid-day rest. At two o'clock I was awakened by George, who suggested that I had better start, seeing that Cantara might possibly be further off than I thought.

Georgie, when helping me to mount, said his reason for trying to discourage me was because he feared I should be overcome with fatigue. I told him that I should have all Sunday to rest, and that I would not fail to turn, if, after riding for three hours, I found myself still far from Cantara. So we left, I, George, Aristides, and the local guide, Georgie, in the meanwhile, muttering that he had always heard people speak of going to Cantara and back as of a day's excursion.

We rode very quickly, for it had become a point of honour with me to accomplish it. We went by a mule track over hills covered with thick clumps of *arbor vitæ* dotted with olive-trees and sheltering patches of splendid barley and wheat. We passed a village named Arinyan, where the streets were red with the blood of slaughtered lambs, then crossed some more hills whose lentisks and thyme reminded me strongly of Greece. After passing a village named Ernani, we began to ascend some hills covered with like foliage, the offshoots of the mountain range whose tops we could see crowned by fantastically-shaped rocks. We discerned the white convent of Cantara a little below one of these summits, and I repeatedly asked the guide how long it would take to reach this.

'Half-an-hour,' was the invariable reply.

'Are you quite sure?'

'Yes. ἡμίσειαν ὥραν piano.'

At 4.30, we were only at the foot of the mountain, and our eyes told us that it would require at least two hours to reach the convent. So I determined to retrace my steps, having no fancy for being overtaken by darkness on a rugged mountain path. The only alternative would have been to sleep at Cantara, and this our lying guide had probably expected that we would do.

I suffered much from thirst whilst riding back, and had to send Aristides forward to one of the villages for some water. We had a glorious view of the plain, with the towers of Famagousta in the distance, and, nearer, the forsaken site of Salamis, with its memories of Evagoras and of St. Paul. We reached the tents about seven; a little more disposed to pay respect to Georgie's opinion in the future.

CHAPTER VIII.

TRIKOMO TO KYTHEREA.

Interview with a Priest—Dress of Cypriots—A Stroll into the Town—Britons or Greeks?—A Gathering—A Great Place for Birds—The Monastery of St. Andreas—Lefkoniko—Marathobouno—Locusts—Visitors—Improvements—Destruction of Locusts—Locust-trap.

We spent Sunday at Trikomo. Soon after breakfast we had a visit from a dirty old priest; and I wish those Greeks who speak of Cyprus as part of ἡ δούλη Ἑλλάς could have heard the tone in which he exclaimed, 'εἴμεθα ἐλεύθεροι.' ('We are freemen.') He insisted that Aphrodite was born at Cantara, and that it was through English influence that Greece has not yet got what was promised to her by the Treaty of Berlin. After he had gone, I asked the muleteers about the church ceremonies, and when they thought that the δευτέρα ἀνάστασις, the Second Resurrection, would be celebrated. They seemed rather hazy on the subject, but at length told me, 'an hour after mid-day.' They cannot manage to count by European time.

I went, therefore, in the heat of the day, accompanied by George and Aristides. We passed along streets which ran between houses of unburnt brick, and which were slightly stained with the blood of lambs. We saw a priest sitting amongst a group of men at a house door, and another amusing himself in a rustic café, where one man was playing a tambourine, and another pirouetting, with outstretched arms, like a dervish. I thought it curious that they should be there during the hours of service, and still more so when some one said the church was not open, giving Aristides, at the same time, a large key. It seemed that they had all misunderstood me; for there was really no service after mid-day. The Cypriots manage to get all their devotions finished very early in the morning; and, as our Saviour rose at that time, they are perhaps more consistent than their brethren of Greece. A δευτέρα ἀνάστασις is hardly logical. It struck me as strange, however, that neither on Easter Day nor on any of the days following it did I hear the phrase, 'Χριστὸς ἀνέστη' ('Christ is risen') from anyone's lips.

The young men of the town were in holiday dress. On week-days, all Cypriots wear the same dress as the Turks, only the full cloth trousers are shorter, and the ankles protected either from the sting of serpents or from thorns by stout leather gaiters. To-day, their trousers were well fastened up at the knee, showing a pair of handsome calves in snowy stockings. The waist was encircled not with a gay silk scarf, like that of an Arab, but with a coarse, black, woollen one; the shirt sleeves were of chequered blue and white cotton, the whole dress being toned down so as to throw into relief the magnificence of the waistcoat, or what would be considered by a woman a sleeveless bodice. The back of this remarkable garment was bright scarlet, open down the middle, and laced with two laces, one blue, the other red. The front was a figured velvet, the pattern of leaves being black and red on a light blue ground, ornamented with sundry tufts of black wool. On the head was a red tarboosh, and the whole appearance of the wearer was enough to turn the heads of a dozen girls.

On reaching the church we entered, and found it, as we had feared, empty. There was a handsome and curious wooden screen, and various pictures on wood with texts from the gospel written in very old characters. Some of these I deciphered for the benefit of twenty nondescript listeners. One of the pictures represented a man on horseback, and this George took to be his own patron saint. It was, however, an Ἅγιος Μῆνας. Could it possibly be he of Crete?

When the afternoon became cooler, Violet wished to take a walk unaccompanied by any of our men. We strolled into the town together, seeking for the post-office, and very soon had a numerous escort of children. The post-office was not easily found; it stood in a humble dwelling within a walled enclosure, and there was nothing to distinguish it from an ordinary house. The post-master, his daughter, and grandson were very intelligent, but they knew no English, none being taught in the school here. They had a collection of school-books for sale, and I examined these, being anxious to know what kind of instruction is being supplied to Cypriot children. They were, without exception, published in Athens, being the same as those that are used in the schools of Greece. I bought a book of songs and poems. All of these breathed a passionate love of country, and a spirit of triumph in the heroic ancestors of the race. Many were in honour of King George, and Queen Victoria was, of course, not mentioned.

This occasioned me much reflection. All children must be taught a love of their country, for it makes them feel that they are something better than brute beasts. English boys are the better for knowing about Boadicea and Alfred, Scotch ones about Wallace and Bruce. But what is there for a Cypriot to be proud of?

The history of the island is not heroic. The great deeds that were done in it were the deeds of foreigners. St. Paul's footsteps have left a track of glory from Salamis on the east coast where he landed, to Paphos, where he disputed with Elymas, the sorcerer. He seems to have followed the road that we took. His companion, Barnabas, was born in the island. But, with this exception, no Cypriot's name can make the pulses thrill except that of Evagoras, the self-made man, the liberator and tyrant of Salamis.

Are the young Cypriots to be brought up as Britons or as Greeks? Many of us say that Cyprus never formed part of Greece. Granted, but can anyone whose mother-tongue is the tongue of Hellas, and who believes himself, not without reason, to have Hellenic blood in his veins, read without a glow of natural pride the story of Thermopylæ, or the tale of Troy, or the imperishable names of more than a hundred philosophers, historians, and poets? I would by no means object to this feeling on the part of our Cypriot fellow-subjects, but I would wish that some one would, at the same time, put into the hands of the rising generation books which should tell them in their own tongue something of the greatness of that empire into which they are now incorporated; tell them how Great Britain has been for centuries the true foster-mother of modern freedom; make them understand that the boast, 'Civis Romanus sum,' is a right and noble one on their own lips; and say, moreover, that if Great Britain received from Greece the lamp of liberty, she has trimmed it anew and rekindled it in the light of a far higher teaching than Themistocles or Socrates knew; that she, indeed, was the first of nations to extend its blessed light to mankind, irrespective of birth, of colour, or of creed.

On returning to our tents we found that nearly all the young women and girls of the town had gathered round them, watching the operations of the cook and of Salîm with great curiosity. George was sorely puzzled what to do with them; he could not persuade them to go away, and they wanted our permission to inspect the interior of the tents. This, of course, we did not give, but I stood conversing with them for about half-an-hour. They were neither so pretty nor so tastefully dressed as the women of Greece, but they had handsome gold necklaces, some of them being composed of Turkish coins. Their manners, too, were different from those of Grecian peasants, their bearing was not so elastic, and they seemed afraid to speak freely. I encouraged them to show me their ornaments, then talked about the locusts and the harvest prospects.

I happened to use the word παῖδες for boys, when an old woman corrected me by saying, 'We call them ἀγοράκια.' Another woman at once put her hand on the speaker's shoulder, cautioning her to be quiet. This was evidently the result of Turkish discipline.

I asked them if they had a good school, and they replied :

'Yes, for boys, but for girls none.'

'Why don't you have a school for girls?'

'Because the boys need to learn, and the girls don't.'

'Well, if your girls don't learn, they will be behind the women of Greece, and of England too.'

'But we're so poor.'

'You always will remain poor if you don't learn.'

George and our muleteers, who were standing near, seemed much struck with this observation. I then insisted on the fact that they would be much happier as wives and mothers if they not only knew how to cook well, but could interest themselves to some degree in their husband's pursuits ; seeing that the Creator intended woman to be man's help-meet, not his plaything nor his slave. I then bade them 'καλ 'εσπέρας' (' Good night '), and they at once dispersed to their homes.

We looked at the muleteers' sleeping arrangements. Each of them had a carpet spread on the ground, and above that the bags of barley which are carried for the mules. On this they lie, with a quilt over them. They had asked George to let them occupy the kitchen-tent at night, seeing that he had taken Ibrahîm into the dining-tent along

K

with the other Arabs. This George had refused, though he meant to let them do it in case of rain.

Trikomo is a great place for birds. A leafless tree near our camp was completely covered by swallows. George brought us in the early morning a little thing he had just caught. It was grey, with a spot of yellow under its chin. It was very tame, and flew about our tent whilst we breakfasted. I tried to deposit him on a thistle, then on a lily stalk, but he clung to my finger. I tried to blow him away, but he only clung closer. At last I laid him on the ground. He spread his little wings, and flew off, only to be caught by Zannetes, and brought back to me.

We started at seven, and rode along the edge of the plain near the mountains with a fresh breeze blowing. Before us loomed Mount Troados, just capped with a little snow; to our left was the great plain, hidden occasionally from our view by low rocky hills; to our right a mountain range, bare of trees, but clothed with small shrubs, the irregular, picturesque outline of its summits standing out clear against the sky. We could also see the white hills round Larnaca. At length we approached a grey village, nestling against a grey hill whose top showed a semi-circular rampart of rock somewhat in the form of an ancient theatre, the proscenium being strewn with large fragments of rock like broken columns. The village is named Kalò Chortò.

We met a postman riding to Trikomo, so we stopped him and deposited a letter in his bag. We passed splendid fields of wheat and barley, and a stream whose waters were fast drying up from its muddy bottom. It is quite impossible for the women of this district to look so well as their Hellenic sisters, for they cannot practise cleanliness either in their persons or in their houses. I should like much to make an experiment on one of those little streams. I would begin by planting some shady bushes for, say a quarter-of-a-mile, on either bank from its source in the mountains. When these had begun to grow, I would plant a further stretch, and so on from year to year till the stream should keep its waters, being protected from the fierce sunlight. Each lessening rill seemed to say, with Bruar water,

> 'Let lofty firs and ashes cool
> My lowly banks o'erspread,
> And view deep-pending in the pool,
> Their shadows' wat'ry bed!
> Let fragrant birks in woodbines drest
> My craggy cliffs adorn,
> And, for the little songster's nest,
> The close embow'ring thorn.'

We passed on our left hand the deserted little monastery of St. Andreas, standing half-way up a craggy hill. Just below it in the rock was a shrine, consisting of a long tunnel-like passage full of water. At the mouth of this was a little stone door-way. Inside the passage, and on a tree above its entrance were hung a quantity of mouldering rags, placed there by people who preferred this way of curing the ailments of the wearers, to the more expensive plan of consulting a doctor. The Cypriot priests have evidently not succeeded in imparting much *nous* to their people. We passed the village of Lapetho, where, as it was still a feast-day, most of the people stood at their doors in holiday dress, wishing us καλό κατευόδιον. The houses were, as usual, of unburnt brick, made with abundance of chopped straw, and were shaded by olives and prickly pears. We noticed a cliff with what we fancied to be a row of rock tombs in it.

We were just approaching the village of Lefkoniko, and the road was as good as we could wish, when a man passed us with a mule and a donkey. I think he must have lifted his stick, for Violet's mule suddenly shied, and in an instant she rolled over its head on to the stony road. The mule walked on, lifting his hoofs carefully over her upturned face. It was a moment of intense suspense. George leaped down, and I kept groaning out something or other, fearing she might be seriously hurt, and blaming myself for having opposed a proposition that Ibrahim should walk beside her. I could not see why Violet, who had been accustomed to riding for years, and was once more courageous than I am, should need such an escort when on a level road.

George helped her to her feet, she walked a little, then lay for a few minutes on the grass, and said she thought she had only got a few bruises. She would not hear of my exchanging mules with her, but re-mounted her own, and we rode to the village, where we took luncheon under some olive-trees. We felt deeply thankful to the Almighty for her escape, especially from having been struck by the mule's hoofs.

At two p.m. there was a breeze, so we rode for two hours to the village of Marathobouno. The country was very uninteresting, being covered with corn-fields whose monotony was unbroken by tree or hedge. George led Violet's mule, and the road, called by the natives an ὁδός carrozzabile, was sometimes crossed by a stream of water, or rather of mud. The only variety in the prospect was the range of hills on our left, whose summits grew more and more fantastic. After passing the grey village of Dipsala, embosomed in olive-trees, we caught sight of the grey village of Marathobouno, perched on a low bare hill; the only break in the dead grey of field and town being the large, white, many-domed church. We rode through the dull streets, greeting the people whom we passed, and found our tents pitched on a slope above the village on the best spot that could possibly have been chosen. Violet was very patient, although badly bruised. I applied arnica compresses, and George brought her a baby bird, which stuck to her hand like glue. She thought the scenery about Marathobouno very beautiful, but I could not tell what she saw in it.

Next morning we were awakened by the voice of many nightingales, singing to welcome the rising sun. On opening the tent door we saw the beautiful outline of the hills against the brilliant red of the eastern sky. Violet thought at first that she could not move, but, on making an effort to dress, she found that she could do so without too much difficulty. I was anxious that we should get on to Nicosia, that Violet might, if necessary, have the benefit of a doctor's advice.

Marathobouno is exactly half-way between Trikomo and Nicosia, and our original plan had been to do the whole distance in two days. Georgie agreed to this, but, finding that I meant to go on the following Monday from Nicosia to St. Chrysostom, a journey of two hours, and on Tuesday by way of Buffavento and Bellapais to Kyrenia, he objected, saying that this would be to retrace our steps. He and Georgie II. strongly advised us to sleep at St. Chrysostom on our way to Nicosia. We agreed to this, but, in consequence of Violet's accident, arranged to make a shorter stage, and sleep at Kytherea.

Locusts sometimes came into our tents, and midges made the candles gutter in a circle of their dead bodies. I had, however, abolished my mosquito curtain as useless. I did not see a mosquito during the whole of our stay in Cyprus, except a very few on the last night, when we slept in the hotel at Larnaca. Our greatest plague was the multitude of impudent ear-wigs. The natives call them ψαλίδα, from the scissor-like form of their antennæ. We used to drown them, and beetles, in a mixture of Keating's powder and water. Soapy water was, however, more effectual.

Violet at length mounted her mule, and we started, George walking by her side. We passed betwixt hedgeless, treeless fields of waving yellow corn. The country was evidently drying up quickly. The hills to our right were getting more and more denuded of herbage, and in the plain to our left we could see Nicosia, with apparently no tree about it.

Georgie had said that it was four hours to Kytherea, but we did it in two hours and a half, walking very slowly. Kytherea is a fine village, embosomed in fine olive-trees, and well-watered by the river Pedios. It is perhaps the most beautiful spot on the southern slopes of the Kyrenian mountains. Had we crossed to the northern side, we should have found ourselves amidst some of the loveliest scenery in the island, but this we did not then know.

On finding ourselves at Kytherea, we decided to let the tents go on to St. Chrysostom, and to proceed on the following morning to Leucosia. We rested in the meantime beneath some olive-trees.

Georgie was in a very bad humour with George and with Ibrahîm. He called them βάρβαροι, because the former had said something depreciatory of my mule, and had asserted that it would be a less important event were one of the animals to get its leg broken than were a like misfortune to happen to one of us. During all our ride little nightingales sat by the side of the road with their mouths open, pouring out floods of melody at us as we passed. We wondered where their nests could be, and were told that they fly down from the mountain slopes.

The ruins of ancient Kytherea are half-an-hour's walk east of the village. De Cesnola discovered there the site of two temples, several Greek inscriptions, and many fragments of pottery and sculpture. He did not, however, excavate much, owing to the necessity which would have been imposed upon him of purchasing the well-cultivated ground. There is possibly something below the soil worth digging for, though we know little of the place's history excepting that it possessed a fine temple to Aphrodite.

As we rested during the noontide heat, two women and a man, above the rank of peasants, approached us. George wished to send them away, but we forbade him to do so, and, as they invited us to come and see their house, I went with them. The back of this dwelling was turned to the street, and looked no better than a wall of mud mixed with bits of clean straw. I was therefore agreeably surprised at being ushered under a trellised vine into a spacious inner court paved with stone and opening into a garden containing a fountain. On either hand wide doors gave access to lofty rooms, in one of which I seated myself on a divan which occupied the further side. It had three windows looking into the court and two into the street. These had no glass, but were filled in with lattice work of pine wood in the Cairene fashion, and furnished with strong shutters. The walls were at least two feet thick. The lofty roof was composed of round beams over-laid with straw matting, and the floor paved with broad flag-stones. The proprietor, his wife, one or two of their married children, and twelve grandchildren, mostly girls, gathered round me, sitting on chairs in a wide circle. They said that we were welcome to rest there during the heat of the day, instead of out of doors; and I apologised for our not doing so, saying that I believed Violet to be already asleep under a tree, and that I did not wish to awake her; the truth being that, when travellers are really tired, they may talk for half-an-hour with strangers, but not longer. I found that the girls were attending school, and one of them read to me some passages from a Greek history about the life of Aristides. I told them about the Trikomo people having no girls' school, and said that I thought it must be the will of the Almighty that we should all learn letters, seeing that He has revealed His will to us by means of a Book. I also said that He surely meant that woman should learn the same as man, when He said that she was to be a help-meet like unto him,* and how could she possibly be so if he were educated and she ignorant? They told me that the English were doing a great deal for the island schools, giving twenty, fifteen, or ten pounds per annum to each village for the purpose, according to its size.

'Have the English made many improvements in the island?' I asked.

'They have, on the roads. But it is rather hard about the trees. It is forbidden now to cut down a single pine or a single cypress on the mountains.'

'But don't you think that is quite right?' I asked. 'The great thing you complain of is want of rain. We know that trees not only help to bring rain, but they shelter the little rills, and encourage the rivers to flow at an equal pace, instead of being torrents in winter and disappearing altogether during the hot season? Now, how are the trees to grow if you are allowed to cut them down?'

My audience smiled at this, and acknowledged its truth. I understood them to complain of the tax on flour, and of that on some of their animals, but not at all of that raised for the purpose of destroying the locusts.

After conversing for about an hour, and telling

* This is, in the Septuagint, Βοη θὸς ὅμοιος αὐτῷ.

them many things about England, I returned to our olive-tree. I had only, however, been seated for a few minutes, when a widow woman, her little sister, and four children accosted us, inviting us to visit their home. A constant succession of such visitors is the penalty one must pay for resting near a village. The only alternative is to allow your dragoman to keep them off; but, as he is sure to do so indiscriminately, this would involve your making a bad impression on the villagers, and shutting yourself out from any knowledge of them.

The widow's children all attended school. Violet asked the boys what games they played at, and this set them a-leaping and throwing sticks.

A third party came up and described to us how the locusts are caught in nets and burnt in fires. This is explained very clearly and fully by Mr. Hamilton Lang.

'An ingenious plan,' he says, 'was adapted for the destruction of the locusts when in march, before they are able to fly. The inventor was Mr. Richard Mattei, an Italian gentleman, and large landed proprietor, who has rendered immense service to Cyprus by his labours. He had observed that in their march the locusts never turned back, whatever was the obstacle in their way. When they got into a town they would spend days in climbing over the walls of the houses if the direction of their march required it, rather than follow the streets and go round corners. This led him to conceive the following plan. Canvas cloths of twenty-four inches in breadth were attached by ribbons to small stakes stuck into the ground and stretched across the march of the locusts on either side at an angle of about one hundred and thirty-five degrees. To the top of the canvas cloth was sewn three inches of oil-cloth. The locusts, whose march was within the stretch of the oil-cloths, at once set to work to climb the obstacle presented to them; but when they got to the oil-cloth their feet slipped on the smooth surface and down they fell to the ground. A little further, and always a little further down the angle they tried to mount, but in vain. At a distance of about one hundred feet apart were dug pits of five feet in length, three feet in depth, and two feet and a half in breadth. Round the mouth of one of these pits a wooden frame-work covered with zinc four inches in breadth was fixed on the inside. The cloths came close to the ends of the pits, leaving no space for the locusts to pass between the cloth and the pits. After vainly trying to surmount the cloth barrier worked down to the pits the locusts jumped into them, but could not get out, for in climbing up the sides they came to the zinc, over the smooth surface of which they could not pass. The pits would fill in about four hours, and so thoroughly would they be packed that I have seen peasants jump upon the mass, and not sink more than a few inches.'

A model of this locust-trap, exhibited in 1886 at the Colonial and Indian Exhibition, seems to have excited greatly the interest of the British public. The most effectual means of destruction is, however, by the collection and burning of the locusts' eggs.

These destructive creatures are now indigenous

to the island, from whatever source they may have originally come. They lay their eggs on the mountain slopes, and, as they cover them with a glutinous matter which glitters in the sunlight, it can be no difficult task for the shepherds to gather them. They used to be paid for doing this by the Turkish government; a tax being levied on the islanders for the purpose. But for a long time the locusts throve and multiplied, the so-called eggs being much mixed with earth. An honest governor, named Said Pasha, was at last appointed, who took the trouble to superintend in person the weighing and destruction of the eggs; and to him, therefore, belongs the merit of having freed Cyprus from an intolerable plague. This occurred ten years before the British occupation, and it has rendered the efforts of those who succeeded him much easier.

CHAPTER IX.

KYTHEREA TO LEUCOSIA.

In a Labyrinth of Hills—Perplexity—Trusting to a Boy-guide—The Convent of St. Chrysostom—Interior—History—First View of Leucosia—Besieged by a Crowd—Leucosia Improved under British Rule—A Greek Priest—Still Besieged—A Prison—Cathedral of St. Sophia—A Tragedy—A Priest Photographer.

WE had talked much about the propriety of taking a local guide from Kytherea to St. Chrysostom, our confidence in Georgie's knowledge being somewhat shaken, owing to his exploit in the bog. It happened that amongst the group who conversed with us there was an intelligent boy who spoke Italian, having picked it up during a six years' stay in Alexandria. Violet, being delighted at finding some one to whom she could talk without the aid of an interpreter, asked this boy if he knew the road to the monastery. He replied in the affirmative. Violet asked if he would take us there, and he replied,

'Certainly.'

Some of the bystanders remarked in Greek that he would show us the way out of the village, but this Violet did not, of course, understand. Suddenly, at a turn of the road, we missed Georgie, who was leading two of the animals; and, fearing that he might have taken another path, we sent George back to look after him. The boy then said to us that Georgie wished to take us a very dangerous way, which ran up and down steep hills, where we might easily be killed; that he had refused to come the way he (the boy) was showing us, and had gone off on his own road. This seemed strange, as Georgie had repeatedly said to me that there was only one road.

We walked on, Ibrahîm leading our two mules, and we trusting to the boy. At length a man on horseback rode over the fields towards us, and said that he would guide us to St. Chrysostom. He was a gigantic fellow; but, as he was a total stranger to us, we would have nothing to say to him.

George at length appeared, followed by Georgie, and they said that the man whom we had sent away was a guide whom Georgie had engaged.

We soon got amongst a labyrinth of hills composed of loose earth, whose dreary aspect was hardly enlivened by the few young pine-trees that here begun to sprout since they have been protected by law. The path wound amongst them, sometimes narrowing itself over their tops, and becoming so uncertain that I dismounted and walked.

So we went on, Georgie and the boy sometimes agreeing and sometimes disagreeing as to which path we were to take. At length our guides lost the way altogether. There was no vestige of a path to be seen, nor any trace of our baggage animals, nor of any living creature having been there before us. We dreaded the prospect of darkness overtaking us in such a spot, so far from any human habitation. Georgie went forward, leading his old white horse and two mules, in order to try to discover the best path. The two Arabs walked beside Violet. I took the opportunity of questioning our boy-guide in his native tongue, the only one, notwithstanding his professions, which he thoroughly understood.

'Can you show me where the monastery of St. Chrysostom lies,' I asked, ' in what direction ?'

' It is over the top of the mountain,' he replied. ' You have to pass through that gorge ' (pointing to the *right* hand) ; ' at least I think it is so, for I have never been up here before.' ('τὸ νομίζω, δὲν εἶμαι ἐδῶ ἄλλην φορὰν, ἀλλὰ τὸ ἀκούω.)

'My mother,' he continued, 'will be anxious about me. She does not know I have come with you.'

I turned back, and told this to Violet. We paid the boy three francs, and sent him home.

Then we were in great perplexity. Georgie threw his staff on the ground, and said that we had sent away the only man, his friend, who knew the road, and that he would not move a step further. George scolded him passionately for having brought us here at all, but I ordered him to be quiet. I then said to Georgie,

'The fact is, we *are* here, and you had better do your best to get us on, and find the path before it becomes dark.'

So Georgie set off with the mules, stopping on the top of every little hill to shout. George and

Ibrahîm followed his example, calling out, 'Ya, Salîm! ya, Salîm!' Violet and I echoing it in shriller tones and waving our handkerchiefs. We halted to take a little wine, and George again began scolding his Greek namesake. I ordered him to be quiet, and he explained to us in English that he considered Georgie to have been guilty of impertinence to him in engaging a man as guide without consulting him, or asking either his or our permission.

'He had plenty of time to speak about it at Kytherea,' added George; 'we were four hours there. He has always insisted that a guide is not necessary, as he himself knows all the roads perfectly.'

'No doubt he is to blame,' we replied; 'but we are dependent on his sagacity at this moment, as he is the only one of us who has been here before. So it would be very foolish to quarrel with him.'

Violet pacified Georgie by the offer of some wine and biscuits, and then began to discuss with me what we should do in the event of darkness coming on. We thought we might find a grassy place to sleep; we had a few rugs, and a small supply of biscuits. The air was not cold, so a worse thing might happen to us than having to spend a night out of doors. We then ascended away from the nasty little bare hills into a mountain corn-field, where still there was no sign of a path, and looked along the line of craggy summits in search of a building or a tent. At length, about six o'clock, we espied some sheep near a distant peak, with their shepherd looking down at them over the rocks. We shouted more vociferously, and I waved my handkerchief until I perceived that Georgie, who had gone far ahead, was exchanging some words with him. The man did not offer to come down from the heights, but Georgie waved back to us a signal that he had found a path. Ibrahîm and I climbed up to it, whilst Georgie went back to Violet and George, who were still in the rear. As Ibrahîm and I stood on the path, we saw in the distance a little boy wearing a high cap, riding on a mule and driving two donkeys. I shouted and waved. Ibrahîm ran towards him and brought him up to me. George, in the meantime, striding through the corn and calling out,

'πληρόνω, πληρόνω, ἔχομεν μίαν Κυρίαν, ϛοβεεται.' ('I will pay, I will pay; we have a lady who is afraid.')

I found that the boy was a servant in the monastery, and was returning thither, so we had nothing more to do but to follow him. He guided us to the left, making us at once perceive how far the Italian-speaking boy would have misled us. The path at first ran over mountain turf, and was fairly good, but, as it soon got full of rocks, I foolishly dismounted, and Ibrahîm allowed my mule to run away. Down it galloped into a deep gorge, where it was impossible for the nimble Arab to follow it. He tried to frighten it by throwing up his arms and screaming, but I suggested that he had better just leave it alone, the probability being that, after a few capers, it would run back to George and the old white horse, who were far behind with Violet. So we sat down and waited patiently till they all came up, the runaway mule being with them. I re-mounted, and, pushing on as fast as I could, again left Violet in the rear. The daylight faded more and more, till it hardly sufficed to show us the convent nestling against a cliff on *this* side of the mountain-top, amidst a grove of young pine-trees, old olives, splendid cypresses, and caroub trees which were perfect specimens of their kind.

Our tents were picturesquely situated on a grass-plot near it under the shelter of the heights. The wind was making their canvas heave up and down; plenty of tiny locusts were jumping on the grass and popping their parched-looking little bodies into everything. I sent Salim and two of the muleteers down with lanterns to look for Violet, who arrived some fifteen minutes later in very good spirits, although she had been walking continuously for more than six hours. She was, however, too fatigued to start next morning for Leucosia, so we had to remain at St. Chrysostom till the afternoon.

After breakfast Georgie came and asked pardon for having mistaken the road at the very beginning of our ascent of the little hills. We told him that the first mistake was his presuming to engage a guide without our dragoman's permission or knowledge. We told the latter that we might perhaps have to dismiss Georgie and engage another muleteer at Leucosia, but that in the meantime he had better say nothing on the subject, as it would only lead to useless quarrelling.

Salim left with our tents and baggage at half-past eleven, although the sun was intensely hot. We sat under the shade of an old olive with a hollow trunk, reading and gazing on the remnant of a convent, with its two round towers, one of them shaded by a fine palm-tree, its belfry, and its tall cypresses. We climbed up to a spring which gushes from under a picturesque crag, and observed near it a little bush hung with rags and an infant's cotton pelisse. We then went into the convent, which is by no means an imposing building, being a mere shadow of its former self. It was founded at a very early date by a certain Mary of Molino, who it seems was a Bavarian by birth. There is a tradition to the effect that she was a leper, and was advised by St. Chrysostom to bathe in the brooklet which runs through the monastery garden. She did so, and was healed. Whether this be so or not, Von Löher tells us that two hundred years ago crowds of lepers visited the spot, but that these pilgrimages have ceased, either because the supply of water has run short, or because the dreadful malady is now less common. The same Mary of Molino built the neighbouring castle of Buffavento, on a peak three thousand feet above the level of the sea.

We saw some pictures in the two churches, talked to one of the two married priests who now reside there, got some lemons from the lovely little garden where a fig-tree, a vine, some orange and lemon-trees nestle beneath a dripping crag. This garden stands thirteen hundred feet above the sea, and the steep, rocky mountains behind it rises to a height of two thousand feet.

We saw some nice rooms with iron bedsteads in them for the use of strangers. It only needs a little more cleanliness to turn the place into a paradise of beauty and comfort. The two priests are very hospitable. One of them accompanied us for a short distance down the path. We asked him what was the meaning of the rags hung on the bush near the fountain, and he replied that people liked to come there because St. Chrysostom was a very powerful saint. I could not help thinking that if he of the golden mouth were permitted to return to earth, no one would thunder against such a practice more than he.

We rode downwards by a lonely path, taking a guide on foot from the first hamlet we passed, and following the course of a little stream as it wound amongst the range of bare hills over which we had followed such a wretched track on the previous day. In an hour we reached the plain, with its rich corn crops, and followed the new carriage road, Leucosia rising before us with its minarets, its palm-trees, its cypresses, and its substantial brick wall, reminding us very slightly of Damascus.

We did not know where our tents were, and the sky was not only overcast but a few raindrops had begun to fall. We had to compass half the city by riding round the southern wall before we espied our camp within the gates at the south-west corner. But what a crowd was round it! All the idlers of the town were there gathered, conspicuous amongst them being a priest. George proposed to get a soldier to send them away, but Violet said he must not do so, so long as they did nothing but stare; that the Cypriots were our fellow-countrymen, and she would not have the English made unpopular. We were beginning to change our dresses when George, coming to our tent-door, said,

'El Wali, el Wali.' We hastened out, and found two young gentlemen, one of whom was Mr. Cade, the governor of the prison, and a Mr. Smith. Seeing the crowd, they had come to offer the services of the constabulary to disperse it. We told them Violet's objections, and they said:

'Very well; but the moment they get troublesome you have only to tell the nearest policeman, and you will get rid of this annoyance at once.'

Next came Mr. Blattner, inspector of the island police, who introduced himself as a friend of Mr. Joseph Mezher, and offered to tell us all about the roads, to lend Violet one of his ponies, and to provide us with a safe guide. He, too, wished to send the crowd away. We did not consent to this, but later on they got troublesome to the cook, and the police interfered of their own accord.

I was anxious, while at Leucosia, to obtain Violet's consent to our undertaking the route which would lead us by Lefka to Kykko. Mr. Watkins, the banker at Larnaca, had told me that there was not a bad road in the whole island, so I felt certain that there was now no danger near these places, whatever there may have been in Miss Ripley's time. I saw no other way of crossing the Troados district to Paphos, the only alternative being to return to Leucosia from Morphou, *i.e.*, to renounce seeing the finest half of the island. St. Paul is supposed to have gone from Lefka to Paphos along the western coast, but the roads there are probably worse than the one which Violet wished to avoid.

I therefore questioned everyone I met about this road from Lefka to Kykko, and everyone gave me the same answer, viz., that it was over a wild mountain pass, but that there was no real danger about it; and that it could not be so bad seeing that camels occasionally traverse it. Violet agreed to attempt it, on condition that no one should try to dissuade her from walking over the worst bits.

Our camping-ground swarmed with earwigs and hornets, but otherwise it was not unpleasant.

Leucosia is one of the prettiest towns that I have ever seen. It must have greatly improved under British rule, for most travellers, Mr. Lang amongst the number, represent it as being dirty and ill-paved. The streets are, in comparison with those of other Oriental towns, good and clean; the houses, though of sun-dried brick, are mostly white-washed, the upper floors project; and the bazaar streets are roofed over with ragged canvas and straw matting. It has the picturesqueness of an Eastern town with the order and cleanliness of an English one. Mr. Jolly, of the Imperial Ottoman Bank, showed us his garden, a perfect paradise of roses, gigantic geraniums, and other flowers which attain a size unknown in England. We were particularly struck with the huge ivy-leaves. I mentioned to him my idea about planting the banks of the Cypriot streams from their sources, and he said it would not be at all a bad plan, as it would save trouble in watering the trees, a duty which is accomplished in Leucosia by convict-labour.

A Greek priest had presented himself to us in the morning with some photographs for sale. I, without consulting anyone, made a bargain with him, that he should photograph ourselves and our tents for the sum of three pounds, and we arranged that this should be done in the evening, about sunset.

All the afternoon we had a succession of visits from English residents, ladies and gentlemen, who were most kind in giving us every information in their power, and in pressing us to prolong our stay in Nicosia. Our camp was still besieged by a crowd of natives, but the only way in which they disturbed us was by squatting in the shade of the dining-room tent, and occasionally tumbling against it so as to shake it. George and Ibrahim were much worried with the work of keeping them from doing this; the scoldings of the latter, delivered in sonorous Arabic, were by far the most effectual. Violet at length hit on an original way of getting rid of the nuisance. She purchased for four francs the entire stock of an itinerant cake-seller, and got George to distribute the cakes amongst the crowd; thus changing a source of trouble into one of amusement. At length Mr. Blattner came bringing with him a fine little Baffo pony, named Derwish, which he kindly offered for Violet's use. He escorted us to the prison of Leucosia, at whose door we were received by the governor, Mr. Cade.

The prison building was, in Turkish times, a caravanserai; but it is well suited for its present use. Some zaptiehs were going through their evening drill in the large, open court which forms its interior, and which has in its centre a *tsesme*, or covered fountain. A covered gallery runs round the court. Mounting to this by a staircase, we found some of the convicts engaged in weaving very dexterously the coarse linen, which others were making into white summer jackets for the zaptiehs. Others were sewing (a work for which their fingers were evidently ill-adapted), and others making boots. Most of them were there on life sentences and on sentences of ten to fifteen years; many for murder, and some for burglary. We then passed before the cells on the basement floor, to which light is admitted by means of a window, with a strong iron grating. In each was a plank bed, and a loaf of excellent brown bread. In some the occupant stood in his blue blouse, saluting us in military fashion as we passed. Such looks of utter hopelessness I never before witnessed. We saw two 'dark cells,' which are used for the punishment of the disobedient, and which had each its occupant. We also saw an old fellow who had just murdered his son, and was awaiting trial. Violet thought that he must be insane, but she was told, 'No; he had calculated on the saving he was effecting in being relieved of his child's maintenance.' Cells and passages were paved with stone, and were so scrupulously clean that Violet said she would much prefer to sleep there, in case of bad weather, than in any of the native houses. They are, of course, washed by the convicts' own hands.

We saw the armoury, which was in apple-pie order; tasted the brown bread; looked at the bowls of *yaioûrti*, or sour milk, and smiled at the thought of the convicts having precisely the kind of supper which we have often ourselves relished when in Southern Germany. We asked what the prisons had been previous to the English occupation.

CHURCH OF ST. SOPHIA, NICOSIA.

'Simply indescribable,' was the reply.

'Surely they must appreciate the difference?'

'Possibly; but what they feel to be a great hardship is the deprivation of drink and of tobacco, and the not being permitted to speak to each other, which is particularly severe on Greeks. They are allowed the services of their priests, and are forbidden to read any books, except religious ones. They get regular exercise twice daily. There are one hundred and eighty of them in this prison.'

'Surely that is a large proportion of serious crime,' we said, 'for a population of one hundred and eighty thousand.'

'True; but you must remember that many of them are legacies to us from the Turks; and that since the occupation crime has steadily decreased every year. Last year we had only two cases of murder.'

We next visited the cathedral of St. Sophia, now a mosque, with a covered fountain before its entrance. It is in the early English Decorated style, and has three naves; but its old Gothic towers have been replaced by minarets. For three centuries the kings of Cyprus were crowned within its walls, and here, too, they were buried.

De Cesnola thinks that Leucosia is built on the site of an ancient city; of which, however, we know nothing. It was called Leucosia in the very earliest times, and in Christian ones, Καλλινίκησις. The Italians blended the two into Nicosia. The most important event in its modern history was the siege it sustained for seven weeks in A.D. 1570, when Selim II. led an army of one hundred thousand men against it. Venetian knights defended its walls. They alone represented the wealth and valour of the island, but they had failed to gain the love of their Cypriot subjects, who were too broken-spirited by their oppressive rule to help them in fighting, and are actually supposed to have welcomed the Turks.

After being twice heroically repulsed, the foe stormed the city on the night of the 9th September. The Venetians fought till they were overpowered; their women flung themselves from the roofs of the houses, and many girls were slain by their parents. The work of slaughter and pillage lasted for eight days, and when it ended, the whole town, with the exception of the cathedral, was a heap of ruins.

The tragedy was not, however, ended. An enormous quantity of booty, together with a thousand fair maidens, were placed on board three frigates, to be sent to Constantinople, the first tribute to be paid by Cyprus to the Sultan. But a courageous Greek lady, Maria Suncletiké, managed to convey a spark to the powder magazine, and all three ships perished in the flames. The tribute of Cyprus reaches Constantinople more safely now, for it is carried thither by British hands.

We then rode a little way outside of the walls, past the newly-consecrated and prettily situated English church. Derwish, the pony which Mr. Blattner lent to Violet, had two virtues, it was easy to make his acquaintance, and he never kicked. A pony is considered safer than a mule for ladies. Both are equally sure-footed; but the mule is more timid, being too often treated to knocks, and, as its mouth is hard, it is somewhat difficult for a lady to pull it up when it shies.

The priest came to photograph us just as the sun was setting. It was difficult to keep the camp clear of the crowd after we had all disposed ourselves in order. We found that by far the best plan was to explain the matter to the trespassers, for they withdrew from amongst our servants when they once fairly understood it. Still it was tiresome to learn, after allowing the priest to make two trials, that neither were successful, and that he must return and repeat the experiment at six in the morning, with a result more creditable to his perseverance than to his skill.

CHAPTER X.

FROM LEUCOSIA TO LEFKA.

The Turk, Mustapha—Nicosia, very Warm—The Dreaded Kofi—Lovely Landscapes—Bellapais Abbey—Kyrenia—Mr. Maurogordato—Crime in Cyprus—The Fort—Country Round Kyrenia Lovely—Along the Coast—Lapethus—Monastery of St. Pantalemoni—Encampment and Sunday Rest—The Bishop—Prospects of Union between Greek and Anglican Churches—The British Government and the Schools —At Morphou—An Archimandrite—Lefka—The Feast of St. George —Queen Victoria's Mistake—The Queen's Birthday.

WE started from Leucosia at 7.30. Violet had engaged a guide, on Mr. Blattner's recommendation, who professed to be well acquainted with all the roads in the island. He was a Turk, named Mustapha, and his presence was at first very irritating to George and the other Cypriot muleteers, who were never weary of telling us that he knew nothing about the way. I could not speak much to him, as he pronounced Greek words *à la Turque*. When he was very anxious to make me understand anything, however, he contrived to do so by coming quite close and speaking slowly. George got on with him in Turkish, after a fashion; and Georgie, after he had conquered his ill-humour, got on very well. But at first the poor man was isolated, all our other servants giving him the cold shoulder.

Nicosia is one of the warmest parts of Cyprus, being sheltered on all sides from the sea-breezes. Fortunately for us, a strong wind blew from the mountains, and our way was along a fine new road, where every mile is marked with a mile-stone, V. R. being inscribed on the top. It took us easily over the range of little clay hills, then over corn slopes and thyme slopes, past the village of Dikomo, and up a mountain side, where we soon found a grove of mulberry-trees on the right, and on the left a grove of young fir and pine-trees interspersed with olives. Here we dismounted for lunch, gazing at the row of serried crags above us, and enjoying the shade until three p.m., when we again started, and rode along the high-road to the top of the pass. All at once a wide expanse of sea burst on our view, with a country entirely different from that which we were leaving. The northern slopes of the mountains are covered with fine trees, and far down on the sea-shore the picturesque fort and white houses of Kyrenia nestle amidst the greenery of orchards. A mile-stone indicated that we had only five miles to ride in order to reach it, when suddenly Mustapha struck into a mountain path amidst the lentisks and caroub-trees. Violet, who dislikes such paths, got off Derwish and walked. I did not wish to creep beside her on my mule, so telling Mustapha to remain near her with George and Ibrahim, who, of course, did not know the way, I followed Georgie on his white horse, for which my mule had a great affection. We had not gone far before I saw a huge snake creep into a lentisk bush, where it quietly lay hidden. I had asked Georgie some days before what he would do if he saw one of these creatures. 'Why, kill it with my staff!' was the prompt reply. But he made no effort to disturb this creature.

Georgie had told us about the dreaded kofi, or asp, so-called from the word κωφός (deaf). The Cypriots say that it is deaf for one month, and blind for the next, and that it has a stone in its head. It is small, and of a dark colour.

We rode over many a lovely wooded hill-slope, admiring the large caroub-trees, and looking down on the white, winding high-road that led to Kyrenia, till at last the ruined church of Bellapais came in sight. It surpasses in beauty of situation anything we had seen for a long time. It reminded me of Heidelberg, on a small scale, perched amidst scenery like that of the Riviera, and embosomed in luxuriant olives, figs, caroubs, lemons, and oranges. The style is Decorated Gothic. The church is in tolerable preservation, and is used as the village place of worship. At one end of it is a curious wooden screen, behind which the female part of the congregation worship. The ruined cloisters are the most beautiful part of the edifice. The large Synod hall, one hundred feet long, is intact, and the crypt, to which I descended through a simple hole in the ground, is extremely fine. I talked for an hour with the custodian; then Violet arrived, and, as George expressed his opinion that Bellapais was like Baalbec, I quite gave up hopes of turning him into an antiquarian.

This abbey was founded by a Lusignan king, Hugh III., about A.D. 1280, and was destroyed by the Mamelukes in A.D. 1425. The name is a corruption

RUINED MONASTERY AT BELLAPAIS.

CALIFORNIA

of the French 'Belle Abbaye,' and not of the Italian 'Bel paese,' as is commonly supposed. It is easier to understand how an *s* could attach itself to the end of the one than how an *a* could creep into the middle of the other.

We descended the hill amidst groves of olives and caroubs, beneath whose shade bloomed myriads of scarlet anemones. The road was crossed by numberless rivulets; vines were sometimes trellised over our heads, and the vegetation waxed even more luxuriant till we entered that little paradise of a town, Kyrenia, standing amidst a wealth of pomegranates, lemons, and blooming geraniums; the white houses peeping from a wondrous greenery, and Salim, standing at a street corner to welcome us amidst a group of friendly English people. We found our tents pitched by the sea-shore on a grassy slope close to the fort. How different from our last night's quarters in sultry Leucosia, all overrun with ear-wigs! We sat down to a delightful dinner at 8.30, and were just at dessert, when Mr. Maurogordato, governor of the prison, appeared, accompanied by a Syrian doctor and his wife. They were quite astonished at the idea of our leaving Kyrenia in the morning.

'Why, it is the finest part of Cyprus, and its prison is superior to that of Leucosia, and contains one hundred and forty criminals, mostly murderers! What more could we want?'

'How is there so much crime in a thinly-populated island?' we asked.

'It is mostly among the Moslems,' replied Dr. Fulcihan. 'They are not a third of the population, and yet they furnish eighty per cent. of the crime.'

'How do you account for that?'

'Poverty.'

'But the Moslems had the upper hand for so long that they ought not to be poorer than the Christians.'

'True; but, both having equal advantages, the Moslem always does become poorer than the Christian, because his wife does not work, nor help him.'

Next morning we rose at five and went to see the fort. It looks beautiful on the outside, but I was not allowed to cross the draw-bridge, not being provided with a pass.

Kyrenia was the capital of one of the nine kingdoms into which Cyprus was once divided. It possesses the only haven on the north coast of the island, and the solitary steamer which we saw there was said to be laden with materials for a new harbour, to be built by convict labour.

The streets of Kyrenia now boast English names, and close to the fort is the entrance to a nice quiet bathing-place for ladies. The change which has come over the town may be imagined if the reader will compare our experiences with those of General de Cesnola in 1876.

'The village,' he says, 'with the exception of the citadel, is a small, dirty place, almost exclusively inhabited by Mussulmans, who, with the garrison, enjoy a very bad reputation, second only to that of their co-religionists at Neo-Paphos. I would not have stopped at Kyrenia had I been alone, but, having with me General Crawford, I thought it would afford him pleasure to inspect these old fortifications.'

Nor did he manage to escape without the preliminary of a stone-throwing fight betwixt his servants and the proprietor of the ground, in consequence of which the Governor provided him with a strong force of soldiers and police.

' We spent one night at Kyrenia,' he says, ' and it seemed to us to be old times again, when, encamped on the Potomac river, we were on the *qui vive* for some night attack of the Confederates.'

Ten years later, we two English ladies slept on the same ground, guarded by our servants, whose only weapons of defence were their staves. Nor did we hear a whisper of danger. Yet it is said that the English have done nothing for Cyprus!

We left our encampment at half-past seven, and soon found ourselves amidst scenery like that of the Riviera, but much finer and fresher. We could not help wondering why our countrymen do not come here in winter. Kyrenia is in the same latitude as Algiers and Cashmere, it has lovely excursions, good roads, and excellent water. Its groves of olives, so much esteemed by consumptive patients, are all unenclosed, so that one does not need, as at Mentone. to fear the snarling dogs, nor the peasants who bar the mountain paths and tell you, ' C'est ma campagne.' It has abundance of shady woods and a vegetation like that of Cape St. Martin,* extending for miles and miles; it has wheat-fields and bean-fields aglow with the red anemone, and, above all, a range of mountains crowned with crags and pierced by

* A favourite resort of visitors to Mentone.

wild valleys. I was so impressed with the idea, that I wrote to Mr. Maurogordato, asking if he could furnish me with any particulars about the climate of Kyrenia, what accommodation the town can offer to European visitors, and what opinion the local doctors hold as to its suitability for invalids. His answer will be found in the chapter on the climate of Cyprus.

We rode for two hours along the coast amidst scenery of this kind, passed the convent of Acheropiti on the right, then toiled up to the village of Lapithus, with its two pretty churches, its gushing streams, and its horribly bad roads. Two poor beggars, who stood with tin plates in their hands at a church door, were, I feel sure, lepers; but this I could not ascertain, as both George and Georgie professed not to have seen them.

Lapithus was once the capital of one of the ten kingdoms. It was founded by Phœnicians, and colonized by Spartans. Its name was synonymous with stupidity, and it contained a fine temple to Aphrodite.

As we went on, the trees became less numerous, and the corn-fields being already reaped, the country was a little more open. At half-past eleven we rested beneath the shade of some old olives. Starting again at half-past three, we descended to the sea-shore, along which we rode, and then struck into a mountain-pass at the lowest part of the range.

Here were not many trees, but a luxuriant growth of lentisks, small caroubs, and pines; with wild roses peeping from under every thicket. The sun was oppressively hot, and we crossed and re-crossed a small stream, till at last we came into a wide valley whose sides were dotted with corn-fields. Passing through this, we ascended the hills by a broad, stony, winding path till at last the northern sea seemed far beneath us, and we had a glorious view of the crags on the southern side of the mountain range. On we wound till at last we espied our tents beneath one of two groves of tall pine-trees, about twenty yards from the large monastery of St. Pantelemoni; behind which nestles the grey village of Myrti. No spot could have been better chosen for our Sunday rest. It was on an upland plain, commanding a view of the lofty Troados mountains in front, whose valleys we hoped to explore in the coming week, and of the smaller Kyrenian range to the east. Our tents were pitched beneath branching pines, on fresh green grass apparently free from insects, half-way betwixt the monastery and the village. We reached them at a quarter to six, so that the distance from Kyrenia to Myrti may be calculated as six-and-a-quarter hours.

Next day being Sunday, we rested, the village-women and children gathering about our tent-door. About two o'clock the Bishop of Kyrenia, who resides in the monastery, sent his servant to ask when we were going to visit the church. We replied at half-past four, and accordingly walked there at that hour, accompanied by George.

It was an occasion on which ordinary dragomans would have got themselves up magnificently; ours, on the contrary, seemed to have made himself shabbier than usual. The monastery consists of a large oblong enclosure, with the church in its centre, and the dwellings of the monks all round. Near the entrance-gate is a large room devoted to the feeding of silk-worms, millions of which feast on mulberry-leaves in the usual bamboo frames. We were met by a priest at the foot of the staircase, and by the bishop himself at the top of it. The bishop is a handsome, intelligent man of middle-age, who was formerly priest and schoolmaster at Larnaca, just before the English occupation. We conversed for a little in his reception-room, Violet in French, and I in Greek; and then descended to the church, which contains some curious old paintings, chief of which is one, in embossed gold, of St. Pantelemoni, dated about A.D. 1719, and another, in silver, of later workmanship. Violet having expressed a wish to see the garden, the bishop accompanied us thither, offering us specimens of all its products for our table, and apologising for the state of neglect in which we saw it. He and the priest then walked with us back to our tents, and we asked them to remain and dine with us. The priest scarcely spoke when in the bishop's presence, but, whilst walking with me, he lamented the disposition displayed by both Greek and Cypriot peasants to despise manual work whenever they have got a little book-learning.

Some Maronite monks from St. Elias arrived whilst we were at the convent, and seemed to be quite at home with their Greek *confrères*. There is a small Maronite village near Myrti.

Salim having placed chairs for our two visitors outside of the tent-door, the cook and each of the muleteers came up in turn to kiss the bishop's hand.

Each was spoken to in fatherly tones, interrogated as to where he lived, and enjoined to take great care of us. Georgie II. caused much amusement by replying that it was the anxious desire of himself and his brethren to do so, but that we were under the immediate charge of the Arabs, who disliked any interference with their duties.

We discussed, after dinner, the prospects of a union between the Greek and the Anglican churches; and here I had the advantage over Violet, the bishop preferring his own tongue when treating of such a theme. I explained that, though a native of Scotland, and a Presbyterian, I was deeply interested in the Church of England, and often partook of the Holy Communion with her members, there being no difference betwixt the teachings of the Churches of England and of Scotland which would prevent my doing so. I said that I thought the greatest want in the Church of England was the lack of a synod, or governing body, which would make her independent of Parliament, and that I really did not see how she could open negotiations with another church until she possessed a representative assembly, composed either of prelates, like the Greek synod, or of clerics and laymen, like ours.

The bishop, who has a clearer view of the subject than most Greek ecclesiastics, replied that on the side of the Greek church there were two very practical difficulties. The first is, that the Church of England does not accept images.

'You must know,' he said, 'that with us the higher clergy are extremely well educated, but the lower clergy are as yet very ignorant. We do not give to these images anything in the least approaching worship (λατρεία) but we think it good for the people to see pictures of good and great men, and to be told that they ought to take these men for an example. It is true that the ignorant do not quite understand this. The second difficulty is that the Church of England does not insist on fasting. We observe it in sympathy with Our Lord and His apostles.'

'The Church of Scotland favours it still less,' said I.

'With you, I suppose,' said the bishop, 'anyone can be a pastor?'

'In that you are mistaken,' I replied. 'You are confounding us with some other body of Protestants. We are quite as particular on this point as the Church of England is. Our pastors all receive a university education, and no one can presume to administer the sacrament unless he has been ordained, like Timothy, by the laying on of the hands of the presbytery. We consider them all bishops, in fact; but no one has the pre-eminence, excepting what Nature may have given him through his superior talents. Our church government is vested in a synod or assembly.'

'Well, that is thoroughly Apostolic,' said the bishop.

'May I ask,' said I, 'how your archbishop is appointed?'

'The people meet together, and elect him.'

'And who consecrates him?'

'The three bishops.'

'And who appoints them?'

'They are elected in the same way, and consecrated by the archbishop. The Cypriot church is thus quite independent of foreign interference. How are bishops appointed in England?'

I told him by the prime minister, who issues a *congé d'élire* for the election of a man whose name is already determined on. This he seemed to think a great abuse.

Cyprus has now an archbishop and three bishops, who take their titles respectively from Paphos, Kyrenia, and Citium. In former times, it had thirteen bishoprics, whose dioceses could not have been much larger than an ordinary English parish.

'I have been told,' I said, 'that English rule is not quite popular with the Cypriot priests, because you find it hard that your lands should bear their share of the taxes, and also that you think the valuation of land by the government is too high.'

The bishop smiled.

'These are matters on which I would rather not give an opinion,' he said. 'But it is true that we find it harder to live than formerly. In the old times we got a *Berat* from the Turkish Government which empowered us to levy contributions on our flocks. This has not been renewed by the English, and, as the people are left free to give what they like, they give very little. How are your Presbyterian pastors supported?'

'In Scotland some of them have glebes and tithes, because they belong to the Established Church,' I replied. 'Those who have not this advantage get their income from two sources. First, from pew-rents, which are not very high, and secondly, from a plate which is always placed near the door of the church, and into which everyone puts a coin of some kind on Sunday morning, in obedience to the Apostle's command that everyone should lay by in store as God has prospered him (Corinthians I., xvi, 2). They are taught to look on the support of Gospel ordinances as a privilege, as well as a duty.'

'That is really a capital idea,' said the bishop. 'How much does your pastor get?'

'His income is a thousand a year,' I replied, 'and it comes entirely from the liberality of his people, who have built the church also at a cost of fifteen thousand pounds.'

The bishop was much astonished.

'We never dream of our people doing anything like that in Cyprus,' he said.

'Do you ever preach to them?' I asked. 'I mean, do you ever give them a sermon from the pulpit?'

'Only the bishop preaches,' he replied, 'when he makes his annual visit to a parish. He does not preach every Sunday. I ought to tell you that there is one thing for which we are very grateful to the English Government, and that is for the help they give to the schools. The only thing we fear is that with the spread of education materialistic ideas will have more liberty to creep in.'

'Do you think Cyprus is unhealthy?' asked Violet.

'We who live here never find it so,' replied the bishop. 'I believe it has got a bad name with some people because the English soldiers first came here in a summer of exceptional heat. They exposed themselves to the sun at mid-day, and then rushed into cold water.'

Next day I did not feel very well, so we remained at Pantelemoni. The bishop kindly invited us to luncheon, but this we were obliged respectfully to decline. He and Father Iakobos called after dinner, and we had a long discussion on homœopathy. During the day we received many presents from him in the shape of wine, cheese, and honey. We sent on our tents next morning, and followed ourselves in the afternoon. We rode down a range of hills covered with young pines and thyme, both of which filled the air with a delightful fragrance. At the top of a little hill the blue gulf of Morphou, or Soli, burst on our view. We descended to the plain of Messaria, and espied the village of Morphou embosomed in trees, and before us the long, majestic line of the Troados mountains, with just a tinge of snow on the highest peak. We crossed many a little stream, and wondered at the abundance of white-shelled snails which hung in clusters on every bush and stalk of tall grass.

At Morphou our tents were pitched in a newly-reaped field close to the town under spreading mulberries, where the clods beneath our feet seemed like big stones under the carpets. The whole population of Morphou crowded about us.

'Do these people never see tents?' we asked of Georgie.

'Oh! yes, they do,' he replied, 'but they are military ones, not quite so luxurious as yours.'

I could not see what he meant by luxury, unless it was in the gay embroideries of the interior, or perhaps in the presence of a cook.

There was a monastery close at hand, and a well-dressed priest stood amongst the crowd. I accosted him, and, as he said he was an Archimandrite, we invited him to dinner. He told us that he resides alone in the monastery, and superintends the two village priests, who eke out their small incomes by manual work on their farms.

'Do you find any improvement here since the English occupation?' we asked.

'Assuredly,' he replied.

'Were not the Cypriots delighted when they first heard of it?'

'To tell you the truth, they were most of them too ignorant to understand the change. What opened their eyes was this: They had till then suffered much from the exactions of the Zaptiehs, one of whom would come down on a family, and make them give him food and lodging for nothing. Now, not only does this never happen, but there are actually Christian Zaptiehs in the force. The grants to schools are also very highly appreciated. Tomorrow is a feast-day with us. It is the birthday of St. George, and we hold it in honour of the King of Greece.'

'How many sovereigns do you acknowledge in Cyprus?'

'Three—the Sultan, Queen Victoria, and King George. Man's duty consists in three things—viz., that he obey God first, the king second, and the priest third.'

I asked the Archimandrite to repeat this, and he did so; but seemed a little shaky in regard to the third point, for he substituted the word θρησκείαν (religion) for ἱερέα (priest); probably because he had remarked a little surprise on my face. I should have thought that θρησκεία was included in his first proposition.

We left Morphou about half-past seven in the morning, our baggage being packed, and our mules loaded, with some difficulty, owing to the pressure of the people around us. The Archimandrite, who came to say good-bye, made many apologies for their conduct, saying that it was because they knew no better, and they very seldom saw travellers. Our way lay for two hours across the almost treeless plain, past the villages of Asellia and Aghagivera, nestling in mulberry and palm-trees. Then we dived into a grove of olives, crossed some streamlets more or less muddy, and one good, broad burn; then came in sight of the village of Lefka, a perfect oasis of verdure on a spur of the mountains. We wound amongst its pomegranate-gardens and crossed its many streams, till at last we found Salîm busy pitching our tents above the village close to some threshing-floors, where oxen were busy treading out straw for their own consumption. Foolish beasts! I thought; if you were less fastidious, you would not need to work so hard. Mr. Hamilton Lang tells us that the Cypriot ox will not touch straw until it has been chopped quite small for him, and that farmers consider the process of doing this to be the hardest labour to which their animals are put. But human beings are, after all, just as fanciful, and make more trouble for themselves and for others than is at all necessary.

I sat down on the roots of a tall lime-tree, with a rushing stream at my back, and gazed over the green groves of the village and the grassy hills on to the bay of Soli, where the sea was all curling with white waves, its brilliant blue shading into opal as it washed the shore. Down there once resided one of the greatest of Greece's lawgivers, a man the influence of whose intellect and ripe judgment we still feel. How wonderful it is that we English should, in these latter days, be privileged to bring the blessing of good government to a place which once gave shelter to the aged Solon!

Plutarch tells us that the great lawgiver visited Cyprus as the guest of Philocyprus, or Cypranor, King of Aipeia, a town whose site has lately been identified on the crest of a steep hill to the west of Lefka. Solon observed the fruitful plain below, and advised the king to transfer his people to it. Philocyprus did so, and named the new town after his friend, Solon.

The name Soli, however, unfortunately for Plutarch, has been found to occur a century earlier amongst the names of the Cypriot kingdoms which sent presents to Esarhaddon.

The bad Greek spoken by its inhabitants has given us our word 'solecism,' from σολοικίζω, to speak badly.*

* Soli in Cilicia has disputed the palm of this derivation with Soli in Cyprus. But it is to the latter that the epigram of Ammianos refers :
'Επτὰ Σολοικισμοὺς Φλάκκῳ τῷ ῥήτορι δῶρον
πέμψας, ἀντέλαβον πέντε διακοσίους
καὶ Νῦν μὲν, φησι, τούτους ἀριθμῷ σοι ἔπεμψα,
τοῦ λοιποῦ δὲ μέτρῳ πρὸς Κυπρον ἐρχόμενος.

De Cesnola found, on the site of Soli, what appeared to be the remains of a theatre, and also the foundations of a little circular temple, consisting of blocks of limestone, quarried from the neighbouring hills. Within the area of this temple he discovered fragments of columns and capitals in marble and granite, and a slab with a Greek inscription, much injured, but containing the names of Soli and of the Pro-Consul Paulus, most probably the Sergius Paulus who is mentioned in the Acts of the Apostles as the deputy of the country, and who, when Paul and Barnabas arrived at Paphos, desired to hear the Word of God, and was nearly wiled away from doing so by the subtilty of Elymas, the sorcerer. (Acts xiii, 6.)

The day of our arrival at Lefka was the Feast of St. George, being May 5, according to our calendar, but April 23, according to the Greek one. It was, therefore, the fête-day of our dragoman, of two of our muletcers, and of the King of Greece. The villages through which we passed were decorated with small flags in honour of the king, and it was evidently being observed as a national holiday.

Now, when did this custom begin? St. George seems to be popular in Beyrout as well as in Cyprus, if I may judge from the difficulty I had in distinguishing between several Arabs of that name. I suspect that the dragon-slayer has been made up by a combination of three individuals, one a bishop of Antioch, in Pisidia, who seems to have had a great liking for the veneration of holy images; one, a native of Cyprus; and one who was born in Cappadocia, and inherited from his mother property in

Palestine. The latter was a tribune and soldier under the Emperor Diocletian, but resigned his commission when that emperor made war against the Christians. He was thrown into prison for remonstrating against cruel edicts, and was afterwards beheaded at Nicomedia.

The first and third of these Georges were, I suspect, the most distinguished; but the existence of the second enables the Cypriots to claim the mythical saint as their countryman.

St. George was the especial patron of soldiers. He is said to have appeared to the army of the Crusaders before the battle of Antioch, which was won by Godfrey de Bouillon, and he also appeared to Richard Cœur de Lion, in his campaign against the Saracens. The dragon which he is represented as slaying is only an emblem of the old serpent, the devil, whom he resisted in spirit.

I wonder whom the Cypriots do look on as their legitimate sovereign? There would have been no use in our putting the question to them, for we should probably not have got a sincere answer. But I could not help recollecting an opinion which my late beloved father often expressed to me.

'I consider,' he said, 'that Her Majesty, during the course of her eventful reign, has made very few mistakes, and that the most serious of these is the alteration of the day on which her birthday is kept. I well remember, from my earliest childhood, how the birthdays of her uncles George IV. and William IV. were celebrated; not in Scotland only, but from one end of the kingdom to the other, in the most remote corners. There was an enthusiasm evoked by the recurrence of the day which was simply indescribable. Where do we see a trace of such enthusiasm now? I would be very far from saying that the feeling of loyalty does not exist. Her Majesty is, in fact, more deeply loved than were her immediate predecessors, but the annual expression of it was unmistakably cooled when people found that the festival was not to be observed on the right day. The custom of keeping it at all is in many places dying out. Her Majesty may have had good reasons for the change, but I say that it was unwise to interfere with a celebration which had existed for centuries.'

If this consideration has any weight when applied to the inhabitants of the British Isles, how much more does it apply to alien races, in whom the sentiment of loyalty to the British throne has as yet to be created?

I again thought of my father's words while at Larnaca, when we were told that Her Majesty's birthday would be celebrated by a grand ball, to be given at Nicosia by the Governor on May 26. Foreign sovereigns may not win the love of their subjects as our beloved Queen has done, but they know better than to alter the day on which their fêtes shall be observed.

Salîm interrupted my reverie by bringing in some lemons grown in the village, each of which was nearly as large as his own head. He and George, however, were never tired of depreciating the Cyprus fruits, comparing them unfavourably with those of Syria. 'These lemons are large,' said Salîm, 'but they do not last so long as ours do.' In proof of this he produced one which he had rescued from destruction at the Custom-house. It had not decayed, but there was hardly a drop of juice in it.

The wind was very high, and we had some slight fear of our tents being blown down. In the afternoon we had a visit from the Mudir, the doctor, and other notabilities of the village, which is inhabited almost exclusively by Moslems. Only one of them, a young Christian, could speak Greek fluently, but the Mudir, fortunately for me, knew some Arabic. I ascertained from him that there are two hundred families in the town, that there is often sickness in the interior of it, owing to the abundance of water about the gardens; that there are schools for boys and for girls, and that they all study the Kurân.

'But in what language do they study it?' I asked.

'In Arabic.'

'Have they a Turkish translation?'

'No, they have not; they read it in the original.'

'Then do they learn Arabic?'

'No, they don't. They just learn the words.'

Poor children!

We could not get any precise information about the road between Lefka and Kykko, which, it will be remembered, was the one that Violet so much dreaded. Its length was variously stated as two hours, three hours, eight hours, ten hours, and twelve English miles. The Mudir of Lefka said it was seven hours, but added that, as it was uphill, the journey would be a trying one for our mules. We therefore decided to take George's advice, and break it by sleeping at Campos. The Mudir told us that many English travellers had passed through Lefka shortly after the cession of the island, but that very few had come since.

CHAPTER XI.

FROM LEFKA TO KYKKO.

A Case of Overloading—Deep Solitudes—A Pleasant Resting-place—A Testimony to British Rule and Improvement—Campos—Polite Reception—A Pleasant Road—Kykko—The Monastery—Reception there from Monks—Conversation with Them—Present of Wine—Monks come to Tea in the Tent—'Resurrection of the Virgin'—The Monks Chanting—A Scene of the Middle-Ages.

The Mudir came in the morning to see us off, pointed out the situation of Kykko on the top of a high, pine-covered mountain, and said that we should be four hours in reaching Campos. To my surprise, we followed a road that led between thick green hedges downwards to the sea, till I began to think they were taking us by a roundabout way, instead of by that mysterious defile about which we had heard such horrors, and about whose length no two people who have passed through it seemed able to agree.

We started at 7.15, and at 8.15 were just above the village of Karabastagi, when we turned our faces towards the mountains and entered the stony bed of a winter torrent. For an hour we followed a path which wound amongst the gravel, crossing and re-crossing the thin thread of a stream which was all that remained of its once swelling waters.

Georgie said that people passed here on horseback all the year round, even when the torrent-bed was quite full.

At 9.30 we entered a narrow defile between green hills, half clothed with dark pines and grey olives, brightened by the yellow of the broom, and the pink of the wild rose. We were reminded slightly of the valleys betwixt Damascus and Baalbec. The path ran winding along the mountain side, now on the right, and now on the left of the stream. It was sometimes narrow, and often we looked over a precipice, but everywhere it showed the marks of a careful hand, for at the dangerous places the stones had been gathered out of it, and piled up so as to form a low fence, or boughs of prickly shrubs had been laid along the edge wherever there was no natural rampart growing. It averaged about four feet in breadth, and few indeed were the spots where two laden mules might not have passed each other. We should have been thankful for a few yards of such a path betwixt Andritzena and Olympia, or at Bassæ, or betwixt Megaspelion and the Styx; or even in the neighbourhood of Delphi. My only source of discomfort was that whilst riding behind Georgie, I saw that he had over-laden his old white horse by placing on it, in addition to its usual burden, two enormous bags of barley. We had all remonstrated with him about this before starting, and had received the usual answer of δὲν πειράζει. Now, though he walked in order to relieve it whenever we came to a steep place, the three sets of things on its back worked their way towards its tail, and not only did it often look unable to move on, but I was in fear lest its whole load should tumble off on to the nose of my mule. Georgie suddenly made it stop at a most inconvenient spot, untied one of the bits of cord which did duty for garters to the leggings of his big leather boots, caught hold of the end of one of the saddle-bags, and tied it together, letting me see how nearly he had precipitated our medicine-bottles on to the road. George remonstrated with him for this careless loading, and received the usual answer: 'τί νὰ κάμωμεν;' ('What can we do?') Violet, however, insisted on the barley being transferred to Mustapha's mule.

We passed on into even deeper solitude, seeing no trace of man save our path and an occasional rustic mill turned by a foaming torrent. There was a peculiar softness in the scenery, owing to the abundance of young tufted pines, which, as we afterwards learned, have all been planted by the English Government.

At eleven o'clock we rested in a more open spot, where was a mulberry-garden, with a large old olive and some rocks in the centre, the stream below, and a water conduit above. Here the mountain slopes were of a red colour, and were in some places planted with vines, even in spots which seemed to us inaccessible. We heard the cuckoo's cry, and I thought I saw a little yellow snake run into a clump of lentisks, at which we poked for some time in vain. We re-mounted and rode for nearly two hours through a scene of great sylvan beauty. The mountains were clothed with young pines to their summits, save where the tender bright green leaves of the vine were just bursting forth on their steep red slopes. The path wound about, now far above the stream, now diving down to it by a steep rocky incline, now passing between shrubbery of caroub and arbutus that reminded us of an English nobleman's pleasure-grounds, now leading up a rough hill where the mules hardly seemed to have a foothold. But it was tolerably free from loose stones. At one place the broad bed of the winter torrent was occupied by twelve large old sycamore-trees; and here we were strongly reminded of the entrance to the vale of Tempe in Thessaly, or of a well-remembered spot in the Peloponnesus, half-way betwixt Andritzena and Kreki. At length we espied far up the valley a picturesque little stone church and a hamlet clustering behind it; all perched on a hill, and shaded by lofty walnut-trees. As we approached, the sound of a clanging bell issued from the modest belfry, and, as I happened to be first, I rode up to a little group of people near the church door. A woman stepped forward with a pan of incense; then appeared a picturesque old man leaning on a staff, then the school-boys standing in a row on either side of the path, their hands folded across their breasts and making deep obeisances as I passed them.

As I rode along the narrow way betwixt the chasm of the stream and the houses, white-robed peasant-women greeted me from every doorway. I found our tents pitched on a grassy bank in the dry bed of the stream close to the village well, and underneath the spreading branches of the walnut-trees. Seldom have I seen a sweeter spot. The music of waters was all round it, and the group of little, square, stone houses above, their roofs thatched with withered boughs, had quite the outline of an old Norman castle. Corn and mulberry-trees abounded on the mountain slopes, which were studded likewise with white, wild roses and scarlet anemones. Violet had dismounted just before she arrived at the village; she was well fumigated with incense and had scented water poured over her hands. She arrived at the tent-door accompanied by the schoolmaster and some women, whose welcomes I had to interpret for her. The air was filled with the notes of the little nightingales, and we felt as if we were in the very home of the Naiads and Dryads. The ground was so sloping that we could hardly make our chairs stand straight, and preferred squatting on the ground.

The schoolmaster sent us a bottle of Commanderia wine. After dinner, we invited him into our tent, and found him a most intelligent man.

'Before the English came,' he said, 'we were in a state of utter barbarism; no better than the horses, the beasts. But our Lady, the Queen, took possession of us and our minds began to develop. Our Queen wishes us to learn letters. May the years of your Queen, our Queen, and of Mr. Spencer,* be many! Εἴμεθα ἐλεύθεροι! (We are free!)'

'Where were you educated?' we asked.

'At Nicosia. I have been here for two-and-a-half years, and I see an improvement already in the juvenile population.'

* Rev. J. Spencer, M.A., English Chaplain at Nicosia, and her Majesty's Inspector of Schools.

'Is it true,' asked Violet, 'that your priests are not quite favourable to the English Government because they have to pay taxes?'

'But they don't pay the military tax;' (*i.e.*, the tax for exemption from military service).

'I mean the tax on their lands.'

'Well, but *we* want them to pay that. Before the English came, the priests paid nothing, and a rich Turk in Leucosia, he would pay nothing either; whereas the poor man had to pay to the uttermost farthing.'

'Do many travellers pass this way?'

'Very few, excepting on the twentieth of September, the fête day of the Virgin. Then we have crowds.'

'How often have you a post?'

'For letters, do you mean? Never.'

'Then if you wish to write a letter, what do you do?'

'I get some one who is going to Lefka or to Baffo to take it.'

'Well, that is curious,' said I. 'I hardly think you could find a village in Greece without a post-office. But then every young man there can read; and, I suppose, it would not pay to have a post-office here for you alone.'

'When the spring rains cease,' said the schoolmaster, 'all the villagers, old and young, turn out to repair the road.'

'The road,' I said, 'might be better, but we had infinitely worse in Greece.'

'Why, they tell us everything is so perfect in Greece!' said the schoolmaster, laughing.

'Are you not afraid of serpents?' asked Violet.

'No,' he replied, 'they never come near houses, for they dread the cats. Pussy catches them in her claws, kills them with her teeth, and makes a good meal of them.'

Campos is most inappropriately named, for it stands in a valley far too narrow to admit of much cultivated ground. In the morning, when we came out of our tent, the village people had again assembled to greet us. Some presented us with bouquets, one fumigated us with incense, and one poured over our hands a fragrant water made from the wild roses of the country.

They all stood and looked, but did not annoy us, as the people at Leucosia and at Morphou had done. The schoolmaster evidently taught them manners. We gazed with great interest on this man. He had only thirty-five pupils, but he represented the principles of progress, which it is the privilege of our country to impart to the Cypriots.

We waited whilst our mules were being loaded, George having arranged that they should precede us, in consequence of all the tales we had heard about the difficulties of the ascent. As we waited we had a curious illustration of what travellers must expect who can only converse with the natives by means of a dragoman. We had given a small contribution for the school on the preceding evening, and now Violet, having noticed some very poor women, pulled out a few francs and said to me that she wished it divided amongst them.

'How are we to manage that?' I asked, 'if we have no smaller coins? Shall we give it to one woman and let the others hear us tell her that it is for them all?'

'Better ask the schoolmaster to do it,' suggested George.

The schoolmaster, who stood near, was accordingly called. Violet offered him the money, and said in English that it was for these poor people. George explained that it was 'διὰ τὴν ἐκκλησίαν' ('For the church'). I said, 'No, διὰ τοὺς πτωχούς' ('For the poor').

The schoolmaster's black eyes sparkled.

'Διὰ τὸ σχολεῖόν μου,' he said, as he took the money. I nodded assent, thinking that he had indicated the best use for it. But I could not help being amused; for I had already remarked the wonderful alterations that took place in Violet's sayings whenever George acted as her interpreter. Here is a specimen:

'Georgie,' she would say, 'you have been very attentive to me, and it was very kind of you to come back and help me over that brook. But I really do not need you when George and Ibrahîm are near. I should prefer that you remained with Miss Smith, and see that no harm happens to her. Will you explain it to him, George?'

'How dare you do such a thing, Georgie?' the dragoman would say. 'Don't you see, you are leaving Miss Smith alone. The lady is very angry indeed with you. Go away from her instantly.'

This kind of thing irritated me at first, until I discovered that George really did not know enough of English to understand all that Violet said.

After leaving Campos, our road ran at first up

a little watercourse betwixt blooming hedge-rows. It then continued by an easy ascent in a deep hollow, whose sides were thickly planted with caroubs, hazel-nuts, wild roses, and occasionally hawthorn. At the top of it we overtook our retinue. We halted under the shade of a great, old olive till they had again distanced us. The sky was much overcast, and we feared rain, which, happily, did not come. Whilst we were passing the village of Kanistra a woman poured some rose-water over our hands. The house-roofs were thatched with twigs and branches, over-laid with earth. On this grass sometimes grows, as in Norway. Sometimes the roof is strewn with gravel, and, where built against a declivity, it is hardly to be distinguished from the road, and the traveller must be careful not to ride on to it.

We now began to ascend the hills by a steep, winding path, at first bordered by shrubbery, but afterwards carried along the bare mountain-side. The view was extremely magnificent. We looked across hill-tops dotted with the dark green of the pine and the light green of the almond-tree down to the blue bay of Soli. On our left, a wilderness of such summits separated us from the snow-streaked Mount Troados. In front was another vista of wooded mountain tops and deep valleys; but it seemed to end in plains, and not in the sea. Georgie and I got on far before the others, and he began to talk about the load on one of Aristides' mules, which load consisted of the canteen and a box of kitchen things to balance it. All the muleteers had objected to it when they started from Larnaca, and it had been arranged that each should carry it on one or other of his beasts for three days in succession. To-day it was Aristides' turn, and they were all pitying him for having got it at such a steep place. The canteen was a nasty box. You could not divide it; it must all go together. It was suitable for a waggon, or for a boat, or for a camel's load, but not for a mule. I asked Georgie what our mules cost per day, and he replied, half-a-crown each. Our fifteen must, therefore, have cost thirty-seven shillings and sixpence.

After winding round numberless hill-sides, we came in sight of the monastery, a two-storied building, partly of grey stone, and partly white-washed. I was far in advance, Violet having dismounted, and, as I turned the last corner, I saw quite an array of monks at the door. The bells rang a merry peal; and I knew this was to welcome us, a letter from the Bishop of Kyrenia having preceded us. I rode up to the door, dismounted, and shook hands with all the reverend fathers.

'Where was the other lady?' they asked.

I felt that the dignity of our approach was somewhat marred by Violet's absence, but I put the best face I could on it, and said that she was very cautious and liked to walk at every steep place, having been much frightened since she fell off her mule near Lefkoniko. I had then to relate all the circumstances of that accident. One of the monks preceded me into the convent.

The moment I placed my foot on its threshold a great bell added its voice to that of the other bells, and went boom, boom as I ascended a flight of stairs, all scrupulously clean, into a long room with white-washed walls, a book-case at one end, and a lovely blue and gilt candelabra depending from the ceiling. A large bronze church candlestick displayed a solitary lighted candle. At the end of the room opposite the book-case was a raised divan, and all along the side walls a row of canechairs. I was asked to seat myself on the divan, and place my feet on the rail of a chair, whilst twelve monks seated themselves on the other chairs. I asked for the Hegoumenos, and was told that he lives at Leucosia, being too old to come up here. I talked with them for about half-an-hour, and young boy servants with long hair and tall caps presented me with sweets and coffee. There were not many monks in the convent at that season, most of them being scattered over the country superintending the harvest. Every Cypriot comes here once at least in his life, on the Virgin's fête day, and he is then considered a Hagi.

None of the monks had ever been in Greece. They thought it more likely that the English residents will learn Greek than that the Cypriots will learn English, an opinion which they are by no means alone in holding. They asked me if there was war between Greece and Turkey, and I replied that they were much more likely to know than I was. Just then the little bells began to sound, and I knew that Violet had arrived, the boom of the great bell announcing her entrance into the monastery. She was in very good spirits, and the chief monk set all his brethren laughing by saying 'Good-morning' to her in English. We invited two of them to dinner; but, as it was Friday, they could not come. They promised, however, to take tea in our tents in the afternoon. They showed us their guest-chamber, which was, of course, at our disposal, but we declined to occupy it, on the plea that we had got accustomed to our tents. These were pitched in a most romantic spot on the brow of a cliff close behind the convent, looking down a precipice into a deep wooded valley. We both agreed that we never saw anything quite so charming. We should have liked to stay for a few days, but that was impossible, as we did not wish to lose the French steamer at Larnaca.

The monks accompanied us to the tent door, and asked if there was anything we should like. Violet suggested wine, and accordingly there appeared on our luncheon-table one bottle of black wine, one bottle of Commanderia, and one of a sweet liqueur, like curaçoa. Violet gave a glass to each of our servants, Mustapha alone declining to take it. The only drawback to our pleasure was the high wind.

About four p.m. two of the monks came and had a cup of tea. We had a long talk about Greece and Turkey, and they were much interested by our descriptions of Thessaly. They took us into the monastery, and showed us two deep wells which they have for rain-water, which are filled by means of conduits in winter time. Their spring would soon fail were all the pilgrims who come in September to drink from it. We were then taken into the church, which is a small building in the interior of the monastery, but on a lower level, the ground being uneven. It contains some fine old paintings, and is in the same state as when built in the time of the Byzantine emperor, Alexius Comnenus. There are many curious paintings on wood, representing saints whose hands, faces, halos, crowns, etc., are of silver. But the chief glory of the church is a portrait of the Virgin, said to be the work of St. Luke. The original is, unfortunately, not to be seen. It was already covered up with silver gilt, and with uncut gems when it was sent hither from Constantinople by Alexius Comnenus. But perhaps this is not to be regretted, for the black image of the Virgin by St. Luke, which is exhibited in the Convent of Megaspelion in the Peloponnesus, is really very ugly.

The canopy round this picture is exquisite. It is of some kind of precious wood, inlaid with ivory. There is also a picture of the Virgin looking at her own portrait after St. Luke has finished it.

Violet returned to the tents, but I said that, if they would kindly furnish me with a prayer-book, I should like to be present at evening prayers. I accordingly placed myself in one of the stalls. A young man with long hair began by repeating prayers of which the first words were Κύριε ἐλέησον, Δόξα Θεῷ and Χριστὸς ἀνέστη very often and very fast, until I gave up in despair the attempt to follow him. I employed myself in reading about the resurrection of the Virgin; how it took place three days after she was buried, how she appeared to the disciples, who, when they looked into her grave, found that it was empty, and how after that they were in the habit of saying, 'Μήτηρ Θεοῦ βοήθησον ἡμῖν' ('Mother of God, help us').

The monks then chanted what was supposed to be the 83rd Psalm, but it was in tones more nasal than those of the Arabs. Then the folding-doors of the screen were opened, and two priests, robed in white silk brocade studded with bunches of red roses and green leaves, with long curls of hair hanging down below their high black caps, marched round the shrine in the inner sanctuary, then came out and went round the church swinging a censer with which they incensed every picture and every person, bowing to the pictures, and occasionally chanting in unison with the priests. Each of our muleteers came in, crossed himself, and bowed before the pictures until his head touched the ground.

Whilst this was going on, George, our dragoman, appeared without any head-covering, and, walking up to me, began showing me a photograph which Violet had sent him with for the benefit of the monks. In vain did I remonstrate with him for this irreverent conduct during a religious ceremony. It was a thing, he said, that was quite usual here.

The service ended by some of the monks repeating prayers, and a little boy repeating others with great rapidity.

It seemed as if I had witnessed a scene of the Middle-Ages, and indeed I fear that the spirit of these times is not yet exorcised from Cyprus. It required a great stretch of charity to believe that there was any trace of spiritual worship in these hurried prayers, or that they had nothing to do with the vain repetitions which our Lord reproved. Whilst the old monk explained the various pictures to us, I not only thought that he and his brethren

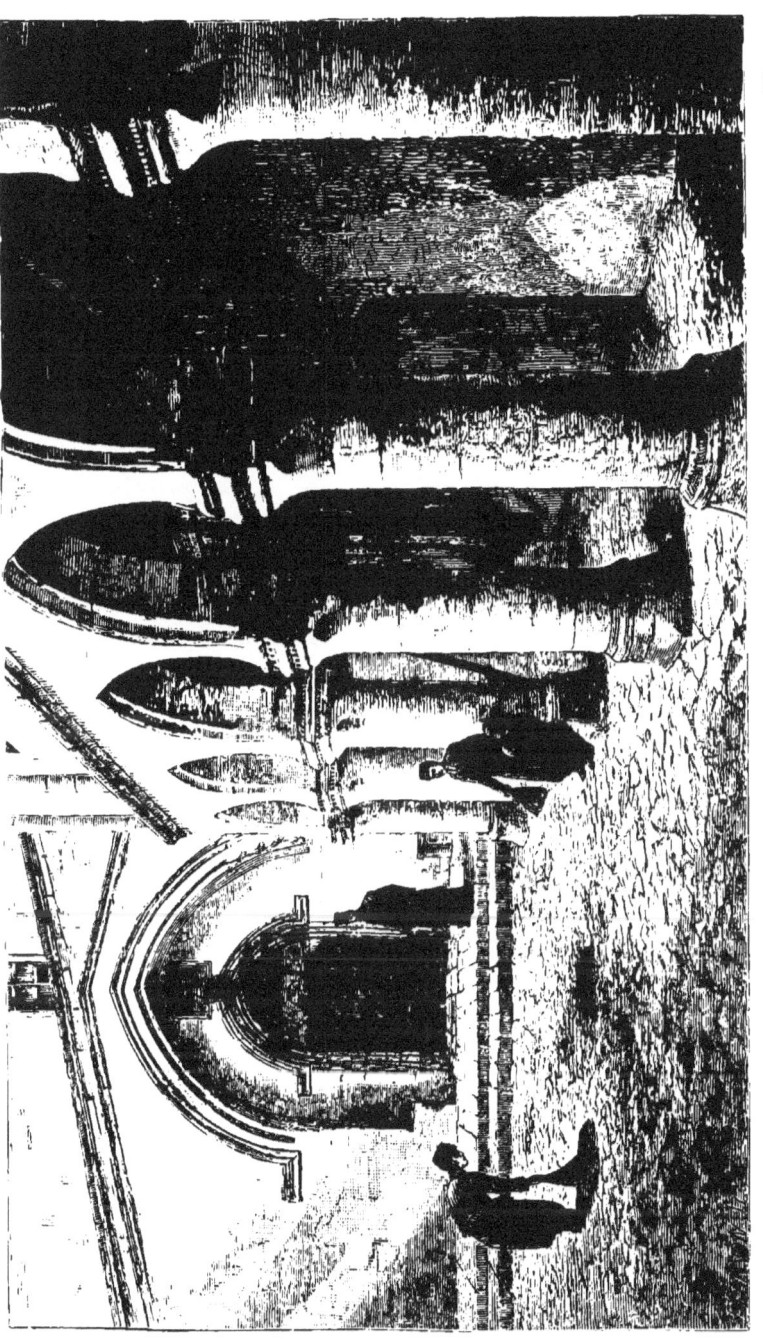

COURTYARD OF MONASTERY AT KYKKO.

were making the Word of God of none effect by their traditions, but that they are open to the suspicion of enriching themselves not a little by making people believe a lie, there being no doubt that the votaries who flock to the place attribute miraculous powers to the Virgin's portrait. Let us hope that they are themselves deceived.

Salîm showed us a short reaper's scythe with a very heavy handle, something like that of a gymnast's club, and furnished with three bells, which made a dreadful clatter whenever the scythe was used, in order to frighten away the serpents.

CHAPTER XII.

FROM KYKKO TO CHRYSOROGHIATISSA.

Bad Roads—Arabic for the Mules—Chrysoroghiatissa—The Monks' Welcome—Heavy Rains—Conversations with the Monks—Collapse of Tents—Lodgings in the Monastery—High Winds—The Village School—Advice to the Children—'Time is Money'—A Glimpse of Sunshine.

THE night we spent at Kykko was very cold. We said good-bye to the monks, and then pursued our way over a road not nearly so good as that of the previous day. We rode for about an hour, looking back on the convent perched on the mountain-top with the precipice below it, and wild vistas of pine-clad hills and deep valleys. Then the road ran so steeply down hill that we both dismounted and walked for an hour till we reached a little stream where I re-mounted and rode along a path which wound along the mountain-sides, and was often narrower than I could have wished. I soon got far in advance with Georgie, and met no living creature except a cow, who must have found it hard to get any sustenance out of the scanty grass. At half-past ten we rested, and lunched under the shadow of a cherry-tree on the bank of a running stream in a deep narrow valley.

We started again at half-past two, and rode for two and a half hours, the path being quite as bad as it had been in the morning, through the same kind of forest scenery. The pine-trees became at last less thick, and the ground more covered with white wild roses. At length we saw from an eminence the green mountain on which Chrysoroghiatissa stands. Diving into a valley where the trees were still fewer, and where the pines were soon replaced by oaks and blooming hawthorn, we found ourselves on a chalky soil, and a turn brought us in sight of the village of Panagia, whose square houses are built of stone without mortar. Passing through its narrow streets, we saw the monastery on a height some fifteen minutes' ride distant, and on a grassy slope above it our three white tents, with the red British ensign fluttering above one of them. We had to descend and to ascend by rather a giddy path before reaching the monastery door, where some poorly-clad monks bade us welcome. Our Turkish guide rode in first. He had encouraged Violet's pony all day by continually calling back to it, 'Allah Derwish, Allah Derwish, taîb Derwish, ma-sh-Allah.' The Greek muleteers caught up these expressions from the Arabs, and George advised me seriously to say, 'Allah ma'ak,' or 'Allah ma 'nâ,'* to my mule whenever it was going down a difficult place, as it would understand, and be thereby admonished to be careful. It is difficult to say whether this savours of reverence or of blasphemy. I declined to do it on the ground that my mule was more likely to understand Greek.

* 'God be with thee. God with us.'

Salim was not a little surprised to see us arrive at five o'clock, instead of at midnight, as he had fully expected, after hearing of Violet's determination to walk. Some of the monks welcomed us at the door of our tents, and we invited them to dine with us on the day following, which was Sunday. As the ground was sloping, our table had to be supported with stones, and its furniture was sent sprawling over the floor by a mule touching one of the tent-ropes.

The views around were magnificent. On the right a lofty white hill, chequered with green hedgerows, and dotted with trees, stood out against the wild range of lofty, pine-clothed, dark mountains behind it. On the left, the sun was sinking over a wide expanse of grassy hills—sinking down to the shining, silver sea at Poli, a village which occupies the site of the ancient Arsinöe.

Rain fell heavily next morning, so we remained within our tent until one o'clock, when some of the monks called, and we went into the dining-tent to receive them. They told us that their monastery is very poor, and became so at the time of the Greek Revolution, (when, it will be remembered, Cyprus rose in insurrection). The Turkish governor of the island came to this district, and, finding a Moslem village near, he asked if they had a mosque.

'No,' they replied.

'What is that building there?'

'A church.'

'Take it, and make it a mosque.'

He gave the Moslems some of the lands belonging to the monastery, and the monks have been ever since engaged in a lawsuit to get these back, and have borrowed money to carry it on.

The monks asked if our parents were living, and were evidently pleased by the way in which we expressed our hopes of meeting them in another world; for they at once asked for our visiting cards, and told us that they intended setting these up in their church, so that our names would always be included in their prayers to the Kyria Panagia. They pressed us to occupy a room in the monastery, but this we declined, saying that our tents were waterproof.

'If the rain should get so heavy as to make the mountain-sides run with water, you will be obliged to come,' they said.

'There is little fear of that,' I replied. 'I trust that we shall see you here to dinner.'

We sat down to luncheon when they were gone, and as it was very cold, and I did not wish to go through the rain to our sleeping-tent for a hat, I pinned a table-napkin over my head. As we ate, I noticed that the rain dripped pretty fast through part of the tent-roof, and some of the sides were getting wetter and wetter. I made a remark about this not being quite conformable to our contract; and Violet asked George if he would not recommend us to go into the monastery.

'No,' he replied; 'the tents will stand, and your sleeping-tent is very strong.'

A little goat came in to take refuge. Violet was feeding it, and I eating dates, when all of a sudden a great gust blew in the side of the tent, and the pole came down, carrying the table with it, and sending plates, wine-bottles, water-bottles, etc., flying.

'Run out, ladies!' cried George, whilst Salîm and he tried to hold up the tent.

We rushed into the pouring rain. I had on thick boots, and a little sealskin cloak, with the dinner-napkin pinned round my head. Violet had thin boots and goloshes, and a velvet jacket, with nothing at all on her head. There was no time to think of the waterproofs and umbrellas, which were all in the sleeping-tent. We ran into the kitchen-tent, where the cook was looking not a little disconcerted. No sooner had we entered it than its pole began to give way. The cook and a boy from the monastery tried to hold it up, the former saying, δὲν θὰ πέσῃ ('It won't fall'), and the latter, 'θὰ πέσῃ' ('It will fall'). We got out, for we did not wish to have the pole on our heads. A glance at the sleeping-tent showed us that it, too, had collapsed, so that there was nothing to protect us from the fury of the elements.

I caught Violet's arm.

'Come at once to the monastery,' I said.

'You don't know the way,' she replied, looking quite confused.

'But I *see* it,' I exlaimed.

She was very pale, and half blinded by the rain. The boy from the monastery took her one arm and Salîm the other. I ran down the white, dripping pathway, and these two brought her after me. We crossed the inner court, and were met by the twelve monks, and taken upstairs to a little room, where Salîm left us, going back to give the help of his strong arm and ready wit to the task of collecting the scattered tents. I asked the monks for some fire, or means of drying ourselves; and they at once ordered a servant to bring in the lower half of a broken earthenware *stamna* full of burning charcoal. Whilst we dried ourselves over this, I explained to the Hegoumenos that we were paying George a fixed sum per day for everything, and that, if he was kind enough to make us presents of meat and cheese, he was not to imagine that we would get any benefit from this; and that it would be far better for him to accept payment from George for everything of that kind. He replied that the muleteers got as much barley and as much food for themselves as they required gratis, and that no one paid for anything in a monastery. I replied that this was a very bad plan to pursue with dragomans, who were likely to take all they could, and give little in return.

The Hegoumenos then asked our permission to retire and finish luncheon, we having interrupted him at that meal. Soon after Zannetes came, carrying my Greek Testament, followed by Aristides with a sponge-bag. After that, one article appeared after another in incongruous succession; and George asked us to go and look at the room which the monks had set apart for us. Violet desired that it might be swept out before our baggage was deposited in it; but this they neglected to do. The room was a large one; its three windows, though destitute of glass, were furnished with strong wooden shutters, and its only furniture was three large wooden settees, or bedsteads. George proposed that we should sleep on the top of these, but we, being more accustomed to Greek monasteries than he was, declined; and Violet suggested that one of them should be taken out, so as to make more room for our iron bedsteads. The twelve monks and six muleteers, eager to comply with her wishes, lifted the huge piece of furniture, and I sat on my travelling-bag highly amused, whilst they made an honest effort to get it out at the door. There, however, it stuck, having evidently been constructed in the room. So it had to be brought back. There was, however, plenty of space for our own beds, and we eventually got our things together, the cork mattresses having escaped wetting owing to our having folded their mackintosh flaps well over them in the early morning. We had some trouble to persuade the troop of monks and muleteers to leave the room; we then got Salim to sweep it a little, and he raised the dust of ages in so doing. Our afternoon was spent in drying the bedsteads and ends of blankets by placing a *stamna* of charcoal beneath them.

We went down to see the church. There was nothing remarkable about it; it seems to have been founded in A.D. 1152. The monks, who are very uneducated, showed me their gospels, which had all been printed in Venice in 1799. I then had a consultation with the muleteers about our route. They advised that our next stage should be Ktima, a large village near the site of Neo-Paphos, which they all said was six hours' distant, excepting Georgie, who said it was eight. He agreed with them, however, in saying that it would be quite impossible for us to go next day, as, even if it ceased raining, the roads would be wet. The sleeping-tent was stretched out to dry within the covered part of the courtyard. We were very thankful that a similar accident did not happen on the previous night at Kykko, as in that case our things would all have tumbled over the cliff into an inaccessible valley. George declared that he had never seen such a hurricane in all his life; but we who have slept on the top of Mount Tabor during a thunderstorm, and have heard the February winds at Athens howl as if they would blow down the houses, could not at all agree with him. The cook said to Violet, 'Nous avons perdu la tête,' and I believe this was true of everyone, excepting Salîm.

When the sun shone out for one brief half-hour in the afternoon, the effect of the flitting light and of the cloud shadows on the green hill slopes below us was extremely grand. The counterpane of Violet's bed caught fire from one of the stamnas just as we were retiring to rest. I made a rush for the water-jug, but she put it out by popping the blazing end on the stone floor and pressing the rest of it on the top.

Next day we had alternate sunshine and hail showers. The wind was exceedingly high, and it was very cold, so that travelling was impossible. We felt quite out of spirits, as the delay involved our having to work rather hard in order to reach Larnaca in time for the boat. We had no books, the monks had no fund of conversation, and it was difficult to pass the time.

A murmur of voices fell on our ears. Monotonous voices they were, but they conveyed to us the assurance that we need not suffer from *ennui*. Their sound reached us through the wall, and we at once knew that the village school had located itself in the room adjoining ours.

I soon found my way in. There were only twelve boys, the usual number of twenty-five having shrunk on account of the rain. The eldest was thirteen years old. They were reading a simple little book on sacred history, and as none had been more than a year at school their progress was creditable, though they were sadly behind English or Arab boys of the same age. One only, who, being several years older than the others, was in a class by himself, professed to know the rudiments of arithmetic and geography. He did several sums correctly on the black board, and told me the capitals of the various European countries.

Whilst I was thus engaged, the Hegoumenos, Violet, and George came to listen. I asked if they had had a school in Turkish times, and was told 'no.'

'Did the Turks forbid you to have one?'

'No, but we were poor, and we never thought about it. When the English Government offered twelve pounds a year for the teacher's salary, of course we took advantage of it.'

I then felt that I ought not to lose the opportunity of giving the small rustics some advice; so, with the teacher's permission, I made them a little speech. I told them that they ought to consider themselves very fortunate in having the opportunity of learning letters. Times were changed since their parents were young. All the world was learning. If they were idle, and unable to read, it might perhaps not matter so much to them if they always stayed in Cyprus. But if they went to Greece when they were grown up they would feel very much ashamed of themselves, for all the people there could read, and would look down on them. They would find the same thing in England and at Beyrout too. Reading would help them to do their daily work better, and I really thought it must be the will of the Almighty that every person in the world should learn letters. Why I thought so was because He has revealed His will to us in a Book. It was a great advantage to listen to the words of that Book when the priest read them to us, and to know how Jesus Christ, the Son of God, loved us and died for us; but it would be far better if each of us could read the story of His life and His teaching for ourselves, without anyone's help.

I turned round to the Hegoumenos after saying this, and saw a pleased smile on his face. The teacher was delighted, and proceeded to tell them that they ought to follow the example of the English in never wasting their time, and that we have a proverb: 'Time is money.'

I then said that I hoped they would be very attentive and obedient to their master, as he was imparting to them so valuable a faculty.

'The man,' I continued, 'who knows letters and knows how to use his fingers at some handicraft, is worth more than twice as much as the man who knows neither; in fact, without both, no one can be considered a perfect man' ('τέλειος ἄνθρωπος').

No sooner had I uttered this last sentiment than I felt a chilling want of sympathy, and, looking at my adult audience, I perceived that the Hegoumenos and George had both wondrously long faces, and that the only one who thoroughly agreed with me was the young schoolmaster. Violet, of course, did not understand my Greek; George, though I did not then know it, was himself quite unlettered, and I suspect that the Hegoumenos was nearly so. I certainly would not have said all I did had I known this. I had been constantly teasing George by writing down things in English and Arabic for his benefit, and it had never once occurred to me that he could not read them.

Violet then distributed a few coins amongst the children. We felt much gratified by the thought that our country's name will hereafter be associated with the beginning of education in Cyprus.

The monks, whatever their head knowledge might be, always showed great reverence when speaking of the weather. When we asked: 'Do you think it will be fine to-morrow?' they replied, 'God knows, we do not know.'

In the afternoon a glimpse of sunshine encouraged me to go with one of the monks to the top of a hill, whence we looked down over a succession of green hill ranges to the bright little bays of Poli and of Baffo. There was a belt of clear blue sky along the western horizon, but betwixt that and us was a bank of heavy clouds which my guide said were carrying hail, although he thought that the 'weather was opening.' We came down in time to escape a heavy shower, and all the afternoon was spent in watching the clouds as the wind drove them over us towards Mount Troados. The sun, in battling with them, sometimes bathed all the green uplands and valleys in a golden mist, sometimes flung them all aside, and sometimes allowed them to gather and march towards us, dropping hail as they went. The pleasantest sound we heard was that of the boys at their lessons. The girls do not attend school at Chrysoroghiatissa, it being considered too far for them to walk.

CHAPTER XIII.

FROM CHRYSOROGHIATISSA TO PAPHOS.

Baffo—Highly Picturesque—Paphos—Welcomed by Mr. Thompson—
'Aphroditissa'—History of Neo-Paphos—Temple of Paphos—
Hieroskipos—A Cave—De Cesnola's Views—Apples of Cyprus—
Old Paphos—Legend of Cinyras—A Ruined Castle—'The Great
Temple of Venus'—Claudian Quoted—Augustine Quoted—Virgil.

WE left Chrysoroghiatissa at eight a.m., under a cloudless sky, a guide from the monastery accompanying us, so that we might keep as much as possible out of the mud. Our way ran betwixt cornfields, over little streams and small, thymy hills, always descending, till at noon we passed through the very dirty, stone-built village of Polemo, and with difficulty found a spot that was not too wet to squat on under a mulberry-tree.

After talking with some of the village women, we re-mounted at half-past two, and rode over green hills covered with juniper, and past a gigantic old oak-tree, leaving to the right a grove of olives, which we were told sheltered a village named Upsala. It certainly cannot boast of a university. A few yards further, and we stood on the brow of a steep, lofty hill. An expanse of sea lay before us, with a broad strip of plain betwixt it and the foot of the hill. In the plain were several little olive-oases, and in each oasis a village. Two of these, close to the sea, are Baffo, once Neo-Paphos, and Ktima, whither most of its inhabitants have migrated to escape fevers. A very steep, white path led down to this plain. On the right, as we descended, I observed a fine rock tomb, and in the sea, just a little off Baffo, a very curious rock. It is white, and in the form of a Maltese cross, and is probably only seen at low tide. I wondered if there were any tradition about it. On reaching the plain, I found that Violet was far behind, so I trotted on fast with Georgie, and reached Ktima about half-past six.

The first view of this village is highly picturesque. A solitary minaret rises like an obelisk above a luxuriant mass of olives, lemons, oranges, and pomegranates. The houses stand mostly in gardens, and are built, some of stone and some of sun-dried brick, the whole place having an air of wealth and comfort about it. We had some difficulty in finding our tents, but discovered them at last in a most extraordinary spot. Not the smooth turf, nor the thymy hillside, nor the stubbly corn-field had Salîm chosen. No, our canvas flapped over the mould of an orange-garden right below the windows of a house which bore at its back the inscription, Club Papho Λέσχη Πάφος.

There is no accounting for tastes, but I was too tired to suggest a change of camping-ground, and was, moreover, anxious to have a peep at the village church, having read somewhere or other of the existence of an image known as the Panagia Aphroditissa. The idea is ludicrously incongruous, and I was anxious to know if it had sprung from the dense ignorance of Cypriot superstition, or from the grotesque fancy of some French traveller. No sooner had I dismounted than I was welcomed by Mr. Thompson, the Commissioner of Paphos. He kindly invited us to dinner, saying that we should meet the only other two English residents at his house. I was obliged to decline this with the suggestion that the party should take coffee in our tents afterwards.

Mr. Thompson accompanied me to the two churches, but neither had anything remarkable to show; and, as he had never heard of the Panagia Aphroditissa, I was led to suspect that I had made her acquaintance in my dreams. I had not at that time read a work entitled, 'Cyprus, Historical and Descriptive,' by Franz von Löher; but no doubt I must have seen the following passage quoted somewhere:

'How at the present day do the Cyprians name the Mother of God? Simply " Aphroditissa." She is often represented in the oldest pictures with her dark features veiled and glittering with gold and silver; exactly as in ancient time the great black meteoric stone—the idol of Venus—Astarte, was solemnly veiled by her priestesses. From the very ground upon which formerly stood the temple of the Cyprian Venus, little images of the Madonna are frequently dug up, as, for example, the five goddesses, sitting upon throne-like seats, each with a child upon its bosom, obtained from the excavations at Idalion, and now preserved in the Ambrose collection at Vienna. Here, indeed, the figures are altogether of an antique character; nevertheless, every one of the five has so completely the character of a Christian Madonna that the observer involuntarily thinks them counterfeits. The conversion of the Aphrodite into the " Aphroditissa " occurred during the earliest days of Christianity, when the sensual culture of Venus gave place to the pure worship of the Virgin Mother.'

Violet arrived at seven o'clock, and Mr. Thompson re-appeared at a later hour with Mr. R——, the judge, and a charming young lady, his wife. They all like Paphos extremely, and have kept their health well, notwithstanding its evil reputation. Four serpents had been killed in one of the gardens on the previous week. They said that the educational efforts which are being made in the island have hardly as yet begun to tell on the population, and they quite agreed with me that the English here will learn to speak Greek much sooner than the Cypriots will English. Two young men who were at Paphos on government business called also, all wondering at Salîm's choice of a camping-ground. We went to sleep to the sound of billiard-balls. I rose at five next morning, and, having arranged to meet Violet at Hieroskipos, rode with Georgie to the ruins of Baffo, or Neo-Paphos, whither the inhabitants of Paphos migrated after their city was destroyed by an earthquake.

Neo-Paphos is said to have been founded by Agapenor,* chief of the Arcadians in the siege of

* Pausanias, viii, 5, 2.

Troy.* His contingent seems to have been recruited both from Northern Greece and from the Peloponesus. Agamemnon lent them ships, as they were quite unused to maritime pursuits. We may suppose that this defect in their education would soon be remedied after their settlement in Cyprus.

Baffo is only ten minutes' ride from Ktima. It is a straggling village, in a grove of caroubs, pomegranates, and palms. The vestiges of the old city are extensive. They appear to be tombs in the rocks, and portions of temples with broken columns

---

* οἳ δ' ἔχον Ἀρκαδίην ὑπὸ Κυλλήνης ὄρος αἰπύ,
Αἰπύτιον παρὰ τύμβον, ἵν' ἀνέρες ἀγχιμαχηταί,
οἳ Φενεόν τ' ἐνέμοντο καὶ Ὀρχομενὸν πολύμηλον
Ῥίπην τε Στρατίην τε καὶ ἠνεμόεσσαν Ἐνίσπην,
καὶ Τεγέην εἶχον καὶ Μαντινέην ἐρατεινήν,
Στύμφηλόν τ' εἶχον καὶ Παρρασίην ἐνέμοντο,
τῶν ἦρχ' Ἀγκαίοιο πάϊς κρείων Ἀγαπήνωρ
ἑξήκοντα νεῶν· πολέες δ' ἐν νηὶ ἑκάστῃ
Ἀρκάδες ἄνδρες ἔβαινον, ἐπιστάμενοι πολεμίζειν.
αὐτὸς γάρ σφιν δῶκεν ἄναξ ἀνδρῶν Ἀγαμέμνων
νῆας ἐϋσσέλμους περάαν ἐπὶ οἴνοπα πόντον,
Ἀτρεΐδης, ἐπεὶ οὔ σφι θαλάσσια ἔργα μεμήλει.
                                    Ἰλιάδος Β. 603—614.

'They of Arcadia, and the realm that lies
Beneath Cyllene's mountain high, around
The tomb of Aepytus, a warrior race;
The men of Pheneus and Orchomenus
In flocks abounding, who in Ripa dwelt,
In Stratia, and Aenispe's breezy height,
Or Tegea bold, and sweet Mantinea,
Stymphalus and Parrhasia, these were led
By Agapenor brave, Anchæus' son,
In sixty ships; in each a num'rous crew
Of stout Arcadian youths, to war inur'd.
The ships wherewith they crossed the dark blue sea
Were given by Agamemnon, king of men,
The son of Atreus: for th' Arcadian youth
Had ne'er to maritime pursuits been trained.'
            Lord Derby's Translation. Book ii, 700—714.

scattered about. Many of these are in the orchards, or built into the walls of the gardens. We asked which was the traditional pillar to which St. Paul was bound, but no one on the spot seemed able to tell us. It mattered little, however, seeing that the tradition has never been strong enough to travel beyond the Greeks of Ktima. We fancied that it must be one of two columns which stood upright in a garden in front of a church. They had no flutings nor capitals, though some of the fragments which lay near them had spiral flutings.

De Cesnola tells us that the name of this city, before the immigration of the Paphians, was Erythrae, and that it was probably changed to Neo-Paphos on account of its being the starting point of the processions to the temple of Aphrodite at Paphos.

Pausanias tells us how Laodice, daughter of Agapenor, sent a peplum to the goddess Athena Alea at Tegea with the epigram:

Λαοδίκης ὅδε πέπλος ἑῇ δ'ἀνέθηκεν 'Αθηνᾷ
Πατρίδ' εἰς εὐρύχωρον Κύπρου ἀπὸ ζαθέας.

This peplum is Laodice's, and to her native land
She sent it for Athena's self from Cyprus' holy strand.

De Cesnola found it impossible to excavate much on this very tempting site, partly owing to the high value of the ground, and partly to the hostility of the Turks in Ktima, who seem to have been, in 1868, as ill-conditioned as the Moslems of Kyrenia, and who compelled the diggers to run for their lives. The only small objects discovered during a week's excavation were a silver coin of Vespasian, with the temple of Paphos represented upon it; but whether meant for a temple at Paphos or at Neo-Paphos could not be ascertained, and a few Roman lamps.

Far more interesting, in Georgie's eyes, was the old Turkish, or Venetian, fort, whose walls are about four feet thick. I climbed to the top of it by a steep ladder, a rope, and a broken stone staircase, and had a lovely view. Ktima, as seen from this point, stands picturesquely on the crest of a craggy ridge, strewn with boulders and surrounded by trees. Behind it are the treeless spurs of the Troados range. The remains of the old harbour are now under water, and a new, wooden quay has been built on them. We had some difficulty in leaving the village, owing to the overhanging branches of caroub and other trees. We rode over some corn-fields, and along the waterless bed of an oleander-fringed stream, and passed a spot containing many rock tombs, which was quite unapproachable, by reason of mud. We reached the high-road, and trotted quickly, till we found Violet and her attendants sitting in front of a house in the little grey village of Hieroskipos. Here two of our last night's acquaintances appeared, riding in one day to Limasol, a distance of more than fifty miles, on government business. What a contrast these young Englishmen must appear in the eyes of the natives, to the lazy Turkish pashas and effendis! These must have felt, just after the cession, as if they had exchanged the rule of King Log for that of King Stork. One would like to know which they hold in the highest respect. Certainly, in Cyprus, a British subject cannot help feeling that Nelson's famous injunction is being fully complied with.

One of these young men told me that our slow friend Georgie had been more than once in his employment.

'Perhaps you can hardly believe it,' he said, 'but there is no end to the amount of work that fellow will do, if you once manage to stir him up sufficiently. He has actually ridden from Baffo to Limasol in one day, to oblige me. Besides this, he is thoroughly honest and good-natured.'

Georgie, however, did not know where the Bath of Aphrodite was. We got an old villager to conduct us down a steep stony little path just below the church, and then we saw a shallow cave with a lofty roof about fifty feet long. A caldron stood over a blazing fire near its centre. Its smoke had blackened one half of the roof, whilst the other retained the whiteness of the limestone. A stream of water, issuing from a sort of tunnel on the left side, poured itself into a large stone reservoir. The place was filled with about twenty women and girls, washing and beating clothes. Oh, Aphrodite! how prosaic thy haunts have become! But it is doubtless infinitely better for the world that thou shouldst be forgotten.

Yet if any Cypriot women are pretty, these were. The scarlet of their head kerchiefs and other garments, their white skirts and flashing black eyes, the rippling water and glittering white rock, would have made an incomparable subject for a painting, whilst the smoke-begrimed roof and boiling caldron lent to the scene a witchery that was hardly enhanced even by the misty associations of tradition.

De Cesnola thinks that this cave has been artificially scooped out of the rock. It was, as the name of the village indicates, within the 'Sacred Garden' of the 'Diva potens Cypri,' the goddess of love and of flowers. Here Cupid lived with her, and here Grecian eyes first observed the flush of returning spring as it came over the earth.

There was another garden, hardly less famous, sacred to Aphrodite, in one of the loveliest and most fruitful parts of Cyprus. This was at Tamassus, near Idalium, or Dali, about fifteen miles northwest of Larnaca. There stood the golden trees from which she plucked apples for her favourites. From it she also took those with which Hippomenes deceived and conquered Atalanta.*

Apples were symbols of love, a favourite pastime of lovers being to throw them at each other. There is, therefore, a deep significance in the legend of the marriage feast of Peleus and Thetis having been disturbed by the goddess of discord throwing an apple amongst the guests. Yet the poet exaggerates who says,

> 'For with the dearest female friends
> When Love begins, all friendship ends.'

We cannot tell whether the legend refers to the apple of our English gardens, or to the pomegranate, or golden apple. The former does not thrive in

---

* Est ager, indigenæ Tamassum nomine dicunt,
Telluris Cyprii pars optima, quem mihi prisci
Sacravere senes, templisque accedere dotem,
Hanc jussere meis.
                      OVID, Met, x. 644.

Cyprus, so we think it must have been the latter, more especially as its beautiful rosy flowers still adorn the heads of Eastern brides, and the many seeds of the fruit have made it from the earliest times symbolic of wishes for a progeny like that promised to the Jewish patriarchs.

Though Cyprus now produces indifferent apples, it was the home of a legend which tells us how the fruit got its name. A certain Melos fled from his native island of Delos and took refuge in Paphos with King Cinyras, who received him hospitably, and not only made him the companion of his son Adonis, but gave him a relative of his own, named Pelia, in marriage. They had a son, who was named Melos after his father, and who was brought up as one of the Cinyradæ, or priests of Aphrodite. After Adonis had been killed by the boar, old Melos could not overcome his sorrow, but hanged himself on a tree, which was forthwith called after him the μηλέα, or apple-tree. Pelia, his wife, followed his example, and Aphrodite changed the one into an apple-tree and the other into a dove. She also caused young Melos to return to his father's country, Delos, with a troop of picked men. Having recovered his kingdom, he there founded the town of Melos, and as he had probably learned from Cinyras in Cyprus the art of shearing sheep and of turning their wool into garments, he taught it to his subjects, and they named the sheep μῆλα in his honour, on the same principle that leads us to speak of Mac-Adamized roads.

It is somewhat remarkable that the apple should have been fixed upon both by Pagans and by our own ancestors as an instrument of temptation. I must not say 'by the Hebrews,' for revelation is quite silent as to what kind of fruit 'brought death into the world, and all our woe.'

We re-mounted, and rode for two-and-a-half hours betwixt hedgeless corn-fields, whose monotony was relieved here and there by a village nestling in its foliage, or by a patch bright with the golden blaze of yellow marguerites. We then ascended a tree-dotted spur of Troados to the site of Kouklia, or Old Paphos, and there we took luncheon beneath a shady caroub, amongst boulders of conglomerate rock.

Paphos is said to have been founded by Cinyras, father of Adonis, and the Cinyradæ, his descendants, were chief priests of Aphrodite. Cinyras' fame rests chiefly on the memory of the suit of armour which he gave to Agamemnon. Homer tell us how, at the siege of Troy,

> Ἀτρείδης δ' ἐβόησεν ἰδὲ ζώννυσθαι ἄνωγεν
> Ἀργείους· ἐν δ' αὐτὸς ἐδύσετο νώροπα χαλκόν.
> κνημῖδας μὲν πρῶτα περὶ κνήμῃσιν ἔθηκεν
> καλάς, ἀργυρέοισιν ἐπισφυρίοις ἀραρυίας·
> δεύτερον αὖ θώρηκα περὶ στήθεσσιν ἔδυνεν,
> τόν ποτέ οἱ Κινύρης δῶκε ξεινήιον εἶναι.
> πεύθετο γὰρ Κύπρονδε μέγα κλέος, οὕνεκ' Ἀχαιοὶ
> ἐς Τροίην νήεσσιν ἀναπλεύσεσθαι ἔμελλον·
> τοὔνεκά οἱ τὸν δῶκε, χαριζόμενος Βασιλῆι.
> Ἰλιάδος, xi, 15—23.

> 'Atrides, loudly shouting, called the Greeks
> To arms; himself his flashing armour donned.
> First on his legs the well-wrought greaves he fixed,
> Fastened with silver clasps; his ample chest
> A breastplate guarded, given by Cinyras
> In pledge of friendship: for in Cyprus's isle

> He heard the rumour of the glorious fleet
> About to sail for Troy, and sought with gifts
> To win the favour of the mighty king.'
> <div align="right">LORD DERBY. <i>Iliad</i> xi, 15—23.</div>

Cinyras was the hero of many Cyprian songs. Pindar tells us that he, the gentle priest of Aphrodite, was a special favourite of the golden-haired Apollo,* and cites him as an example of a man who had become laden with riches through the favour of the gods.†

Cinyras was probably devoted to the service of the goddess from his earliest years, and grew up in her temple as the little Erechtheus did in that of Athena.‡ His beauty is celebrated by several ancient authors, and his wealth became as proverbial as that of Midas and Crœsus. Tradition represents him as the pioneer of Cypriot civilization, the mythical inventor of the roof-tile, the hammer, the anvil, the tongs, and the crowbar. He was supposed to have introduced into the island the art of mining (for copper), and of preparing the wool of sheep. To him were probably transferred the deeds of many others, until he became the national hero in the arts of peace. He was even credited with the invention of a musical instrument named

---

* κελαδέοντι μὲν ἀμ—φὶ Κινύραν πολλάκις
φᾶμαι κυπρίων, τὸν ὁ
        χρυσοχαῖτα προφρόνως ἐφίλησ' Ἀπόλλων,
ἱερέα κτίλον Ἀφροδί—
        τας· ἄγει δὲ χάρις φίλων
        ποίνιμος ἀντὶ Ϝέρ—γων ὀπιζομένα·
Pythia, ii, 15.

† σὺν θεῷ γὰρ τοι φυτευθεὶς ὄλβος ἀνθρώποισι παρμονώτερος·
ὅσπερ καὶ κινύραν ἔβρισε πλούτῳ ποντίᾳ ἔν ποτε κύπρῳ.
Nemea, viii, 17.

‡ <i>Iliad</i>, ii, 548.

the κίνυρα, and he thus seems to have united in his person the functions of a Jubal and a Tubal-cain. The κίνυρα was a kind of flute, used chiefly in the θρῆνοι, or wailings for Adonis, who, it will be remembered, was Cinyras' son.

The flute was particularly hateful to Apollo, whose favourite instrument was the κιθάρα, or lyre, with its more tranquil and stately music. Hence arose the story of Cinyras entering into a contest with Apollo, by whom he was overpowered and slain. According to another account, the god punished him for his treachery to Agamemnon in supplying inferior armour, and in neglecting to give the help which he had promised.

Cinyras was said to have married Metharme, daughter of King Pygmalion, a man whose best title to fame rests on the fable of his having fallen in love with a statue, and under whose auspices mankind was said to have first acquired a taste for animal food. It happened on this wise. For a long period no animals were offered in sacrifice to the gods, and the altars of Cyprus remained free from the stain of blood. From what quarter sacrifices were at length introduced we are not told; but one day a piece of flesh from a victim fell upon the ground. The officiating priest took it up; it was hot, and burnt his fingers, causing him such pain that he raised them to his mouth. From that hour he and his wife enjoyed a repast of meat in private. Pygmalion, hearing of this, ordered both of them to be hurled from the top of a cliff, and gave the priestly office to another man. This man allowed himself to be tempted also, and was condemned to a like punishment. But a love for the forbidden food spread amongst man, till Pygmalion himself was obliged to approve it.*

It is noteworthy that these traditions differ from the Homeric ones on one point. If Cinyras was a real person, he was presumably of the epoch of Agamemnon. Now, in the *Iliad* there is no well-defined priestly caste, though we undoubtedly meet with augurs or seers. It is the king's hand who cuts the throat of the sacrificial victim. In Cyprus, the priests are guardians of Aphrodite's temple, and seem sometimes to be identical with the kings, but sometimes also distinct from them.

I was much puzzled to know where were the remains of the ancient town, and the hole in the wall from which it is thought that the oracle spoke. I had no resource but to apply to Mustapha and to Georgie, both of whom were intent only on leading their mules to water. Mustapha knew nothing about it, and Georgie looked sulky at the very mention of an antiquity. He at once retired to a little distance, and became quite absorbed in his pipe. So I walked back a little way with George to a spot where I had seen two little pillars, but, after examining the ground well, I could see no vestige of what had been described by our English friends at Ktima. George then took up the matter, and, walking deliberately up to his reflective namesake, said, in an insinuating tone,

'You have passed this way hundreds of times. Are you sure that you have never seen anything

---

* Porphyrius iv, 15.

very, very old, παλαιὸν 'ateeq πολὺ, παλαιὸν 'ateeq katheer.'

Georgie no doubt reflected that, as wilful folk must have their way, he would save himself neither time nor trouble by ignoring my wishes.

'It's up there,' he said, pointing to a ruined castle.

The old fortress was approached through a growth of rank grass. Georgie took us by a stony path and up the side of a hill so steep that we felt certain it was part of the castle wall. On reaching its summit, however, we saw nothing but mediæval architecture.

'This is old,' I said, 'but it is not what we want.'

So we returned to the road and rode a few steps beyond the castle. Suddenly, on the brow of the hill, we saw what there could be no mistake about, a wall of gigantic stones that could be referred to no age save to that of the Titans. Of this fragment De Cesnola gives a most interesting description.

'The great temple of Venus,' he says, 'was situated on an eminence, which at present is about twenty-five minutes' walk from the sea. Some parts of its colossal walls are still standing, defying time and the stone-cutter, though badly chipped by the latter.

'One of the wall-stones measured fifteen feet ten inches in length by seven feet eleven inches in width, and two feet five inches in thickness. The stone is not from Cyprus, but, being a kind of blue granite, must have been imported either from Cilicia or from Egypt. The temple, as rebuilt by Vespasian, seems to have occupied the same area as the former temple, and was surrounded by a peribolos, or outer wall. Of this a few huge blocks only are now extant. On the west side of this there was a doorway, still plainly visible. Its width was seventeen feet nine inches. The south-east wall I ascertained, by excavating, was six hundred and ninety feet. The west side I could only trace for two hundred and seventy-two feet, the remainder of it being hidden by the houses of Kouklia. I was able to trace the walls of the temple itself correctly. Though very little is seen above ground, strange to say, the four corners are still standing. The northeast corner-stone is cased in a house of Kouklia, the north-west one stands by itself in a cross-street of the village. Some travellers have mistaken it for the emblematic cone of Venus. The south-east corner stands in an open field, where the Christian population of Kouklia burn lamps and little wax-candles, in honour of whom I did not inquire.

'The temple was oblong. Its eastern and western walls each measure two hundred and twenty-one feet, and the two other sides one hundred and sixty-seven feet. The corner-stone of the north-west side has a hole in it thirteen inches in diameter; a similar hole also exists in the south-west corner of the outer wall. As the temple at Paphos possessed an Oracle, Dr. Friedrichs thinks that these strange holes, which go through the entire stone, may have been connected with it. From this spot, if a person stands upon the large, perforated stone, he can produce a clear and fine echo of a phrase of three or four words, pronounced in a moderate tone of voice.

' In the area of the temple, about two feet below the surface, I found a mosaic pavement wrought into stars, meanders, and other designs, prettily combined for effect, and composed of variously-coloured marble tessellæ, white, yellow, red, brown, and rose. Some three feet beneath these mosaics I found several large pedestals of colossal statues, with Greek inscriptions engraved upon them. The inscriptions are all of the Ptolemaic period. From this I argue that Vespasian may, after all, have only repaired the temple of Paphos, or, if he rebuilt it entirely, he did so partly with the former stones.

'From the elevated position which the city of Paphos occupied, its famous temple must have been visible many miles out at sea. Gently sloping from Kouklia towards the shore, there is a fertile plain belonging to the castle; this plain must formerly have been thickly wooded, and was, doubtless, the grove spoken of by Homer. A few hundred yards from the coast are the foundations of another temple, the foundations of which are also oblong. This must have been the Temple of Venus, built to commemorate the spot on which, for the first time, she appeared to the Cyprians. It was here that the annual procession of pilgrims, coming from Neo-Paphos to visit the great shrine, stopped to sacrifice before ascending the hill to visit the Sanctuary. Of this temple there are two upright monoliths remaining, five feet apart.'

One cannot help recollecting that the Parthenon at Athens was also visible from the sea, and that its bronze statue of Athena Promachus had a helmet, which, glittering in the sun, served as a beacon to sailors. May we not legitimately suppose that some statue of Aphrodite at Paphos may have served a similar purpose, more especially as the goddess was credited with the power of calming storms?

> 'Te, dea, te fugiunt venti, te nubila cœli,
> Adventumque tuum.'
> LUCRETIUS, i, 6.
>
> 'Cingitur, impulsos pluviis quo mitigat amnes,
> Quo mare, quo ventos, irataque fulmina solvit.'
> CLAUDIAN. *Npt. Honor et Mar*, 125.

Tacitus tells us, however, that the really sacred image of the goddess was not in human shape, but was a round, white stone, tapering upwards like a cone or pyramid. Why such a shape should be adopted he could not explain. We may be permitted to suppose that it was an aerolite, like the statue of the Mother of the Gods, which was brought, in B.C. 204, from Pessinus, in Galatia, to the temple of Cybele, in Rome; and like the image of the Sun, which was worshipped at Emesa, in Syria. Meteoric stones frequently assume a pyramidal shape. We have a suspicion that the image of Diana, at Ephesus, which was said to have fallen from Jupiter, was of the same character.

The presence of this stone made Paphos the centre of the earth ὀμφαλος τῆς γῆς for the worshippers of Aphrodite, just as Delphi was for those of Apollo, and as the Church of the Holy Sepulchre at Jerusalem still is for idolatrous Christians.

The Roman poet Claudian seems to have understood the configuration of the ground where the temple of Aphrodite stood. His description may be compared with that of De Cesnola.

> A steep, broad hill in Cyprus fronts the couch
> Where Pharos sleeps, and Proteus. None may tread
> Its cliffs, which see the seven great horns of Nile.

The hoary frosts forbear to clothe its crest;
The wild winds fear to smite; the rains to hurt.
'Tis free to luxury and love; the year's
Most bitter part is banished; gentle Spring
Reigns ever. Like a plain its summit spreads;
A fence of ruddy gold protects it round.
'Tis said that Vulcan kissed his wife within
Its walls, and built their towers a pledge of love.
There verdant lawns, untrimmed by human hand,
Perpetual bloom, content if Zephyrs till.
The shady groves admit no winged bird,
Unless the goddess first approve his song.
These feed among the boughs, their rivals flee.
The leaves are Venus' guests. Each happy tree
Its neighbour loves. There palms by nods assent
To union; poplar sighs at poplar's touch;
And plane to plane, and elm to elm responds.
Two fountains flow, one sweet, and bitter one;
They mingle honey with a poison dire,
And give to Cupid's arrows great renown.
A thousand quivered boys beside them play,
Alike in words and dress, the tribe of Loves.
These, nymphs adorn, and golden Venus one
Declares her own. He rules the host of heaven
With little bow, and mighty kings subdues;
They wound plebeians and the lesser gods.
Here Liberty may dwell without restraint,
Wraths light to move, and, o'er the flowing wine,
Night Watches, artless Tears, and Paleness dear
To lovers; Boldness trembling at its thefts;
Fears full of joy; and Pleasure not secure;
And Perjuries that fly on lightest wing;
And there capricious Youth, with lofty brow,
Shuts out Old Age. The goddess' palace stands
Distant, but dazzling, midst the greenest woods;
Built by the Lemnian god with gems and gold.
He mingled art with splendour, emerald beams
He placed on pillars cut from jacinth rock;
The walls are beryl, and the threshold glows

With jasper; agates form the trodden floor.
Amidst the fragrant clods a threshing-place
Hath scented harvests; hath amomum sweet;
Hath cassia ripe; hath cinnamon that swells
Panchaian; costus' branches green with buds,
And balsams trickling from the sweating wood.
Here Cupid paused, and fluttered o'er the roads
On nimble wing; then walked with haughty step
Where Venus, on a glittering throne, arranged
Her hair. The Idalian sisters stood
On either hand; one sprinkled bounteous showers
Of nectar; one with bite of ivory comb,
Ploughed through her tresses; whilst the third behind
Plaited and parted all in order due,
Careful to leave what seemed a slight neglect;
For wandering locks were fairest; mirrors none
She needed, every wall her likeness showed.*

Auguries were obtained here, the most trustworthy being those from the entrails of goats. The sprinkling of blood on the floor of the temple was forbidden, and the altar was purified with prayer and fire.

The altar, though it stood in the open air, was never wet with rain. St. Augustine† speaks of a candelabrum which stood near it, in which was a light which no tempest could extinguish, a light which was therefore named the λύχνος ἄσβεστος. A similar superstition still prevails in the Church of the Holy Sepulchre at Jerusalem; where, also, abundance of incense is burnt, just as it has always been in temples of Aphrodite, and in churches of the Panagia. It would, indeed, be difficult to estimate how many Pagan rites have been incor-

---

* Epithalamium on Honorius and Mary, 49.
† De Civitate Dei. Lib. xxi, cap. 6.

porated in the Greek and in the Roman Catholic churches.*

Augustine tells us also that the temple of Paphos was renowned for the practice of magic arts. This would account for the presence of Elymas the sorcerer. It was finally overthrown by an earthquake, and a new one was built by Vespasian on its site.

I was determined not to leave without seeing the two monoliths near the sea, of which De Cesnola speaks. George and Georgie were both of opinion that they existed only in my imagination. Seeing a woman standing at the door of her cottage, I asked if she had seen anything of them. She at once held up both hands.

'Two stones as like each other as these,' she said.

Several people were willing to guide us to them. We went by a narrow path through the corn-fields across a river (once the Bocarus), and found the stones a few hundred yards from the shore. De Cesnola excavated about them, and found that, though they now stand about eleven and a half feet above the ground, their real height from the base is nearly eighteen feet. They are of a brown-

---

* A curious confirmation of this was brought under my notice during my recent visit to the little museum at Smyrna. The learned and courteous young curator who showed me its treasures, pointed out a statue which has been recently unearthed, I think, at Tralles. It represented a headless priest in full canonicals. 'This statue has perplexed us,' he said. 'It is that of a Christian priest, yet we know that the early Christians did not make statues. We have come to the conclusion, therefore, that the dress of Christian priests has been copied from that of heathen ones.'

ish granite, which is not to be found anywhere on the island.

Had we seen these stones in Great Britain, we should have supposed them to be Druidical. Aphrodite is supposed, or I should rather say is known, to be identical with the Semitic Astarte. Her worship passed into Greece by way of Cyprus. May it not be that an image of Astarte was carried ashore here by the priests who accompanied the earliest Phœnician colonists; nay, may it not have been brought by Chethim himself?

These stones are not pyramids, as Murray calls them; but monoliths, each having a curious oblong hole pierced through the middle.

Few cities have been more sung by the poets. Æschylus calls it the βαθύπλουτον χθόνα καὶ τᾶς 'Αφροδίτας πολύπυρον αἶαν the very rich ground and the land of Aphrodite abounding in wheat.* Homer describes how Aphrodite was here bathed and anointed with ambrosial oil by the Graces, who afterwards robed her with wondrous garments.† Virgil tells how, when she vanished from her son,

> Ipsa Paphum sublimis abit, sedesque revisit
> Læta suas: ubi templum illi, centumque Sabæo,
> Thure calent aræ, sertisque recentibus halant.
> *Æneid*, Lib 1, 415

> 'She through the sky to Paphos moves,
> And seeks the temple of her loves,
> Where from a hundred altars rise
> Rich steam and flow'rets' odorous sighs.'
> CONINGTON'S *Translation*.

And how she said in her prayer to Jupiter,

> 'Est Amathus, est celsa mihi Paphos, atque alta Cythera,' ‡

---

* Æschylus, Suppliants, 545.   † *Odyse.* viii, 362.   ‡ *Æneid*, x, 50.

all of these, excepting the third, being Cyprian towns.

Dionysos, or Bacchus, was also worshipped at Paphos, although his chief temple was on the Cyprian Mount Olympus. This was natural in a spot so famous for the culture of the vine. His festival was blended in some way with that of Aphrodite, the horned centaurs who followed in his train, being either her offspring by Zeus or possibly the priests of Kronos whom she had transformed. Euripides makes his Bacchæ say,

> ἱκοίμην ποτὶ τὰν Κύπρον,
> νᾶσον τῆς ’Αφροδίτας,
> ἵν’ οἱ θελξίφρονες νέμον—
> ται θνατοῖσιν Ἔρωτας·
> Πάφον θ’, ’ἂν ἑκατόστομοι
> βαρβάρου ποταμοῦ ῥοαὶ
> καρπίζουσιν ἀνομβρον
> ὅπου καλλιστευομένα
> Πιερία μούσειος ἕδρα,
> σεμνὰ κλιτὺς ’Ολύμπου
> ἐκεῖσ’ ἄγε με, Βρόμιε, Βρόμιε
> προβακχήιε δαῖμον
> ἐκεῖ χάριτες, ἐκεῖ πόθος·
> ἐκεῖ δὲ Βάκχαισι θέμις ὀργιάζειν.
>
> EURIPIDES. *Bacchæ*, 400.

> Let me fly to Cyprus,
> Isle of Aphrodite,
> Where the hearts of mortals
> Yield to Love, the mighty.
> Paphos, too, where currents
> Myriad, from the ocean,
> Pour on rainless meadows
> Wealth of life and motion.
> Where Pierian Muses,
> Near Olympus gloomy,
> Sit on thrones of splendour.
> Lead me, Brómie, Brómie,
> O thou frantic demon!
> For there do the Loves and the Graces delight,
> And the Bacchæ may revel, and know it is right.

Tennyson puts the following beautiful description into the mouth of Œnone,

> 'O mother Ida, many-fountained Ida,
> Dear mother Ida, harken ere I die.
> Idalian Aphrodite beautiful,
> Fresh as the foam, new-bathed in Paphian wells,
> With rosy slender fingers backward drew
> From her warm brows and bosom her deep hair,
> Ambrosial, golden round her lucid throat
> And shoulder : from the violets her light foot
> Shone rosy-white, and o'er her rounded form
> Between the shadows of the vine-branches
> Floated the glowing sunlight, as she moved.'

But Paphos has far nobler memories. It was the last stage of St. Paul's journey through the island. Here he spoke words of burning eloquence, words at whose sound the blossoms on the altar of the Cyprian goddess shrank and withered. Here he withstood Elymas the sorcerer, and here he probably baptized the Roman pro-consul.

CHAPTER XIV.

FROM PAPHOS TO COLOSSI.

The Cypriots and Cruelty to Animals—Pretty Village of Piscopi—A Storm—A Babel—Retreat from Tents—Still Unsheltered—Ruins of the City of Curium—Colossi—The Commanderia Wine—De Cesnola's Discoveries.

ON leaving the monoliths of Aphrodite, we rode over some ploughed fields near the shore, and then through a perfect wilderness of lentisks and arbutus, interspersed with a few wild olive-trees. Then for two hours we crossed a succession of hills covered with these plants, where no trace of a house nor of an animal was to be seen, excepting a dead serpent upon a wall. It was past six o'clock when we reached our tents, and we were much fatigued, having had about ten hours of fast trotting.

We were therefore glad to see the tall figure of Salîm, robed in white, with a red sash round his waist, standing in a lonely spot amongst the trees, and then our white tents under the shade of some large olives. A little above them was a deep well, from which Aristides was drawing water. The place was named Lakkofranca. It differed from the lonely mountain-side only in having two or three yellow corn-fields and a sheep-cot. Violet was very much afraid of serpents, and laid boxes and other heavy things all round the inside of our sleeping-tent to keep down the canvas, and shut up every hole by which they could enter.

I was annoyed at seeing the younger Georgie give one of his mules a sounding blow on the head with his staff, whilst the poor thing's fore-feet were tied together. He was the owner of the mule from which Violet fell near Lefkoniko, and the reason of its shying habits was now only too apparent. A writer in the *Hestia* of Athens of May 25, 1886, endeavours to make a fool of the English in Cyprus for their efforts to pass a law for the prevention of cruelty to animals. This law was successfully opposed by the Greek members of the legislative council, on the ground that it was premature, inasmuch as the people were not well enough educated to understand it, and that it would be oppressive to the owners of beasts. He recommends us to be philanthropists before we try to pose as lovers of the lower creatures. I can only ask this wiseacre if infliction of a fine in cases of gross cruelty would not have been a powerful help to the influence of moral suasion, and if the man who is merciful to his beast is likely to be unmerciful to his fellow-man. The Greek Cypriots, it appears to me, obtained but a sorry triumph when they threw out the bill in question.

A poor, starving dog came prowling about our tents, driven by the instinct of hunger to seek for a bone. Stones were needlessly thrown to drive it away, and, after we had gone to rest, it set up a howl of agony. Violet completely put me off my sleep by suggesting that perhaps boiling water had been thrown on it from the kitchen tent. Whether Arab or Cypriot did this deed, I cannot tell; but we both may be pardoned for the wish that we could have brought a blush of shame to the bronzed cheek of the delinquent. I do not think that any one of our servants was naturally cruel; it was only because they had never reflected that they are responsible to the Almighty for their treatment of His creatures. The very law which the Cypriots spurn as oppressive has been imposed upon English peasants, who were not at the time a whit more enlightened, and no one doubts to-day that it has done them a great deal of good.

We left our lonely camping-ground at half-past seven, and, after riding for half-an-hour over hills covered with arbutus and huge lentisks, and with caroubs that seemed only a larger edition of the lentisks, we passed the foot of the tree-dotted hill on which Pissouri stands. We then crossed many wooded and lentisk-covered hills, getting an occasional peep at the sea, until at ten o'clock we came on a pretty valley well-wooded with old olives and caroubs, where troops of brood mares and little foals were browsing and cooling themselves in a rippling stream. We rode for an hour further through the lentisks and caroubs till we came to another stream, a tiny one, but still with water sufficient for our mules. The muleteers could not understand the great attention Violet paid to Derwish, seeing him get water, and giving him his feed of barley in front of our tents in the evening. They said that he was worth only nine napoleons, whereas each of their mules cost twenty-three pounds.

It was very hot, and Georgie said that we had only two hours further to ride; so we did not start again till four. Our path ran up steep hills and down again into little valleys filled with yellow corn and scarlet anemones.

We passed along the brow of a cliff whose base was at first washed by the sea, but which soon overlooked a treeless peninsula connected with the shore by a narrow isthmus. At last we descended by a white path into a valley, where we saw some remains of ancient walls, built of huge stones, and some holes in the rock which we supposed to be tombs, but which Georgie declared were only caves and folds for sheep. Below the hill was the pretty village of Piscopi, with a white minaret amongst its wealth of trees and streams that rushed foaming from mill-wheels, or poured their waters down its streets, a sad waste in such a parched island. We passed between many hedges of prickly pears in flower; our white tents, with their fluttering red flag, being visible from a distance. They were pitched on a grassy hill below the village, and, as we reached them at half-past six, we told Salim to boil the water for tea, and then sat at the tent-door to watch a truly magnificent sunset.

After dinner the wind was high, justifying the epithet of ἠνεμόεσσα which is applied to Cyprus by an ancient writer.* The canvas flew about dreadfully. I asked Salim if he did not think that our tents might collapse, and he replied that it was not the same kind of wind as we had had at Chrysoroghiatissa, that there it was cold, and here it was warm. When we went into our bed-room tent, it

* Orpheus *Argonautica*, 1283.

was blowing so fiercely that Violet said she would not sleep there, but would lie down outside. I was overcome with fatigue, so I said she was talking nonsense. I lay down, however, with my clothes on. No sooner had I done so than it seemed as if the roof and sides of the tent were about to flap in my face. I got up, and we called George. We said that he must take us into a house directly, and that we would pack up our beds and all our things.

'The tent is better than a house,' he replied.

'Have you ever seen such storms in Syria?' asked Violet.

'No, lady.'

'Then how can you speak about what you have no experience of?'

Whilst we were speaking, Salîm busied himself with knocking the tent-pegs firmer into the ground. I looked up and saw an inky-black cloud coming towards us over the sea.

'Where are the muleteers?' asked Violet.

'None of them are here,' replied George. 'They have all gone up to the village café.'

'You ought not to have let them go,' said Violet. 'They should all have remained beside our tents when they saw it was going to be a night like this.'

'George,' said I, 'you know that it is in our contract that you must take us into a room immediately whenever there is any semblance of an approaching storm.'

George at once disappeared, running towards the village. We busied ourselves in rolling up our beds and stowing away in our baggage everything that we could lay our hands upon. I was called away suddenly by Violet saying,

'Agnes, do come out and translate for me.'

I found a singular group standing in the dim moonlight. Georgie and Aristides were there with a mule; George, Salîm, and Ibrahîm beside them, and Violet in her grey riding-habit and a little white tippet, perfectly at her wits' end, arguing with them. George either could not or would not make them comprehend what she wanted. I made matters still more confused, for my head was a perfect Tower of Babel. When I thought I was expressing myself to Aristides in his mother tongue, a flash of lightning showed me that it was Ibrahîm, and, when I said the same thing over in Arabic, the blue eyes of Georgie were suddenly revealed to me. To make matters worse, I could not recollect the Greek word for 'sweep,' and was driven in desperation to use the vulgar νὰ παστρεύεις. However, they all stood near enough to catch something of my meaning, and Aristides assured me that the room was already παστρικά. On the one hand, Salîm kept saying, 'Ya sitti; the tent is better than the house,' and on the other, Georgie repeated, 'Kyria, the house is far better than the tent, and there is a rain storm coming.'

Our beds and bags were being heaped on Aristides' mule. I entreated Violet to come quickly to the village, as our situation would be infinitely worse were rain coming on, and she had neither umbrella nor waterproof ready. But only the two Cypriots could show the way to the house, so we had to wait till they had finished loading the mule, and, as Georgie led it off, I followed, keeping my eyes fixed on its tail. Violet was a few yards behind; she stopped to condole with the cook, who was all alone in the kitchen tent, and I stopped to put on my waterproof, as I felt a few drops. So I lost sight of the mule, but I hurried on, seeing only by the vivid lightning flashes the forms of one or other of our men. We crossed a rushing mill-stream, and passed between garden walls till at last we came to the doorway of a building through which the mule was led, not without bumping its burden.

We found ourselves in a stone-paved, open court, and a coal-black African escorted us up an outside stone stair to a large room roughly paved, having eight windows and a door. The windows were destitute of glass. Five of them had ill-fitting shutters, and three out of the four at the two ends of the room had only half-broken Venetian blinds, letting in every wind of heaven. However, it was large, and did not look bad by the light of a lantern, although it was just over a stable. Aristides said that we might have had a better room over the café, but that they thought we should not like the noise. George said that he had wanted to take us to a Christian's house, but that the Christians were all much further off. This house belonged to a Turk, who did not live here himself, but kept it as a sort of khan.

Salim and the cook were to stay with the tents. George announced his intention of sleeping outside our door. We found Aristides making up a bed of saddle-bags for him in a picturesque corner under a trellised vine. We remonstrated, saying that we were not in the least afraid of being alone.

'But the door does not shut properly,' said George.

'But there will soon be a deluge,' replied Violet. 'Remain as near us as you can, but it must be under cover.'

He promised to seek shelter when the rain came on. We finally retired, long after midnight, to rest, but certainly not to sleep; for all the winds of heaven blew through our room without let or hindrance. Wilder and wilder did they wax, each gust lifting and dropping the blankets as it passed. Violet thought it was an earthquake. She rose, and put all the heavy things she could lay hands on against some of the window-blinds, to shut out the furious blasts; she insisted on moving my bed to a less unsheltered spot, and then lay down again, only to alarm me by saying that she felt as if the floor were giving way. It was no pleasant prospect, that of finding ourselves among the heels of our mules in a Cypriot stable; but I suggested that the walls, though of sun-dried brick, or of mud, were probably solid, and that the roof was more likely to come down than the floor. Nor would its fall be heavy, seeing that it was composed of the trunks of small trees, covered with canes, whose interstices showed the gravel of the earth lying above them. We could not well have passed the night in a more exposed situation. Still it was a degree better than our tents, and we reflected that Salim and the cook must be infinitely worse off than we, especially whilst the rain was falling in torrents. I have seldom passed a more terrible night, the only one, I think, in all my travels when I heartily wished for the comforts of home; and we both felt deeply thankful to Providence that, after twenty-four hours of fatigue and excitement, neither of us became seriously ill.

It was daylight before we fell fast asleep, and we were awakened at five o'clock by George knocking at the door. I believe the inconsiderate man was expecting us to start at seven o'clock as usual. Sleep, roughly driven away, would not again woo me, so I was glad when he again knocked at the door, and offered us the tea-kettle. Limasol, our next stage, was only six miles distant. We thought of staying at Piscopi till the afternoon, but the light of day made our apartment look so uninviting that we gladly adopted Georgie's suggestion, that we should ride for half-an-hour to Colossi, lunch under the trees, and go to Limasol in the afternoon.

Georgie's advice was not altogether good. Had we felt less exhausted, we should have asked one of the villagers to conduct us to the ruins of the city of Curium, which is said by Herodotus and by Strabo to owe its origin to a colony of Argives. According to another tradition, reported by Stephanos, the Byzantine, it was founded by a certain Curcos, son of Cinyras, the high-priest of Paphos, and therefore brother of Adonis. All we know for certain is that it must have been a very strong city, for it was built, as De Cesnola says, like an eagle's nest, on the summit of a rocky elevation three hundred feet above the level of the sea, and almost inaccessible from three sides.

After the night's experiences, we were perhaps

over-anxious to reach a more civilised town; so we cannot pretend to have seen the gigantic rock which has been forced to take a shape in accordance with the wishes of the architects, and was cut on the east and south sides into a perpendicular face.

More vexatious still, we did not see the thousands and thousands of rock tombs excavated within a small space, the 'City of the dead,' of which De Cesnola speaks. Nor did we see the treasure chambers of the temple, where he made his most astonishing discoveries.

We contrived to be ready by eleven o'clock, and rode away from Piscopi, with its rosy pomegranates and its wealth of greenery, to Colossi, another village embowered in verdure. Here there is a fine tower, built by the Knights of Rhodes, who named the place in honour of their Colossus. The proprietor, an intelligent old farmer, took us up a dark, stone stairway into two fine halls, with Gothic fireplaces. I told him of our adventure, and remarked that I wished we could have taken refuge in one of these apartments, with their six-feet thick walls.

'You have come from Piscopi,' he said. 'Did the people there not tell you that the great question about the genuine character of De Cesnola's discoveries was to be decided yesterday?'

'By whom?' we asked.

'By the French Consul from Larnaca,' he replied. 'He has made an examination of the royal tent, and has found that De Cesnola's measurements are correct. May I ask your opinion about it?'

'I have no means of forming one,' I replied. 'I

have seen neither the spot nor the treasure which was said to be found there, and as for the book although I have read it, I was dissuaded from bringing it with me by friends, who said that De Cesnola's discoveries are undoubtedly spurious. All the Americans whom we have met are indignant at the accusation, and no wonder, seeing that their country has secured the spoils. But I am very glad to hear that the verdict is favourable, for it is much pleasanter to believe in a man being honest than in the contrary.'

The old man showed us the armorial bearings of the knights sculptured over one of the doorways. I told him that if his tower could be transported to England, many noble and wealthy families would envy him its possession. It would make a comfortable dwelling-house, though he uses it as a granary.

Colossi is the head-quarters for the famous Commanderia wine, which resembles old Madeira in its taste. The vines were originally transported to Madeira from Cyprus, and were renewed from the same source, after the ravages of disease.

With regard to the discoveries of De Cesnola, we found that the prevailing opinion amongst the English residents in Cyprus is as follows:

De Cesnola was not an archæologist, but simply a man of culture, who had plenty of time at his disposal, his official duties being light. He was seized with a zeal for excavating, and collected many valuable objects of ancient art. Finding that these attracted the interest of scientific men who happened to visit him, he was induced to make a catalogue of them, stating to the best of his recollection the places where he had found each item. But, as he had not make a habit of doing this from the beginning, his memory failed him in one or two instances; and he thus furnished a handle to his detractors of which they have made ample use. His collection has the undoubted merit of having been made in Cyprus, and it is therefore genuine; but much of its value to antiquarians is lost through the want of accuracy in naming the spot where each separate object was found.

CHAPTER XV.

LAST DAYS IN CYPRUS.

'Canning Street'—Limasol—Many Invitations—Hot Winds—The Oldest City in Cyprus—The God Malika—Human Sacrifices—Heathen Miracle Plays—Vases—Sculptures—Pretty Hamlet of Zee—Visitors—Citi—Larnaca—The Royal Hotel—On Board the *Alphée*.

AN easy ride of two hours brought us from Colossi to Limasol, a pretty town which numbered some six thousand inhabitants at the time of the cession. Its streets are clean, and its houses of reddish sun-dried brick afford peeps through windows and doors of occasional flower-pots, tea-tables, and other English comforts. We thought it very funny to cross a stream which ran in the usual careless Turkish fashion through a street, and to see the next moment a lamp-post depending from a mud wall duly labelled 'Colossi Street,' or 'Canning Street.' We found our tents pitched on a little plot of grass near the main road close to the Commissioner's house. Salim had not put up our dining-tent, having taken a room for us in a house near. It was on the ground-floor, with a window which, though small, would have exposed us to the gaze of the numberless women and children who had assembled in the inner court. Our beds and furniture were already in it, and Salim was not too well pleased at having to move them into our tent. Several English families were kind enough to call as soon as they heard of our arrival. They told us that many windows in Limasol had been broken by the storm of the previous night. I cannot help surmising that we had been caught in the outer sweep of the cyclone which burst over Spain on the night of May 12th, a storm which will long be remembered from the fact of Queen Christine having bravely driven out to console her suffering subjects, just before the birth of Alfonso XIII.

There are now twelve English families settled in Limasol, besides the soldiers who occupy a camp in a picturesque spot on the hills. Limasol is the military port of the island; it is an open roadstead, but vessels can approach very near to the shore. Here, on the 1st of July, 1570, the Turks first landed in Cyprus, and ravaged all the country, meeting with little opposition till they reached Nicosia.

Many were the invitations we received to visit the houses of our hospitable fellow-countrymen. But, alas! we were obliged to decline, as it was imperatively necessary that we should move on.

The wind was not yet lulled, but we were protected from it by the surrounding houses. There was a great crowd about our tents all the evening, the curiosity of the people being insatiable.

Violet awoke me at two o'clock in the morning, saying that the wind was getting stronger, and that she fancied our tents were in danger. The canvas was heaving and rolling; but I knew it was the scirocco, and not a storm, and, when I looked out,

I saw the starry sky bathed in moonlight. Violet took the precaution of removing everything from the table to the floor. I told her that, as there was no rain, the fall of the tent would not be a great catastrophe. So we dressed ourselves, and lay down again, thus securing three hours of much-needed sleep before five o'clock.

We started at seven, with the intention of making Mari the goal of our day's journey, riding to Citi on Monday, and to Larnaca on Tuesday morning, thus allowing Salîm and the other Arabs to leave with our tents for Beyrout, their home, in the Austrian Lloyd's boat. Otherwise, they must have remained idle in Cyprus for another fortnight.

The road was a carriage one, not very good. It ran by the side of the sea for some way, and then on the inner side of some sand-hills, all blowing about in the hot wind. The road was white, and the heat greater than anything I ever experienced in Syria. I often tried to put up my white umbrella, but I had always to lower it again, and endure the sun's rays as well as I could. We followed a still whiter road through yellow corn-fields, dotted with fine olives and caroubs, the wind blowing as if it issued from an oven.

We passed near the site of Amathus. This was the very oldest city in Cyprus, but every trace of it has disappeared. It had rich copper mines. Its temple of Aphrodite is supposed by some to be older and more important than that of Paphos, though, in historical times, the latter certainly eclipsed it. The legend of Cinyras was appropriated by both. The Cinyradæ were probably priests in both; but at Paphos they contrived to possess themselves of the kingly dignity, and to extend their authority over the rival city.

A Phœnician or Tyrian god named Melkart was worshipped in Amathus under the name of Malika. He was said to have led a colony thither, and to have had a son named Amathus. The name is supposed to be connected with a place in Syria, named Amatha, or Gadara, near Tiberias, a place which received its name from Hamath, son of Canaan. Thus two towns of ancient Cyprus, Citium and Amatha, are etymologically connected with the grandsons of Noah.

Human sacrifices are said to have been offered here at an early period to Kronos, and to have been abolished by Aphrodite, who changed the worshipping priests into horned men κεραοται. The hand of the fair goddess meets us at every turn in Cyprian history. There is no end to the Protean multiplicity of the names under which she was honoured. She was the Golden, the Genetrix, the Victrix, the Nemesis, the Moira, the Pandemos, the Aphrodite Persephone, the Aphrodite Hera, the Aphrodite Urania, the Aphrodite Athena, and even in later times the Panagia Aphroditissa. She was also the Ariadne Aphrodite. Plutarch tells us that Theseus, when sailing from Crete, was driven by a storm towards the shores of Cyprus. There he left Ariadne, who was suffering greatly from the fatigues of the journey, and sailed away. Cyprian women took her in, and comforted her in her loneliness. They seem to have been fully aware of the influence which mental emotions exercise on the bodily health, for they showed her forged letters, which they pretended Theseus had written. They nursed her in her confinement, and when she died buried her. When Theseus returned to the island, he was overwhelmed with grief, and distributed money amongst the islanders, commanding them to offer sacrifices to Ariadne. He also dedicated two little pictures to her, one of silver, and one of brass. The grave was shown as that of Ariadne Aphrodite. Her festival took place in the month of Gorpiaios, about the end of August, or the beginning of September. The whole story of her abandonment, her confinement, and her death was then acted in a sort of mummery; a young man, dressed as a woman, representing the heroine.* A similar festival was held in her honour at Naxos. It was evidently begun in sorrow and lamentation, but was finished by the rejoicing consequent upon the birth of a son. At Tenedos, at the feast of Dionysos, a cow was treated as the suffering Ariadne. These mummeries appear to us ludicrous; but is it not just possible that the idea of men representing on a sacred stage those events which lay at the foundation of their religious belief may have been carried from the heathen to the Christian church, and have thus given rise to the miracle plays, and perhaps even to the ceremonies of Holy Week? These also begin in sorrow and end in joy. It seems as if some of the early Christian teachers shirked the work of instructing people in the theology and morals of the New Testament, preferring the easier method of winning their assent to Christianity not only by baptising some of the old gods with new names—turning Poseidon

* Plutarch. *Theseus*, xx.

into St. Nicolas, Helios into St. Elias, Athena into the Virgin, etc.—but by gratifying their love of dramatic representation and by substituting the stories of the Nativity and Crucifixion for those of Ariadne and Adonis.

The temple of Aphrodite is supposed by some to have stood near the modern village of Hagia Tychenos. De Cesnola found some beautifully-sculptured sarcophagi at Amathus. If we may trust the words of a gentleman of high position at Limasol, who related to Von Löher an occurrence of which he was an eye-witness, a very disgraceful piece of vandalism was enacted here by the French in 1865.

It seems that there were two gigantic, solid stone vases, finely shaped, with sides almost a foot in thickness, ornamented with four gracefully-arched handles, decorated with palm branches, and adorned by the images of four bulls. The vases were delicately chiselled, about ten feet in diameter, and so deep that a man standing within could just look over the edges. When the spot was visited by the French antiquarians, one of them stood above the ground, and was perfect; the other being partly buried in the earth. The French officers, who were seeking to convey the uncovered vase* to a steamship, commanded by the Comte de Vögue, found that the half-buried vase was somewhat in their way, and thereupon ordered the sailors who were with them to smash it to pieces. Von Löher found some bits of a handle of the broken vase lying on the ground. His zaptieh, Hussein, who had been present on the occasion, spoke with en-

* This vase was deposited in the Louvre Museum.

thusiasm of the enormous size and of the beauty of the vase which was carried off.

Von Löher thinks that the oxen sculptured on these vases had a religious significance, seeing that similar vases stood within the temple at Jerusalem. And indeed the resemblance is very close. The molten sea made by Hiram, the Tyrian artist, for King Solomon,* was doubtless of brass, but it seems to have been of the same character as the Amathian vases, and both may possibly have served for a like purpose.

Feasts in honour of Adonis were held at Amathus. He, the beloved of Aphrodite, was supposed to have been killed by a wounded boar in the forest of Idalium, to the north of Larnaca. Scarlet anemones sprang from the ground moistened by his blood. Adonis is identified with the Tammuz for whom the idolatrous Hebrew women wept.†

In the Wady Afka of Mount Lebanon a similar tragedy is fabled to have taken place. Here, in one of the most wildly romantic spots in Syria, is a rushing fountain, source of the river Adonis, whose waters, after every storm, tear the red soil from the banks, and thus

> 'Run purple to the sea, supposed with blood
> Of Thammuz, yearly wounded.'
>
> MILTON—*Paradise Lost*, 451.

In both places Aphrodite was worshipped with rites so impure that they debased the character of the women of Amathus, and led to the famous resolve of Pygmalion, the Cypriot sculptor, never to marry a mortal of the other sex. His son, by his

---

* 1 Kings, vii, 23.   † Ezekiel viii, 14.

own noble creation, was named Paphos, and was believed by some to have been the founder of the city of that name.* The story of Galatea must, however, be a later invention, the original legend being that Pygmalion fell in love with a statue of Aphrodite.

Amathus was finally destroyed by Richard Cœur de Lion, in retaliation for the insult offered to his queen, Berengaria, by Isaac Comnenus, the last Duke of Cyprus.

At half-past nine Salim and our retinue passed us, and at ten we fairly struck work, and, having reached a small river, halted for our midday meal. We seated ourselves on a carpet below a shady olive, where our sufferings from heat and from thirst quite pass description. Violet took her usual luncheon, whilst I regaled myself with a bowl of *yaioûrti* or sour milk. I should have found this refreshing at any ordinary time, but it tasted only a little less hot than other viands.

About twenty camels passed us. They and their little foals were in fine condition, and much cleaner than those of Egypt. Happening to look up, we saw that dark clouds were gathering over the sea, and we felt sure of an approaching rain-storm. It was half-past twelve, but we thought that we had better start. All our men were asleep, except George, who said that there would be no rain that day. Georgie, being awakened with difficulty, said that the scirocco generally ends in rain, and that we had still three hours to ride; so off we set as fast as we could, my lips being blistered and baked.

* Ovid—Met. x, 243.

At length, just as we reached the brow of a hill, the wind suddenly changed from warm to cold, a moist blast rushing against our faces. Over the sea the storm came marching, black and fearful. Georgie urged us to make haste. Violet, who was behind me, kept calling out, 'Quicker, quicker,' George translating this by 'συγᾴ, ἥσυχα,' ('Slowly, quietly').

At last, on turning another corner, the wind dropped, the dark clouds appeared to travel away towards Paphos, and the sun shone on us. The air was wonderfully still. We felt a little rain, and put on our waterproofs, only to take them off again. At half-past three we came to the turn of a steep road leading uphill to Mari, and a black man met us with the news that Salim had been anxious to obtain a room in the village where we could find shelter in case of rain, and, having been unsuccessful, had gone to a village an hour further on. So we rode on, sending Mustapha to Mari to make sure that there had been no mistake. There seems to be some doubt as to whether Mari, or Arsinoë, alias Poli, is the site of the ancient Marium, a town destroyed by Ptolemy Soter, who removed its inhabitants to Paphos. The balance of evidence seems to be in favour of Arsinoë, Mari having probably received its name in compliment to the Virgin. Marium was one of the nine or ten kingdoms into which ancient Cyprus was divided, but it was never distinguished in any way—at least, not under its original name.

Georgie's hours and half-hours were very elastic, for notwithstanding several stoppages, we reached the pretty hamlet of Zec at half-past four, and found only two tents pitched close to the sea, Salim having engaged a room for us.

I was discontented at this, for I infinitely preferred our tent, and there was every prospect of a fine night. Violet, however, said that she had not slept for forty-eight hours, and that, the next day being Sunday, we could move down to our camp in the morning, weather permitting.

The room was a very nice rough one. It had a little balcony looking on to a little quay and some boats.

We slept from nine p.m. till seven a.m., having long arrears to make up. Our room stood on the roof of a house; the only thing we disliked in it was a kind of white-wash that came off the stone floor on to our things. The weather was very fine, but I could not persuade Violet to return to the tents until the afternoon. About eleven o'clock I took a dip in the sea, making use of the dining-tent as a bathing-machine. I found the water tepid, and the sand and shingle of the shore quite hot to the touch.

After dinner we had a visit from Mr. Hunter, the island post-master. George asked if we were willing to ride next day to Larnaca, a distance of seven hours, Zee being exactly half-way from Limasol. From this fact it derives its name, which signifies, I am told, in Turkish, a balance.

Georgie insisted, as usual, that we should have to ride for nine hours; but George, with unwonted firmness, told him that it must be done.

Next morning we both had a dip in the sea, and started at half-past six. Our road lay across reaped corn-fields, dotted with caroub-trees. After crossing the river Pentachino, we kept along the sea-coast, the wind being cool, and the trees becoming fewer and fewer, till we approached the treeless, uninteresting village of Mazotas, and saw the mountain named Stavrobounó, on whose summit Helena built a convent, and deposited a bit of the true cross.

At half-past ten we came to a rude café by the side of a pretty little stream, where my mule deliberately put her cheek against the wall, expecting me to dismount. This showed no small degree of intelligence on her part; she evidently recognized the place, though she had not seen it for months, and had gone all round the island since the last time she was there. We took lunch beneath some fine flowering olives, the village of Citi being visible about three miles in front of us. This town, which is about two hours' ride from Larnaca, seems to have retained a trace of the ancient name Citium, or Chittim.

We left the olive-grove at half-past two. After we had passed Citi, the trees got more and more scanty, till at length we reached a village, situated in a magnificent grove of cypresses and mulberries, close to the sea. Then Georgie and I struck into a mule path across corn-fields where the reapers were busy, to a spot which in the eyes of Mussulmans ranks just after Mecca and Medina. This is the Tepe of Alat-es-Sultana,* a lovely little mosque, embellished in feathery palm-trees and dark cypresses, standing on the brink of one of the salt lakes which

---

* I do not know if this is the correct spelling. None of our escort could read or write, so it was useless to ask them.

yield fourteen thousand pounds a-year to the
government, and help to defray the heavy tribute
of Cyprus to the Sultan. We dismounted at its
door. Violet had sent Ibrahim after us, and Georgie,
giving himself the airs of a dragoman, motioned to
him to take charge of the horses, whilst he conducted me into an inner court, containing a large fountain and a garden of flowering pomegranates. Here
we were received by a young Turk, who spoke a
little Greek and less English, and who asked us to
sit down in a nicely-furnished room till his brother-
in-law, the sheikh, or 'president,' should be ready
to see us. The sheikh, a young man of about
thirty-five, came and offered us coffee and cigar-
ettes. I took the former, and Georgie, with great
dignity, accepted both. They were not in the least
in a hurry, supposing I had come on a pleasure excursion from Larnaca. At last, in response to my
repeatedly expressed wish to see the mosque, the
sheikh rose, and conducted me with much ceremony
to a garden by the side of the sacred building,
where he amused himself by cutting roses for me,
and doing every polite thing except opening the
door. At last I persuaded him to move towards
it, and, on entering, I put on slippers, and read to
him the Arabic inscription: 'Enter here, and sanc-
tify the place.' I then found that he understood
Arabic far better than Greek. He took me to an
inner sanctuary, and showed me the tomb of the
Sultana, who was either the foster-mother or the
foster-sister of Mohammed. Beside it were three
plain tombs, two of them being those of the sheikh's
father and grandfather, who had charge of the

place before him, the office of 'president' being hereditary.

I bade him farewell, and, riding out of the place, found that I had to cross a causeway between two of the lakes. Violet rejoined me, and at half-past six we were in our tents, which were pitched in their old place.

Mr. Blattner came in the evening. He told us that all the pine-trees which we had seen in the Troados district have been planted by the English. Their age certainly corresponds to that of our occupation of the island. The penalty for cutting down one of them is Draconic. A man had just been sentenced to three months' imprisonment and a fine of sixteen pounds for destroying three of them.

Next morning we rose at six o'clock, and removed our baggage down to the 'Royal Hotel,' a small establishment on the Marina, kept by a retired sea-captain named Gauci. He has not secured as much custom as he deserves, and this owing to the way in which the Levantines persist in misrepresenting everything about Cyprus. Whilst at Beyrout, we met several English families, who were anxious to spend a fortnight in the island, and were deterred from doing so by the false report that Captain Gauci had become bankrupt, and that all the visitors in the hotel had been obliged to hurry out of it, for fear of their luggage being seized by the bailiff. There was not a vestige of truth in the whole story; and I sincerely hope that our countrymen have not introduced into Cyprus the unjust law of distraint, a law which we have inherited from the Dark Ages, and which is, unfortunately, still permitted to blot our statute-book.

English residents in Cyprus were, at the period of our visit, suffering under an intolerable grievance, the abolition of the weekly mail, which had till then been brought by a Government steamer, and the establishment of a fortnightly one, brought by the Austrian Lloyd's from Trieste, by way of Alexandria and Beyrout. The inconvenience was aggravated by the departure of the fortnightly mail-steamer on the day of its arrival; so that letters must be answered within a few hours after their receipt. What this means to bankers and merchants may be imagined. One young man, who had been two years in the island, said to me that the inconvenience of keeping up a correspondence was now so great that his friends, finding that their questions could not be answered in less than a month's time, got one by one disheartened, and ceased to write to him. They would, he supposed, in time forget his existence.

British soldiers who come to Cyprus from Egypt are apt to dislike the island, solely on account of the difficulty they experience of hearing from home during their stay. Postal facilities are curtailed for the sake of economy; but whether this policy be wise, or even just, towards our fellow-subjects, and towards men in the service of Her Majesty, we will not undertake to say.

Our Arab servants sailed on the day after our arrival. George went with them, as we did not wish to detain him for a fortnight after we had gone. We were hospitably entertained to luncheon next day by Mr. Cobham, Commissioner of Larnaca; one of those English rulers who have secured the respect and good-will of the natives, and who adds to his other accomplishments an intimate acquaintance with their language.

We embarked on board the French steamer *Alphée*, taking a rather hasty farewell of our poor faithful muleteers, and brought away with us an intense interest in the future of an island which yields to none of our other British possessions in beauty, in fertility, or in importance.

CHAPTER XVI.

GLEANINGS FROM THE HISTORY OF CYPRUS.

First Notice of Cyprus—Divinities—Worship of Aphrodite—The Nine Kingdoms—Subject to Egypt—To Persia—The Cyprus Contingent for Invasion of Greece—Greek Influence—Evagoras—Abdemon's Plot—Sparta Supreme—Evagoras—Freedom Against Tyranny—Evagoras' Situation Becomes Desperate—Plots—Luxury—Menander's Satire on the Cypriots.

THE first notices which we have of Cyprus are connected with Phœnician commerce. No place in the ancient world was so favourably situated for shipping, its harbours being quite commodious enough for the vessels of those days. It had abundance, too, of the goods which merchants desire. The soil beneath was rich in copper, iron, asbestos, in building-stone, and even in diamonds. The mountains were clothed with cedar and cypress; the pools were reservoirs of salt, and the plains granaries of the finest wheat.

The Phœnicians, however, did not really colonize the island.* Their settlements, some of them, were only places of call. We do not know when the

* The facts related in this chapter and the following one are taken chiefly from the German author Engel, and from the Cypriot Phrancoudi. We have, however, verified them as much as possible by reference to ancient authors.

Greeks migrated thither, but the antiquity claimed for their legends shows that they must have had a footing there a thousand years prior to the Christian era.

Both races, of course, brought their divinities. How the Semitic ones were blended with the Hellenic, how Astarte became Aphrodite, and Tammuz Adonis, has been indicated in our notes about Paphos. There is no doubt that Cyprus was the stepping-stone by which the worship of these deities passed into Greece. She borrowed from Asia and supplied to Europe those influences by which the Eleusinian mysteries were corrupted. Under her auspices, Iacchus was supplanted by Bacchus.

This field of inquiry is a very fascinating one to the antiquarian. To the moralist it may be no less useful to trace the effects of physical causes upon national character.

Here, Nature was lavish in her gifts. The sky was sunny, the air balmy, the sea supplied refreshing breezes, and the earth yielded her fruits readily. Cyprus must have been a veritable paradise before her forests were cut down, and her streams were allowed to spread into marshes or were dried up in their very infancy by the fierce sunbeams. Yet when we turn to her children, how many tales of heroism can they tell us? Onesilos, Evagoras, Bragadino (who was hardly a Cypriot), and the Christian martyrs—that is all. Why has Cyprus a record so different from the rest of Greece?

There can be no doubt that the worship of Aphrodite was debasing. It must have left its mark on the national character, though, happily, after the lapse of two thousand years, no leaven of its influence is to be found amongst the Cypriot women.

Thucydides, in the beginning of his history, traces the renown of Attica, and the independence of her inhabitants, to the lightness and comparative poverty of her soil. The richest lands of Greece, he tells us, suffered the most frequent changes, and were most liable to invasion. We find a striking parallel to this in the case of Cyprus. The greater part of her record is the story of her change of masters. We dissent emphatically from the opinion of Cerrutti, that Cyprus shows us the noblest aspect of Hellenism. Most writers think, on the contrary, that no original development of the progressive Hellenic spirit took place there. The Cypriots, being in constant communication with Oriental peoples, received elements which the Greeks of other places succeeded in repelling. The worship of Astarte Aphrodite took root and grew where the soil was fitting. The character of the people became more and more enervated by luxury, till they ceased to assert their own wills with any effect, and Cyprus became the appanage of whatever power was strongest in the Levant. Intellectual life died out, and material prosperity gradually vanished. It is one of the many warnings with which history supplies us, that the weal of nations, as of men, does not consist in the abundance of the things which they possess.

Cyprus was, at an early period, divided into nine kingdoms, whose capitals were Citium, Curium, Paphos, Amathus, Neo-Paphos, Lapithus, Soli, Kyrenia, Kythera, and Salamis. Of these the first three only are supposed to have been originally Phœnician settlements, and two of them, at least, were afterwards Hellenized. Some of them sided with Athens and some with Persia, according to the proclivities of their inhabitants. They were not always independent, for, in the year B.C. 1000, we find Hiram, king of Tyre, making war on Citium to enforce payment of some tribute due to him; and, about B.C. 707, seven Cyprian monarchs, who are described as coming from a land 'at the distance of seven days from the coast in the sea of the setting sun,' were received in audience as vassals by Sargon, king of Assyria, the immediate predecessor of Sennacherib.

In the year B.C. 594, Cypriot independence vanished. Then Apries, king of Egypt, whilst fighting with Tyre, defeated the united fleet of Phœnicians and Cypriots. Fifty years later the island was completely subjugated and made into a dependency of Egypt by King Amasis, to whom it proved of the greatest possible importance in his struggle with Cyrus, furnishing him with materials for constructing a fleet which were not to be found in Egypt. Amasis seems to have felt the importance of winning the goodwill of his new subjects, for he adorned the temples of Aphrodite with costly offerings. But many Greeks were at that time settled in Egypt, Amasis was their sovereign, and they regarded the conquest of Cyprus much in the same light as they would have done the domination of one Greek state over another. The visit of Solon to King Cypranor of Soli probably took place about thirty years before the invasion of Amasis.

Twenty-five years passed, and Cyprus changed masters. Cambyses succeeded to the throne of

Cyrus, and was assisted not a little in his successful campaign against Egypt by the alliance of the insurgent Cypriots.* In return for their allegiance, the islanders exacted from him the following conditions: They were to retain their own kings and live under their own laws, and were not to be placed under Persian satraps. They were to pay a moderate tribute, and to do service in time of war where it did not conflict with their own interests. This agreement held good until Darius Hystaspes demanded a heavier tribute than the Cypriots had agreed to pay, and excited a series of revolts against Persian authority which often took place in conjunction with the Greek states, and which lasted for one hundred and fifty years. It is supposed that the Cypriot kings had become Persian vassals with the view of checking the democratic tendencies of their subjects; and Persia on the other hand liked to deal with petty sovereigns rather than with a free state. Be that as it may, when the great struggle betwixt Persia and Greece really began, it was impossible to keep Cyprus quiet. Salamis was then the richest and most important town in the island. Her king, Gorgos, sided with Persia, whilst his brother Onesilos was the leader of the Hellenic party. The latter, after vainly endeavouring to kindle some sparks of patriotism in his brother's mind, took advantage of his momentary absence from the town, shut the gates, and took the reins of government to himself. Gorgos fled to Darius, and Onesilos was proclaimed king.

He at once summoned all the other island sove-

* Herodotus iii., 19.

reigns to join in his revolt. The King of Amathus only refused. He laid siege to the city. Then came news that the Persian general Artybios was bearing down upon Cyprus with a fleet and a large army. Onesilos sent heralds to the Ionians, asking them to help in the common cause. But their own affairs were not prospering. Their forces were unequal to those of the Persians, Athens had not done much for them, and they had lost their last chance of holding their own against the ships of Darius, by a fault which seems ingrained in the Greek character, a want of unity amongst themselves. Their forces had been defeated at Ephesus, the Athenians had gone home, and they were in want of new allies, so they welcomed the messengers from Cyprus with open arms. They sent an expedition to Salamis, which arrived just as the Persian forces crossed from Cilicia, and marched over the hills to attack that town. Their fleet was cruising about those little islands near the north-east corner of the island which are known as the Kleides, or Keys, when the princes of Cyprus called their leaders to a council, and asked them whether they preferred fighting with the Persians on land, or with the Phœnicians at sea. If the former, then they must at once come on shore and prepare for battle, leaving their ships to the Cypriots, who would then engage to meet the Phœnicians on their native element. If, however, they preferred the latter course, the Cypriots would cede them their ships. But, whatever was decided, Ionia and Cyprus should both be free in the case of a common victory.

The Ionians replied that they had been sent by

their own confederation to guard the seas, and not to cede their ships to the Cypriots and fight the Persians on land. They would do their best to comply with these orders, and they trusted that the Cypriots on their side would show themselves brave men, remembering what they had suffered from the Persians.

The assembly was scarcely dissolved before the Persian army appeared in the plain of Salamis. It happened that the order of battle placed Onesilos opposite to Artybios himself. The Persian general usually rode on a horse which had been trained when in presence of heavily-armed foot soldiers, to rear up and trample them down. This was known to Onesilos, and he accordingly told his shield-bearer, a Carian by birth, and a veteran warrior, to keep his eye on the horse, and, if it reared, to knock it or its rider down. The brave shield-bearer answered joyfully that he was ready to attempt the overthrow of both, or to do anything else that his king commanded.

'A king,' he said, 'should confront a king on the battle-field, and a general a general. I shall take care that Artybios shall be opposite to none but thee.'

The fight began by sea and by land. Onesilos sought Artybios. The horse reared, and in an instant his armour-bearer hewed off its feet with a sickle. The beast fell, and Onesilos slew his opponent. But in the heat of the fight Stasanor, King of Curium, went over to the Persians with a large body of troops; the chariots of the Salaminians followed him in ignorance of his tactics; the

Persians got an advantage, and the Cypriots were defeated. Onesilos was amongst the slain, and so was Aristocypros of Soli, the son of the Philocypros who entertained Solon.

The people of Amathus got possession of the body of Onesilos, and avenged the siege of their city by cutting off his head and placing it over one of their gates.

The Ionians had, in the meantime, defeated the Persians in a naval engagement. Finding, however, that they could reap no benefit from it, owing to the demoralized condition of their Cypriot allies, they sailed homewards; and all the island cities surrendered, except Soli, which withstood a siege of five months, and capitulated only when the enemy had undermined its walls.

Cyprus thus became entirely subject to Persia in the year B.C. 498. The insurrection of the Ionian states ended, four years later, with the fall of Miletus, and then Cyprus was called on to furnish a large contingent to the army, which was about to invade Greece. Her ships, one hundred and fifty in number, were commanded by the native kings, amongst whom Gorgos of Salamis is mentioned. It seems, however, that Xerxes could not quite trust the fidelity of his island subjects, for one of the arguments which Queen Artemisia employed, when she tried to dissuade him from giving battle at Salamis, was that he could not reckon upon the hearty co-operation of the Egyptians, nor of the Cypriots, nor of the Cilicians, nor of the Pamphylians. It is just possible that the treachery of these people may have supplemented the effect of the successful stratagem of Themistocles; for we find the Persian general Mardonius telling his enraged sovereign, after the battle, that, however badly the allies might have behaved, no blame could be cast upon the Persians themselves. Diodorus states that the Phœnician and Cyprian ships were the first to flee before the Athenians.

The first effort of the victorious Greeks, after driving the hordes of Asia from their own soil, was to free Ionia and Cyprus, and thus effectually to root up the maritime power of Persia. The Spartans, who had then the hegemony, accordingly sent Pausanias, with a fleet of fifty sail, to Cyprus in the year B.C. 577, thirty Athenian ships, under Aristides, accompanying them. Pausanias drove out the Persian garrisons from all the fortified places in the island, but he seems to have been unable to retain his hold on them. The native kings were probably always plotting in the Persian interest; and they must have succeeded in bringing it again under the dominion of the Great King, for we find Cimon, in B.C. 442, sailing to Cyprus with a fleet of two hundred ships, and dying whilst he was besieging Citium.

Notwithstanding the victory of the Athenians on that occasion, and the great naval battle which they won just afterwards near Salamis, they found themselves so much weakened by losses, that they returned home, and sent a votive offering to Delphi made from the tenth part of their spoils, with the following inscription:

Ἐξ οὗ γ' Εὐρώπης Ἀσίας δίχα πόντος ἔνειμε,
καὶ πολέας θνητῶν θοῦρος Ἄρης ἐπέχει,
Οὐδέν πω τοιοῦτον ἐπιχθονίων γένετ' ἀνδρῶν
Ἔργον ἐν ἠπείρῳ καὶ κατὰ πόντον ἅμα,
Οἵδε γὰρ ἐν Κύπρῳ Μήδους πολλοὺς ὀλέσαντες
Φοινίκων ἑκατὸν ναῦς ἐν πελάγει
Ἀνδρῶν πληθούσας, μέγα δ'ἔστενεν Ἀσὶς ὑπ' αὐτῶν
πληγῶσ' ἀμφοτέραις χερσὶ κράτει πολέμου.

> Since first the wave divided Europe's shore
> From Asia's, Mars the fate of man doth sway.
> But never both on sea and land before
> Had wretched mortals such a moil as they,
> Who late in Cyprus slew the Medes, till o'er
> Phœnicia's hundred ships the billows play,
> Filled with her children. Asia wept aloud,
> Wounded in both her hands of war so proud.

History does not tell us clearly in what condition Cyprus was left by the Athenians. Greek influence was certainly not supreme there, neither was Persian. The inhabitants inclined probably to the one side or to the other according as they were moved by the character of some individual prince. The ruling families always favoured Persia; the merchants, on the other hand, must have found it their interest to seek the friendship of Athens, to which there was a great export of corn. One of the scholiasts on the 'Knights' of Aristophanes calls Cyprus an Attic island; but the wish was probably father to the thought. Far better would it have been for Athens had she attempted its complete deliverance instead of wasting her efforts on the ill-starred expedition to Syracuse. Little is said about Cyprus at this period because, for the moment, she fell out of the great march of world-history. In the dim light, however, one heroic figure becomes visible, the greatest, indeed, that

Cyprus herself can show us. Salamis had always been the chief focus of Hellenic culture and influence, and these reached their culminating point during the reign of Evagoras.

Abdemon, the immediate predecessor of this king, seems to have been of Phœnician origin. But whether he was one of a dynasty who had displaced the family of Teucer, or a successful Tyrian adventurer, who had murdered the rightful king of Salamis, with the help of the Persian party, is a point about which ancient historians disagree. All we know is, that his occupation of the throne must have been peculiarly distasteful to the Greeks, showing them, as it did, how vain had been the efforts of Pausanias and Aristides, and the victories of Cimon. Not only so, but Abdemon was constantly occupied in persuading the other island princes to submit to the Persian yoke, and to adopt Asiatic customs. If we may believe Isocrates, the Athenian orator, Cyprus was in a fair way to become a land of barbarians.

Evagoras, who excelled all his contemporaries in the beauty of his person, the splendour of his mental gifts, and the ardour of his patriotism, was born in B.C. 455, shortly before Abdemon ascended the throne. Later legends affirm that his entrance into the world was heralded by dreams, prophecies, and oracles, and that he was a lineal descendant of Teucer. Isocrates tells of him that even as a boy he was distinguished amongst his companions for the strength and address which he displayed in games, and that all these brilliant qualities were enhanced by a kindness of heart by which those who were forced to own his superiority were the more readily won to his side. He was evidently sprung from a race of heroes, and it needed no close observation to predict that he would not rest contented in a private station.

So Abdemon was uneasy, and hired ruffians to take away his life. Evagoras discovered this, and fled to Soli in Cilicia, where his mind and his will were matured and strengthened by the hardships of exile. He secretly formed a company of fifty Cypriots. More he might have had, but he would only enlist those on whose courage and fidelity he could implicitly rely. Like another Garibaldi, he landed in Cyprus trusting more to the justice and the popularity of his cause and to his own daring, than to the means at his command. He gave himself no thought about providing himself with a place of retreat in case of failure, or getting possession of any fortified place, or waiting until he had collected many adherents. On the very night of his arrival he burst open a little gate in the wall of Salamis, led his followers through it, and attacked the royal palace. The city was thrown into confusion. Many who would have joined him were restrained from doing so through fear of the tyrant's anger. For the most part the citizens remained passive, those of their number who had taken up arms, as in duty bound, being awed by the reverence they felt for the spotless fame of the rebel chief. Evagoras, with his handful of followers, fought apparently against great odds, took the palace, killed Abdemon, and installed himself on the vacant throne.

This took place about the year B.C. 410. It is somewhat surprising that the Persian king did not prevent it; but the expedition seems to have been planned with great secrecy and rapidity, and we know that it is not the habit of Asiatics to be very watchful or very prompt. The Goliath of tyrannical power has often been overthrown by a little stone flung by a determined hand, and so it was in this case. Evagoras seems to have been a born ruler of men. One of his first cares was to restore the trade betwixt Cyprus and Greece, and the export of corn, which had for some time been prohibited. His next was to fortify Salamis, to improve the harbour, and to build ships. The town so prospered under his wise management, both in its internal and its external affairs, that no city of Greece was deemed to come second to it. His favourable disposition to the Athenians was soon known, and Conon, after his defeat at Ægospotami in B.C. 405, knew no safer place of refuge than Salamis. Thither he accordingly fled, and was received by Evagoras with open arms. The two were drawn to each other by a subtle sympathy, no less than by common aspirations and beliefs. They were alike in their hatred of Persia, and in their disapproval of Spartan ambition. Many young and eager Athenians flocked to the court of Evagoras, chiefly those who had been banished from Attica at the request of the Lacedæmonians. These had left their own country, like Teucer, only to find another in Cyprus, where they considered the rule of Evagoras to be much more just than that of their own archons. Evagoras was a Hellene of the Hellenes, and the dearest wish of his heart was to draw closer the bond of friendship betwixt Athens and his own city.

Nor were the Athenians unresponsive to his advances. They bestowed on him what was in their eyes the highest of earthly honours, they repaid him for the substantial benefits he had conferred upon them by making him a citizen of Athens.

Affairs now took a curious turn. Sparta was victorious in the Peleponnesian war, she humbled her illustrious rival, and sought to attack the Persian king in his own country. Agesilaos, one of her two sovereigns, actually formed a plan for hurling Artaxerxes from his throne. The latter, in dire perplexity, turned his eyes to all who had cause of quarrel with Lacedæmonia. And they were not few. Whilst some of his envoys went to Argos, to Corinth, and to Thebes, others dangled before the eyes of Evagoras and of Conon the bait of helping to restore the fallen fortunes of Athens. The two prudent statesmen took in the situation at a glance. They saw clearly that the one thing lacking to the Persian monarch was a clever general, and they actually requested him to place Conon at the head of the Persian fleet. Evagoras, knowing how difficult it would be to persuade Artaxerxes that such a proposal, coming from his natural enemy, was meant in good-will, wrote to his physician Ktesias, begging him to employ his influence in overcoming any objections which his royal patient might entertain against this plan. Nor was the precaution needless. 'How?' Artaxerxes must have thought. 'Who is this daring man, who asks me to give into the hands of his close confederate the better half of my armaments? Is it he who drove my vassal from the throne of Salamis? He who has opposed me with a front of brass in all my projects, and has, till now, maintained himself on the throne in spite of me? Only the worry which these Greeks have given me in other places has delayed the hour of his ignominious deposition. True, he has paid me some tribute, but that is only to soften my anger. I know that he is, at the same time, strengthening himself in every way to meet the hour of my just judgment on his contumacy.' Had the electric telegraph existed in those days, it would doubtless have carried a message from Artaxerxes to Evagoras similar in spirit to that lately sent by Alexander III., of Russia, to Alexander I., of Bulgaria.

But necessity has no law. By whatever means it was brought about, an offensive and defensive alliance was actually made betwixt Persia and Salamis. Conon wished to go to Susa in person, but Evagoras dissuaded him from doing so, and sent letters to Artaxerxes, together with a large sum of money, as a token of his submissiveness and good-will. A Spartan embassy which was then at the Persian court, tried to thwart the negotiations, but without avail. Artaxerxes wrote to Conon, and offered him the command of the fleet, but this only as second to his own admiral, Pharnabazus.

Evagoras made great preparations, and supplied a hundred ships, while Pharnabazus brought only forty with him. With this force, Conon sailed along the coast of Asia Minor, and annihilated the Spartan fleet at Knidus, in Caria. This victory restored to Athens the preponderance at sea, and the hegemony of Greece. Filled with gratitude, her citizens loaded Evagoras and Conon with honours, placing their statues by the side of that of Zeus Soter. But Artaxerxes could not dissemble longer. The triumph of the two friends was only the prelude to a bitter war, which lasted as long as the siege of Troy, and taxed the skill and resources of Evagoras to the utmost.

The wise statesman had foreseen this. He knew that the Persian was only using him as a tool, to be thrown away, and he therefore prepared himself in the first place by endeavouring to subdue the other kings of the island. Citium and Amathus, being old Phœnician settlements, gave him most trouble. Soli, too—which, as a town, ranked second in importance to Salamis—was not altogether inclined to yield. He had made some sort of pact with these three towns before allying himself with Persia, but no sooner had victory declared itself on his side, when, the dread of Sparta having passed away, they, in the year B.C. 391, sent ambassadors to Artaxerxes to beg for protection against him. The ambassadors struck a responsive chord in the despot's heart. He was secretly fuming at the hard necessity which had obliged him to place so large a part of his naval force in the hands of his natural enemy. Conon had gone much further than he had anticipated in restoring the power of Athens, and it was high time that a check should be put on his progress. Nor was he blind to the danger of Evagoras getting possession of all Cyprus, and there raising a fleet which would give him the command of the eastern Mediterranean.

Artaxerxes, therefore, sent messengers to the satraps of all his provinces, and to all the maritime towns, commanding them to fit out vessels with all possible speed. He appointed Hecatomnos of Caria admiral of his new fleet, and he sent a large army to Cyprus, of which he intended to take the command himself.

But his orders were only languidly obeyed. Greek ambassadors had arrived, and were negotiating the preliminaries of peace; so that it was highly inconvenient to begin a new war at that moment. His chosen admiral, Hecatomnos, was a Greek by birth, and was possibly only waiting a favourable opportunity to follow the example of the prince whom he was sent to attack.

Evagoras took advantage of the delay. He sought everywhere for allies, and even tried to make an alliance with Dionysius of Syracuse. Now was the time to try what the gratitude of the Athenians was worth. They had not deceived him with empty promises, for they gave him thirty thousand drachmas for the purchase of arms, and ten ships, which, however, were destroyed by a larger Spartan fleet before they could reach Cyprus. Athens and Sparta were at this moment both carrying on a war against Persia; yet their fierce jealousies would not permit them to make common cause, and the Spartans actually destroyed a fleet of their rivals, although it was hastening to the help of Evagoras against their worst enemy.

The Athenians sent a new fleet in the following year, under Chabrias, who gained some brilliant victories, forced the whole island to submit to Evagoras, and erected suitable trophies.

The negotiations for peace betwixt Persia and Sparta proceeded very slowly. They were brought to an end in B.C. 387 by Antalkidas, one of the Spartan kings, who made terms which were very dishonourable to his country, and by which all the Greek cities of Asia became tributary to Persia. Artaxerxes accordingly withdrew the support he had given to Athens, and followed his natural impulses by trying to strengthen Sparta. He could now proceed, with both hands free, against Evagoras. Conon had deeply offended him; for there could be little doubt that he had used the power and even the money entrusted to him by Persia for the service of Athens. The wily Greek soon perceived that he had fallen into disfavour, so he fled, with his wife and his son Timotheus, to Salamis, where he soon after died.

Evagoras knew well the art of war, and was aware that the best way of defending himself was to strike. The victories of Chabrias had left him in possession of all the island fortresses; so he carried fire and sword to the mainland. Tyre, the great city to which Cyprus had once been subject, was taken by storm, the whole of Phœnicia was plundered; Syria and Cilicia were excited to open revolt. Terror reigned in the Persian court. All felt as if the greatest monarchy in the world was being shaken to its foundations. Never, since the sun set on the wreck-strewn shores of Salamis the island, had the dominion of the Great King been in such deadly peril as it now was from that island's victorious colony. The will of one determined man had brought about a strange revolution. It had seemed only a few months previously as if Evagoras was deserted by his friends, for whom he had effected so much, and left, without protection, to the vengeance of his implacable foe. Only the consciousness of their own impotence could have made the Athenians agree to a peace so dishonourable as that which had been concluded in the name of all Greece by Antalkidas. Ionia was by it handed over to Persia, and Evagoras was left to make what terms he could.

But now all was changed. Cyprus, which Artaxerxes had always intended to conquer at his leisure, had developed a power of its own, and was thundering at his gates. The web of Asiatic intrigue was rent, there was no time for further dissembling. Throughout his wide dominions men rushed to arms. The cost of preparation is said by Isocrates to have amounted to fifty thousand talents, or nearly three millions and a half sterling. The land army, consisting of three hundred thousand men, including cavalry, was placed under the command of Orontes, the king's son-in-law, and a fleet of three hundred ships under Tiribazos. When we look at the little corner of earth which Evagoras ruled, an involuntary smile rises to our lips at the idea of so vast an expedition being sent against him. The fleet set sail from Phocae and Cyme, towns on the coast of Asia Minor, near Smyrna, in the spring of B.C. 386.

The army of Evagoras could bear no comparison with this. That of Salamis itself is supposed to have numbered only six thousand men. The rest of

Cyprus, no doubt, furnished more, but, on the other hand, the inhabitants, or at least the rulers of three island towns, were ready to throw in their lot with the enemy.

The disparity was, however, only apparent. Evagoras' army had the advantage of being homogeneous, if not in race at least in sentiment. He trusted, in the first place, to the weight of his own personal reputation, and in the second to secret allies in the Persian camp.

These were not difficult to find. Under an autocracy, especially under one which embraces a large extent of territory and a variety of races, there must always be a great amount of smouldering discontent. Hecatomnos, the ruler of Caria, had been dismissed from his post as admiral. It was with reason that Artaxerxes distrusted him. He dared not help Evagoras openly, but he supplied him with money to hire mercenaries. A certain king of the Arabs sent a considerable body of troops. But the chief external stay of Evagoras was Egypt.

Amyrtaios, the king of that country, had been trying, not without success, to make himself independent. His son Acôris welcomed the idea of an alliance with Evagoras, and sent about fifty ships to augment his fleet.

And there was moral force on the side of Salamis. Its king was fighting for an idea—*the* idea which has nerved the arm of patriots in all ages. Persia's troops were men forced into the ranks, or were mercenaries; those of Evagoras were men conscious of the greatness of the issue. It was, in a word, the eternal struggle of freedom against tyranny. The spirit of Leonidas and of Miltiades was up and awake.

And men fight well who trust their general. Evagoras had done such wonderful things; he had made the little kingdom of Salamis a power; he had displayed the most brilliant qualities of a warrior, and when most hardly pressed had risen superior to circumstances. What marvel if his followers deemed him invincible? Besides this, he had the power of winning men's hearts.

It seems strange that he allowed the Persian army to land. But he was then probably absent in Phœnicia, and he knew that they would find no plain in Cyprus where they would have space to unfold their might, save that close to his capital. Perhaps he meant to confound them by some unexpected blow.

He was by no means weak in naval resources. Besides the fifty ships sent by Acôris, he soon made ready sixty new ones of his own, the whole strength of his fleet being about two hundred sail. Men worked with a will in the dockyards of Salamis, and many a little vessel was fitted out to harass the Persian cargo-boats.

Tiribazos had, in truth, made a gigantic mistake. He should have secured the autocracy of the sea before landing such a host of men on so small an island. They soon exhausted the resources of the places where they were encamped, and then looked wistfully for the boats of purveyors, which had either been captured or were deterred from venturing on a voyage to the island. Mutiny followed fast on the steps of hunger. Many of the Persian officers were murdered, and Gaôs, who was second in command, found that all his efforts to restore order were but as oil cast upon the flames, till the happy thought occurred to him to place the whole Persian fleet betwixt Cyprus and the coast of Cilicia, and to make it a sort of bridge for the transport of provisions. Acôris, in the meantime, was not idle. He supplied Evagoras with money and with arms of all kinds in superfluity.

Gaôs began to suspect his sailors. Many of them were Ionians, and a lively interchange of letters went on betwixt them and their friends at home, who were urging them to mutiny. He accordingly prepared a trireme, and gave out that it was going to sail to Ionia. A goodly number of letters were entrusted to its crew. It sailed, but soon returned to the shore. The letters were opened, and many of those who had written them were chastised with whips.

A few skirmishes took place on land. These were in the mountain passes, and their result was always favourable to the Cypriots, who knew the country. Evagoras, however, saw that the decisive struggle must be on the sea, and he was unwearied in practising evolutions with his ships. By this means he gave them confidence in himself and in each other.

The hostile fleets met near Citium. The Persian ships sailed about at their leisure, without any attempt at order. Those of Evagoras moved forward to the attack in a fair, unbroken line. Victory came to the latter with the first blow. The overthrow of the Persians seemed as great as it had been a hundred years previously at Salamis.

But there was more behind. Evagoras found, to his cost, that he had only dealt with part of the enemy's forces. In the very flush of his triumph, he saw another hostile fleet bearing down upon him. It was led by Gaôs in person. The struggle was both obstinate and bloody. Victory at first seemed to lean to the side of Evagoras; but, whether it was that his sailors were fatigued, or whether they had got scattered in chasing their first adversaries, we know not, the day ended in their total discomfiture.

Evagoras, much disheartened, returned to Salamis, and prepared to pass the winter within its strong fortifications. Tiribazos invested it closely with army and with fleet, having first obtained possession of Citium. He soon left the command to another, and started for Susa, to announce his victory in person to his sovereign.

The situation of Evagoras seemed desperate. But it was precisely in such circumstances that the genius of the man showed itself. Having put everything within the city in order, and appointed his son Protagoras commander, he slipped through the enemy's fleet by night with ten sail, and fled to Egypt.

Acôris received him with honour, and was not slow to believe that the fate of his own dominions was bound up with that of Cyprus. He supplied the fugitive with money, though with somewhat less than Evagoras had hoped for.

Spring came, and Tiribazos returned to the scene of his exploit, with two thousand talents. Evagoras, too, was there, having the less reason to complain of Acôris, inasmuch as his other allies had quite failed him. Finding that Salamis was hard pressed, and despairing of a successful resistance, he entered into negotiations for peace, in the hope that he would now get more favourable terms than when exhausted by a prolonged struggle. The only conditions which Tiribazos could offer were, that Evagoras should confine himself to the town of Salamis, and give up all claim to any other part of the island, and that he should pay a yearly tribute to the Kings of Persia, and demean himself towards them as a servant to his master.

Evagoras replied that he was ready to assent to all this, even to the payment of tribute. But one point he was determined never to yield. He would not submit to the will of the Great King as a servant to his master, but as a sovereign tributary to another sovereign.

The negotiations were broken off, and Evagoras prepared to resist to the uttermost. His allies had all forsaken him, except Acôris, from whom further help would probably arrive when it would be too late. In vain did his friend Isocrates employ the resources of his eloquence in trying to persuade the Athenians that it was alike their duty and their interest to break the peace. Evagoras turned to the camp of his enemies.

Tiribazos had returned loaded with honours, which awakened the jealousy of Orontes, another general; and this man formed a plot to overthrow him. Having conferred secretly with Evagoras, he wrote to Artaxerxes, accusing Tiribazos of treachery, of seeking to attach the troops to himself by bribes, and of having sent to consult the oracle at Delphi about the probable success of his intended revolt. Evagoras also wrote confirming the accusation. Artaxerxes believed them; Tiribazos was sent a prisoner to Susa, and Orontes was appointed to fill his place.

Evagoras now found little difficulty in repelling the attacks of the besiegers, for the Persian soldiers were disposed to mutiny, being discontented at the disappearance of their leader. Orontes was forced by their behaviour to conclude a peace, of which the chief condition was that Evagoras should pay a yearly tribute, and obey the commands of the Great King, as a king.

The ten years' struggle was at an end. For a year Evagoras reigned in all honour, then, it is painful to relate, he and his son Protagoras were both murdered, the victims of just vengeance, having both been seduced into a discreditable intrigue. Thus died the most illustrious man to whom Cyprus ever gave birth, a man whose indomitable courage, political sagacity, love of culture, and energy in misfortune place him on a level with the greatest of the world's heroes.

We have dwelt thus long upon his story because we think it is one which ought to be generally known. The world would not be the poorer were the names of many battles and of many warriors forgotten; but it is far otherwise with those whose determined wills set up even a temporary barrier to the perpetual current of despotism and of ignorant servility which always flows through our poor planet.

Ancient historians who recount the deeds of these heroes, are almost silent as to the social condition of the common people. We think we are not far wrong in surmising, however, that the state of the Cypriots could not have differed materially at that period from that of the Continental Greeks. They enjoyed a certain civilization, and had made considerable progress in the fine arts, as we know from recent archæological discoveries; but they were steeped in heathenism and superstition. And that deterioration of the national character consequent on their having chosen Astarte Aphrodite as their chief divinity must have gradually become more and more apparent.

It is at least a significant fact that the two towns which were the chief seats of that worship, Paphos and Amathus, were the very two whose opposition frustrated the patriotic designs of Onesilos, and which consistently opposed Evagoras. Their Phœnician origin may have inclined them to take this course, but is not enough to account for it, because all reasoning men know the difference betwixt oppression and freedom, and we actually find the Arabs sending a contingent to Evagoras.

We find, too, that Cyprus had at that early period acquired the reputation for immoderate luxury which probably occurs to our readers at the very mention of her name, and to which the present condition of her hard-working inhabitants forms a painful contrast. In all parts of the civilized world this delightful island was esteemed the best place where idle youths might spend their money in the pursuit of pleasure.* The Cyprian kings vied in luxury with oriental ones. Next to them was an aristocracy consisting, probably, in Salamis, of the descendants of Teucer's companions, amongst whom the land had been partitioned, and in the other states of those who had held a similar position to their founders. Any rights which this caste may at first have possessed, were soon lost in the growing degeneration of manners, till at length each king had a body guard, not of Prætorian soldiers, sworn to guard his person and to do him service in the field, but of men nobly born, who had the significant title of κόλακες, or Flatterers. They formed a sort of tribunal whose office it was to punish dangerous persons, without trial. Their chief duty was to go about in the public places and workshops of the town to spy out the disaffected. They were not a little proud of their art, for it advanced them greatly in the favour of their king.

Still more characteristic of the age and of the island was a guild of ladies, who were called κολακίδες, or She-flatterers, and afterwards κλιμακίδες, or Ladders. When the wives of a king stepped into a carriage, or stepped out of it, it was the duty of these females to bend towards the earth, each lower than her neighbour, so as to make a kind of ladder of their backs for the princesses' feet.

A boy, the son of a king of Paphos, is thus described. He lay upon a couch with silver feet,

* ἐκ Κύπρου λαμπρῶς πάνυ
πράττων, ἐκεῖ γὰρ ὑπό τιν ἦν τῶν βασιλέων.
MENANDER. *Meineke*, p. 118.

covered with a magnificent carpet from Sardis. A purple counterpane was thrown over him, shaggy on both sides, and a linen veil from Amorgos covered his head. Three pillows of the finest linen, fringed with purple, were under his head, and two scarlet ones under his feet. He was clothed in a white chlamys. Servants stood at a little distance. Three of these, however, were close to him. One had the charge of his feet, another stroked his hands, extending each finger in its turn, and another, the most esteemed, smoothed the pillows and fanned his master so gently that the very flies were not disturbed. On one occasion, a large fly, sent by an angry god, was so impudent that the good servant lost his temper, and his screams made everyone else flee from the house.

There exists, also, part of a comedy by Antiphanes,* a poet of Rhodes, named the 'Soldier,' in which one of the personages relates that he has spent some time in Paphos, and that the luxury he there saw was unexampled and inconceivable. The king, as he sat at table, was fanned by doves.

'How was that possible?' asks his friend.

'He was anointed with oil brought from Syria,' he replies, 'made from a fruit which doves are very fond of. These fly in, attracted by the scent, and wish to perch on the king's head, but the servants scare them away. Then they rise and flutter about, not too near and not too far off. So they make a current which is moderate, and not too strong.'

Some of the lost plays of Menander are supposed to have contained no little amount of satire about

* Athenæus. Dindorf, vi, 257.

the Cypriots. With the death of Evagoras, the last spark of a wish for anything better seems to have died away. He was succeeded on the vassal-throne of Salamis by his second son, Nicocles, the business of whose life was to out-vie the King of Sidon in the luxurious appointments of his household. Both these princes earned the dislike of their subjects, and the end of their sumptuous lives was a violent death. Some time about the year B.C. 351, Artaxerxes III. undertook an expedition into Egypt, and the Cypriot kings seized the opportunity of making an united effort to shake off his authority. It was in vain. They received but a feeble support from their subjects, who had, during the last few years, profited by the natural riches of their island, and by the constant stream of trade which flowed past its shores, and were becoming less and less inclined to war. The Persians had little difficulty in suppressing this revolt. They sent an expedition, commanded by Phocion, an Athenian, and by Evagoras II., who was probably a grandson of the great Evagoras, and who had been driven from his throne by his justly incensed subjects. All the Cypriot towns submitted at once, except Salamis, which the two generals prepared to besiege. But their mercenary troops were so delighted with their quarters in so rich a country, and the fame of what was to be enjoyed and earned in this war spread so rapidly on the mainland, that adventurers streamed to Cyprus from all quarters, and the Persian army was soon doubled. The Cypriots were in no little trepidation at this invasion of human locusts. But the danger melted as suddenly as it had appeared.

Some one accused Evagoras II. to the Great Monarch, who withdrew his protecting hand, but shortly after found him innocent, and rewarded him with a rich satrapy in Asia. Probably the difficulties he encountered in Egypt induced him to withdraw his fleet from Cyprus.

Twenty years later, events occurred which roused Cyprus from her sleep of degradation. She had not responded adequately to the calls of her own brave Evagoras. She was now to hear the mightier voice of the Macedonian conqueror, summoning her to join him in the work of Hellenising Asia and the world.

CHAPTER XVII.

HISTORY OF CYPRUS (CONTINUED).

Alexander—Cyprus a Persian Province—Cyprus and Alexander—His Gratitude—Part of Macedonian Empire—A Lapse of Years—A Province of Egypt—The Ptolemies—A Monster—Short Dream of Honourable Independence—Cato—Introduction of Christianity—Thirteen Bishoprics—Four Centuries of Peace—Rinaldo of Castile—The Crusades—Richard Cœur de Lion—Cyprus Sold to Knights-Templars—Guy de Lusignan—Saracen Ravages—Venetian Supremacy—Turkish Rule—British Occupation and Rule.

WHEN Alexander began his campaigns, Cyprus was nothing better than a Persian province. Not only so, but her ships formed the most redoubtable part of the fleet of Darius, commanded, as they were, by the most skilful of sailors. But no cords of affection or of gratitude bound these men to their masters; so it is not surprising that, after the decisive battles at Gravicus and at Issus, Cyprus espoused the cause of the victor, being no doubt willingly swept away by the rising current in favour of everything Greek. Her princes contrived to take the decisive step just as Alexander was building a fleet at Sidon, in order to invest Tyre. The Tyrians had great hopes from their Cypriot allies; and their hearts beat high with expectation, when they knew that a fleet of one hundred and fifty sail was approaching under the command of Pnytagoras of Salamis. It arrived, and at once joined the ranks of their enemies. Thus, instead of giving battle with its help, as they had intended, on the open seas, they found themselves shut into their own harbours by greatly superior forces. Not only that, but the Cypriots led the van of Alexander's fierce attack on the famous merchant city; and it was, in a great measure, owing to their zeal in his service that he was enabled to conquer it.

Alexander was not ungrateful. He rewarded the islanders by allowing them to manage their own affairs, and by advancing many of their chiefs to high positions in court and camp. To Pnytagoras he gave the sovereignty of the island, on condition of paying tribute to him instead of to Darius, and allowed him to add the domain of Citium to that of Salamis. Historians are puzzled about this statement; for it seems that there was a King of Citium, named Pasicyprus, who was so devoted to Alexander, as to present him with the famous sword which he used in all his subsequent battles.

Alexander visited Tyre a year after its fall. He had changed the population of the city by slaying many of the original inhabitants and selling many more into slavery; but he had endeavoured to maintain its prosperity and continue its trade by bringing in a colony of Phœnicians and Cypriots. Great were the festivities with which he celebrated his triumph. The most renowed actors of Greece were in attendance. There were sacrifices to the gods, chariot races, and other games of the Stadium, and the Athenian custom of appointing distinguished men as choregi was followed. Foremost amongst these were the kings of Salamis and Soli. The two strove to outbid each other in the splendour of their representations. Thessalos, Alexander's favourite actor, was employed by the king of Salamis, and when the palm of victory was accorded to his rival, Athenodorus, the great conqueror is reported to have said that he would rather have lost half his kingdom than have seen Thessalos vanquished.*

The Cypriots took part in all Alexander's subsequent campaigns, and at his death their island was considered part of the Macedonian empire. It was a coveted prize, for its possession meant the supremacy of the seas. We accordingly find Antigonus, the ambitious satrap of Phrygia, and Ptolemy of Egypt, contending fiercely for it, the kings of Citium, Amathus, Lapithos, and Kyrenia favouring the former, those of Salamis and Soli the latter. Ptolemy obtained possession of the whole island, and Antigonus made several unsuccessful attempts to drive him out of it. It happened during one of these campaigns that the dynasty of Teucer in Salamis came to a tragic end. Nikokreon, who occupied the throne of that still flourishing city, was for a long time the most trusted lieutenant of Ptolemy. Being a man of unstable character, utterly without principle, he accepted bribes from Antigonus, and agreed to further that monarch's plans. Ptolemy, hearing of this, sent two of his friends with a commission to depose the king. They sailed to the island, and having obtained troops from their sovereign's brother, Menelaos, they beseiged the palace at Salamis, and announced to Nikokreon that his treachery was discovered, and

* Plutarch, Alex. 29.

that Ptolemy commanded him to make away with
himself. Nikokreon found that his defence was not
listened to, so he and all his brothers put an end to
their own lives by hanging. His wife, Axiothea,
hearing of it, rushed to the apartment of her
daughter and stabbed her with a dagger; then calling together her newly-widowed sisters-in-law, she
said to them, 'Life is no longer worth having. The
bloodthirsty cruelty of the Egyptians will pursue us
all to death, let us then seek it of our own accord.'
They closed the doors of the women's rooms and
hastened to the roof, whence they could see an excited crowd gathered below; then in sight of all the
people they strangled their babes, and set fire to
the rafters. As the flames rose, some threw themselves upon them, and others slew themselves with
daggers. Axiothea gave herself a fatal wound and
then rushed into the fire. Ptolemy, having secured
possession of the island, proceeded forthwith to
depose all its petty kings, who henceforth are never
mentioned in history.

Antigonus, however, made another desperate
attempt to wrest it from him. He wrote to his son
Demetrius, who was then in Greece, telling him
that the fate of the empire would be decided in
Cyprus. Demetrius accordingly sailed thither with
a large fleet and an army, gave battle to Menelaos
outside the walls of Salamis, and inflicted on him a
severe defeat. Menelaos entrenched himself strongly
within the city, protected the harbour with plenty
of ships, and despatched messengers to Egypt for
help.

On this occasion Demetrius displayed for the first

time that extraordinary mechanical and inventive genius which won for him the title of Poliorcetes, or besieger of cities. He brought artificers in wood and in metal from Asia, he caused the most enormous machines, catapults, and battering rams to be constructed. Most wonderful of these was what appears to have been a kind of movable tower, called a helepolis, seventy-five feet broad on all sides, and one hundred and fifty feet high, divided into nine stories, and mounted on a carriage with four massive wheels, or rollers, each fourteen feet in diameter. From each story stones, catapults, and arrows were hurled at the enemy by a garrison of two hundred men. The walls of Salamis were well sprinkled with Egyptian blood. Fiercer and fiercer grew the combat, enormous breaches were made, and Menelaos saw no hope of deliverance. Then a happy idea struck him. In the darkness of the night he gathered a quantity of dry wood, hurled it at the tower and the battering rams, and flung countless torches after it. The huge constructions were all ablaze. The garrison of the tower were burnt alive.

But Demetrius would not yield. He pressed on the siege with greater vigour, till news reached him that Ptolemy himself had arrived in the harbour of Paphos with one hundred and forty sail, and was marching with ten thousand fresh troops to attack him in the rear. To the message that 'he had better take himself out of the way quickly, and not wait until he was discomfited,' he replied that 'he would allow the Egyptian king to withdraw this time, on the condition of at once removing his garrisons from Corinth and Sicyon.' Leaving a detachment of his army to continue the siege, he took the best part of his men and of his munitions on board ship, with the intention of giving battle at sea.

The two fleets confronted each other. They were manned by the best sailors, and led by the most intrepid commanders of the age. Prayers were repeated aloud and responded to by the sailors on the deck of each ship. The sovereignty of Cyprus and of Syria, and possibly the sovereignty of the known world, were at stake. Demetrius approached to within twenty paces of the enemy, and then hung out a golden shield, as a signal for beginning the combat. Trumpets sounded, shouts rent the air, the hostile ships bore down on each other, seeking to crush their opponents with their beaked prows. Rowers worked for dear life, stones and arrows darkened the air, and the sea was reddened with human blood. Demetrius himself fought like a lion. He stood on the deck of his ship, his spear ready to hurl the clambering foes back into the waves, and his shield to receive the countless shafts which were aimed at his person. His ship led a successful attack against the right wing of the enemy, but Ptolemy did the same against his right wing. The Egyptian centre at length gave way, and Ptolemy retired with only eight ships to Citium.

Menelaos, in the meantime, was not idle. He sent sixty vessels out from the harbour of Salamis; these defeated ten of Demetrius' ships which happened to be lying near, and made haste to reach the scene of the conflict. They arrived there too late, and returned to their own harbour.

So ended the greatest naval battle of antiquity. Demetrius lost twenty ships, sank more than eighty of the enemy's, and captured eighty with their crews. He found himself also in possession of rich spoils, consisting of women, slaves, gold, munitions of war, and provisions. Ptolemy fled to his own country, and Menelaos surrendered with all his land and sea forces.

The young victor did not abuse his triumph. He gave honourable burial to the Egyptian dead, he sent many of his prisoners back to Ptolemy without ransom, and with handsome presents, amongst them Menelaos, the brother, and Leontiskos, the son, of that monarch; he took more than sixteen thousand of the Cypriots into his service, and sent his friends the Athenians twelve thousand complete suits of armour as a gift.

Aristodemos of Miletus carried the news of this victory to the aged Antigonus, who was then in Syria. On seeing him approaching, eager to learn tidings of his son, he stretched out his hand and shouted, 'Rejoice, King Antigonus, Ptolemy is defeated; Cyprus is ours. Sixteen thousand eight hundred men are prisoners.' The crowd took up the shout. 'Rejoice, oh, king!' they cried. 'Hail, king! Hail to King Demetrius!' The officers approached, placed the royal diadem on the old man's head, and carried him into his castle amidst the acclamations of the people. He at once wrote to his son a letter of thanks, tied it up with a diadem, and addressed it, 'To King Demetrius.'

Antigonus of course expected that Alexander's other generals, Ptolemy included, would acquiesce in his accession to the throne of the world. But it was not so. Ptolemy felt himself very secure in his rich kingdom of Egypt, for his people loved him. He responded to the news that Antigonus had been proclaimed king by declaring himself sovereign of his own country. His example was followed by Seleucus, Lysimachus, and Cassander in their respective provinces.

Antigonus, much irritated, resolved to compel them to submission, and sent orders to Demetrius to help him in a campaign against Egypt. Their united forces set sail, but returned without accomplishing anything. Fortune turned against them in the next few years, and after the disastrous battle of Ipsus, in which Antigonus was slain, we find Demetrius taking refuge with his aged mother, his wife Phila, and all his treasure in Salamis of Cyprus. This island now formed the pivot of his power, for its resources were quite sufficient to enable him to continue the contest. Ptolemy, though anxious to wrest it from him, was forced to win him from an alliance with Seleucus, with whom he was then at war, by guaranteeing him its possession, and by betrothing to him his daughter Ptolemais. Demetrius seems to have remained in Cyprus for three years. In A.D. 297 he sailed for Athens with a large fleet. It was scattered by a tempest, and he sent orders to Salamis for a new one. Before it arrived, he conquered the Peloponnesus, and then with his ships laid siege to Athens. Cyprus was in the meantime denuded of troops; so Ptolemy, who was for ever on the watch, swept down on it. The whole island submitted, except Salamis, which contained the mother and the children of his adversary, and to which he laid siege. One town in Asia fell away from Demetrius after another; he staked his whole fortunes on the issue of the contest in Europe, and he left Cyprus to its fate. His wife Phila defended Salamis bravely, but was forced to surrender. Ptolemy treated her and her children with all honour, and sent them to Demetrius loaded with presents.

Cyprus had belonged to Demetrius for ten years. For the next two hundred and thirty it was a province of Egypt, without the shadow of self-government. Henceforward the Cypriots have no history; they are mere servants, more or less willing, in the strong hands of those who hold their country. We have little to write about them; we can tell only what foreigners did with their island.

To the Ptolemies it was a chief source of power and wealth. By means of it they kept up their fleet, and filled their treasury with the produce of its mines. It was their starting-point when they attacked their enemies, and their place of refuge when they were defeated. Their lieutenants bore not only the titles of generals and admirals of the island, but also that of high priests. From this we conclude that the Cinyradæ had either been deposed, or relegated to a subordinate position.

The dynasty of the Ptolemies gradually degenerated, till it produced Physcon. This unnatural monster, who divorced his sister to marry his niece, her daughter, and presented her with the head of his own first-born, her son, left two sons by his last wife, Cleopatra. The elder, Ptolemy Soter II., or Lathyrus, had been banished by him to Cyprus; the younger, Alexander, was placed upon the throne by his mother's influence. The elder brother, however, succeeded in reversing this arrangement, becoming himself King of Egypt, and making Alexander governor of the island in his stead. Three years later the brothers again changed places. Both in turn bore the title of king of Cyprus. During the reign of Ptolemy Soter in the island, he engaged in a war with the Jews, who were then under the leadership of the Maccabees, and with a Cypriot army gained a decisive battle near Asophus on the Jordan. The cruelties which he perpetrated were worthy of his father. He caused numbers of Jewish women and children to be killed, cut in pieces, and boiled in cauldrons, with the view of inspiring terror in the hearts of the fugitives, and making them believe him to be a cannibal. To such work did the countrymen of Evagoras lend themselves.

King Alexander being poisoned, his mother was banished by his subjects, and Ptolemy Soter took possession of the blood-stained throne. Cyprus, after its short dream of a not very honourable independence, was thus re-united to Egypt, and was incorporated along with it into the Roman empire when the illegitimate scions of the Ptolemies called on the mistress of the world to settle their family disputes. The last Ptolemy who reigned in Cyprus had a tragic end. The Roman senate had passed a decree of confiscation against him, and sent Cato as their commissioner to carry it out. Cato did not like the task, for he had joined Cicero in protesting against the decree as unjust. But he had no hero to deal with. This Ptolemy, we are told by Valerius Maximus, did not so much possess his treasures as his treasures possessed him. He was in name the king of the island, but at heart he was the wretched slave of his money. So when he received the decree of the senate, and knew that his goods were confiscated, he resolved that he and they should perish together. He therefore took them all on board of a ship and put off from the shore, intending to sink with them to the depths of the sea. But when the decisive moment came and the waves were about to devour the objects of his love, his heart would not allow him to sacrifice them. He turned his ship towards the shore, saved his treasures, took poison, and died a laughing-stock to friends and enemies. So ended the reign of the Ptolemies in Cyprus.

Cato took peaceful possession of the island, and proceeded forthwith to sell the astonishing quantity of golden vessels, jewels, and ornaments, rich furniture, purple robes, etc., which he found in its palaces. The price of these was a most welcome contribution to the treasury of the republic. To ensure its safe arrival he packed it in little boxes, each of which contained two talents and five hundred drachmas, and was fastened by a rope to a large piece of cork. The transaction was a fine opportunity for the display of his scrupulous honesty, and also for the coldness of heart and the petty meanness by which he alienated his best friends. He boasted of having brought more treasure to Rome on this one occasion than Pompey had done in his many triumphs, after campaigns throughout the whole inhabited world. Clodius, who had urged on the decree of confiscation in order to gratify a private grudge against Ptolemy, had the effrontery to accuse Cato of having appropriated something to himself. When the accusation had been triumphantly refuted, he laid claim to the honour of calling the numerous slaves whom Cato had brought with him Clodians. Some of the Romans proposed that they should be called Porcians, after Cato. Neither name was pleasing to the virtuous Censor, and finally they were called Cypriots. It has been supposed that the Vicus Cyprius in Rome was their first place of residence.

Lentulus, the friend of Cicero, was the first Pro-consul of the island. The great orator interested himself so much in protecting its inhabitants from oppression and robbery, that they wished to erect temples and statues to him, an offer which he declined.

The Cypriots were not a little pleased at obtaining the rights of Roman citizens, rights from which they reaped very doubtful advantages. They had a short and illusory independence when their island and they themselves were presented by Julius Cæsar to Cleopatra. The island of Aphrodite was indeed a fitting gift from the Lord of War to one who seemed to be the incarnation of the Goddess of Love; and it is somewhat singular that, both actually and metaphorically, it probably nourished the asp which was to put an end to her miserable existence. She was confirmed in its sovereignty by

Mark Antony. The island reverted to the Romans at her death, and was divided by Augustus into four districts or sub-provinces, whose capital towns were Salamis, Neo-Paphos, Amathus, and Lapithus. Augustus bestowed great care on the island, and rebuilt the temple of Paphos, after it had been destroyed by an earthquake.

Then a new era dawned for Cyprus. She never regained a shadow of her former independence, nor a tithe of her ancient wealth, but she was quietly annexed to the kingdom which is not of this world, partly by the influence of her own sons, and partly by that of certain Jews who were scattered abroad upon the persecution that arose about Stephen, and travelled to her shores, preaching the Word of God at first to their countrymen only. History tells us very little about it, but we can well imagine the change which must have passed over the face of Cypriot society before the temples were converted into Christian churches; and the worship of Aphrodite was supplanted by that of the Virgin Mary. Many ideas and ceremonies of the old corrupt religion were, no doubt, incorporated into the structure of the new; as the rain-drops from heaven become intermixed with the impurities of earth before they are quaffed by the thirsty souls of men; still the advent of Christianity to an island where the faith of Aphrodite had for centuries reigned supreme, must at first have been an unmixed blessing. Its progress was greatly accelerated by the visit of Paul and Barnabas, and we may safely assert that, to whatever depths of ignorance the Cypriots may have since sunk, nothing has ever equalled the moral degradation in which they lived prior to the era of Augustus.

A modern Cypriot author, Phrancoudi, thinks that Christianity made very slow progress in the island, and that the converts gained by Paul and Barnabas were exceedingly few. In proof of this, he cites the existence of heathen temples where sacrifices were offered as late as the third century A.D.

Cyprus was divided into thirteen bishoprics, viz., Citium, Amathus, Kyrenia, Paphos, Arsinoë, Soli, Lapithus, Kerbeia, Kythereia, Tamassia, Trimethos, and Carpasia. It is now divided into three, which take their names from Citium, Kyrenia, and Paphos.

Salamis was destroyed in A.D. 116, when an insursection of the Jews against the government of Trajan was followed by frightful massacres. The number of those slain in Cyprus alone is estimated at twenty-four thousand. Jews were henceforth forbidden to reside in the island; and, curiously enough, they have respected this prohibition till the other day, when a colony of forty Israelite families, who had been expelled from Roumania, were deposited there, not to settle, but to starve.

Cyprus was visited, about the end of the third century, by a period of drought which lasted for seventeen years, and left the once blooming island almost a desert.

The Romans built a town in Cyprus, named Epidauros, and Augustus repaired the temple of Paphos. With these exceptions, they left no material trace of their rule, having used the island chiefly as a mine from which to replenish the exchequer of the state and the purses of private individuals. Herod the Great derived a great part of his riches from Cyprian copper.

When the Roman empire was divided, in A.D. 292, into four parts, under its two emperors, Diocletian and Maximian, Cyprus was assigned to the eastern division, under Diocletian. Soon after it was attached to the Byzantine empire, under Constantine the Great.

The island must at that time have been totally ruined by the exactions of its conquerors, and by seventeen years of continuous drought. We may conjecture, in the absence of authentic information, that the bulk of its inhabitants never embraced Christianity, but that the temples of the gods were forsaken, because the worshippers were forced to flee to more genial shores. It was recolonized about the year A.D. 325 by the Empress Helena, on her return journey from Jerusalem to Nicomedia. The new inhabitants were brought from several neighbouring countries, many of them being the children of those who had emigrated during the drought, and all being Christians. Helena built two churches, which still exist, one of them being near a stream named Tochne, and the other on the hill of Stavrobouno, near Larnaca. Just before this period rain fell in torrents, whilst trees, grass, and flowers all sprang up with exuberant life; so that doubtless Heaven was supposed to have wrested the island from the stubborn idolaters, and prepared it for the reception of true believers.

A governor of Cyprus, named Kalokairos, having made a futile attempt at insurrection, was burnt alive, and the island was placed under the jurisdiction of the Dukes of Antioch. Twelve of its bishops were present at the Council of Nice in A.D. 325. Salamis gave its name to the archbishop; and we find that a dispute took place betwixt him and the Patriarch of Antioch about the rights of the Cypriot clergy. The Synod of Ephesus, in A.D. 431, declared in favour of the latter, but the patriarch refused to conform to its decree. The matter was finally settled in A.D. 477, during the reign of the Emperor Zeno, when the bones of St. Barnabas were discovered near Salamis, and Zeno thereupon conferred upon the Archbishop of Cyprus the right of wearing a purple robe whilst officiating in the church, of carrying a sceptre, of signing his name in red ink, and of being head of an αὐτοκέφαλος, or completely independent church.

For four centuries Cyprus enjoyed comparative peace, being unaffected by the wars which devastated other parts of the empire. But in A.D. 634 and 656 the whirlwind of Arab fanaticism, guided by the caliphs Omar and Othmar, swept down upon its shores. Syria and Egypt had bent before the blast, and Cyprus could not hope to escape. Mabias, the Arab governor of Syria, sailed thither with a fleet and destroyed all that was left of Salamis. It is supposed that Charàm, foster-mother or foster-sister of the Prophet, died near Larnaca during this invasion. Fifty-five years later the Moslems got possession of the island, A.D. 689. The Emperor Justinian was then fighting with the Bulgarians, and, being unable to assist the Cypriots, he advised them to emigrate to Asia Minor; those who did so seem to have found no great advantage from their change of residence, for most of them returned in A.D. 749. We do not know how long the Arabs remained in Cyprus, but we find them making a third invasion in A.D. 806, under the Caliph Harûn-al-Râshid, destroying churches and towns, and carrying off many of the natives to sell them as slaves. The Emperor Nicephorus first acknowledged the suzerainty of the Caliph over the island, and agreed that it should pay him tribute. It was again won for the Byzantine empire during a successful campaign of Nicephorus II. in A.D. 966. But that empire was falling into decay, and Cyprus came in for its share of civil war. Its duke, Theophilus, in A.D. 1034, took advantage of the weakness of the central government under Constantine VIII., or rather under his daughters, Zoe and Theodora, to declare himself independent. Zoe having married when more than sixty years of age, her husband was proclaimed emperor under the name of Constantine IX., and brought this rebellious vassal to submission in A.D. 1042. Alexius Comnenus had to quell another revolt of the Cyprians shortly after his accession in A.D. 1081.

Towards the end of the twelfth century, Cyprus was laid waste by a Christian prince, Rinaldo of Castile, who was then governor of Antioch, and who had assisted Emmanuel Comnenus in quelling a revolt of the Armenians in Cilicia. The emperor failed to give him the promised reward, and he revenged himself by doing more mischief than the Arabs. Cyprus participated to the full in the throes of the dying empire; and was even for a few years independent of Byzantium, under a rebel cousin of the Emperor Emmanuel I., named Isaac Comnenus.

Then came the third crusade and with it Richard Cœur de Lion, whose betrothed bride, Berengaria of Navarre, was forced by stress of weather to approach Limasol. Isaac Comnenus made haste to take prisoners the crews of her vessels who had already landed, and sent her many gifts with an invitation to visit him, counting, of course, on a great ransom. The shrewd princess declined politely, and, having ascertained that he was preparing to capture the vessel which carried her, she escaped his vigilance, and soon rejoined her bridegroom's fleet.

Richard was not the man to leave such an insult unavenged. He at once landed some of his troops, and the cowardly Isaac sought refuge in the mountains. There was a fight somewhere near Colossi, which resulted in the total defeat of Comnenus, and the capture of rich booty by Richard, who celebrated his nuptials with Berengaria at Limasol on the 12th of May, A.D. 1191; the Archbishop of York placing the crown on her head as Queen of England and of Cyprus. Just as Richard was preparing to pursue Isaac in the interior of the island, Guy de Lusignan, titular king of Jerusalem, arrived at Limasol, and assisted in capturing the fugitive. Richard loaded Isaac with silver chains; laid waste the town of Leucosia, and divided the land into two portions, one of which he assigned to the natives, and the other to his English knights. Having left part of his army to support the latter, he hastened to join his fellow-crusaders who were besieging Ptolemais.

Richard shortly afterwards sold Cyprus to the Knights Templars for one hundred thousand gold ducats, or about £280,000, the relative value of which in our day is estimated by De La Mas Latrie at £320,000, just three times as much as the annual tribute which it now pays to the Sultan. These doughty champions of Christendom lost no time in taking possession of their new purchase, but they held it for little more than a year. The islanders, goaded to frenzy by their exactions, rose in revolt, and forced them to withdraw to Syria, where they persuaded Richard to give them back the first instalment of the price they had paid him. The only trace which they left behind them, besides the deep seated hatred of the natives, was the tower at Colossi, which they ceded to the Knights of Rhodes, and which was probably built by the forced labour of their unwilling subjects.

Cyprus did not remain long in the market, for Richard soon sold it to Guy de Lusignan, for the same price as to the knights, on condition of his renouncing all claim to the sovereignty of Jerusalem and of Tyre. Richard, however, retained for himself the title of King of Cyprus.

Guy seems to have been imbued with some sense of justice to his new subjects, for he gave them some measure of self-government in what related to the internal affairs of the island. He, however, distributed much of the land amongst the crusading adventurers who flocked towards the East, on condition of their becoming liable to military service under himself.

The Cypriots were much irritated by the erection

of Latin churches, and by seeing the Latin clergy take precedence over the Greek,* also by the return of the hated Knights Templars, at the invitation of their new ruler, to assist in garrisoning the fortresses.

Guy was succeeded by his brother Almeric, who obtained from the Emperor of Germany the title of King of Cyprus, and was solemnly crowned in the cathedral of Leucosia. About the beginning of the twelfth century, during the fourth crusade, the thirteen bishoprics of Cyprus were abolished, and four new ones formed, two of which were Latin and two Greek, under a Latin Archbishop of Leucosia.

The dynasty of Lusignan reigned in Cyprus for three hundred years. Its history presents little that is interesting to us, the chief events of the period being the unsuccessful attempt of the Emperor Frederick Barbarossa to obtain possession of the island during the sixth crusade, and the coronation of Hugh III. as King of Jerusalem in A.D. 1269. This Hugh III. was the most distinguished of the Lusignans; he founded the abbey of Bellapais, and was an enlightened patron of letters. But the history of Cyprus can scarcely now be called the history of the Cypriots. The gentry of the island were now exclusively foreigners; society was divided into four castes, the lowest of which was that of the agricultural serfs, who had to give compulsory service to the government two days in the week, and were bought and sold as slaves.

Ammochostos, now called Famagousta, had become the third commercial city of the East after

* This arrangement lasted until the advent of the Turks.

Constantinople and Alexandria. Her merchant princes vied with those of Venice and Genoa. One of these, about the year A.D. 1341, gave his daughter, on her marriage, jewels for her head-dress which exceeded in value all those belonging to the Queen of France. One grocer's shop in Famagousta contained more than five waggon-loads of aloes. The German traveller who reported these things feared to speak of the precious stones, the gold embroidery, and the other articles of luxury which he saw, for fear lest his Saxon fellow-countrymen would not believe him. The Cypriots, he said, spend their wealth in horse-racing, and in all kinds of pleasure. The extravagance which follows upon wealth brought many misfortunes in its train, and prepared the way for the civil and family wars, the rivalries of rulers, and the assassinations which distinguished the last days of the Lusignans.

To the carcase of a weak or badly-governed nation come the eagles of foreign greed. In A.D. 1362 and A.D. 1365, we find the Turks making secret incursions into Cyprus, stealing the harvests and venturing up to the gates of the towns. The Genoese, who were in want of a harbour for their fleets and their commerce, were on the watch for a cause of offence. Their consul quarrelled with his Venetian colleagues at Leucosia for the right of precedence at the coronation of Peter II., and, notwithstanding the intervention of Pope Gregory XII., the two states had recourse to arms. Thus a hostile Genoese fleet appeared before Limasol in A.D. 1373, and landed troops which ravaged the country, capturing Leucosia, and afterwards Famagousta, after a some-

x

what longer siege. Peter himself was made prisoner, and had to submit to the indignity of being slapped in the face by the Genoese general. A shameful peace was concluded, by which the revenues of the island were hypothecated in order to pay the war expenses of the enemy, and Famagousta was ceded to the Genoese.

Limasol was now the chief port which remained to the Lusignans, and it was plundered by the Egyptians in A.D. 1425. Leucosia too was captured by them, and the whole island devastated. King Janus, who tried to make a stand against them on the heights of Troados, was himself carried prisoner to Cairo, where he remained for five years, being only liberated on condition of paying a yearly tribute of five thousand gold ducats. As some of the public revenues had already been hypothecated to pay the debt to the Genoese, this tribute proved an intolerable burden not only to his subjects, but even to the Venetians, who were heirs-presumptive to the decaying dynasty.

The climax of confusion was attained after the death of John II. in A.D. 1458. This king left a legitimate daughter, Charlotte, and an illegitimate son, Jacques. The former having ascended the throne, the latter fled to Cairo, and represented to the suzerain of Cyprus, the Sultan, that he had been wrongfully dispossessed. The Sultan, pleased with this act of submission, and hoodwinked by the crafty pretender, sent an expedition to Cyprus.

The unfortunate island was now ravaged by Saracen hordes in the name of their would-be king, and by the Genoese for their own profit. Charlotte and her somewhat irresolute husband, after defending themselves for a short time in Kyrenia, took refuge in Italy. Jacques managed to wrest Famagousta from the Genoese by the help of a Venetian fleet, after they had held it for ninety years. But his allies acted a part dear to unscrupulous arbiters from the days of Æsop to our own. They were too shrewd not to see that the power of the Lusignans, wielded alternately by women, by bastards, and by babes, was fast waning, and they laid their plans accordingly. Jacques was married by proxy to Catherine Cornaro, the daughter of a rich Venetian senator, in A.D. 1469. Catherine was declared the adopted daughter of the republic. She went to Cyprus four years after her marriage. Jacques died a few years after her arrival; his posthumous son lived for only two years, the Venetians gradually got possession of all the fortresses, Catherine had to seek their aid in quelling the disturbances which the presence of their troops occasioned, and she herself, after being made queen, was persuaded to abdicate in their favour in A.D. 1488.

Cyprus now for the second time fulfilled the purpose for which nature seems to have intended it, viz., to be the station of a commercial and enterprising maritime state. There is a curious similarity of sound in the name of the two countries which have thus held it: Phœnicia and Venetia, but it has apparently no ethnological nor philological foundation.

The ceremonies which took place at Famagousta, Leucosia, Limasol, and Paphos in February, 1489, when Catherine transferred the insignia of power to the Venetian admiral, amidst the good-will of both rulers and ruled, found a curious parallel in 1878, when the out-going Turkish governor hoisted the British flag with his own hands. Both transactions were confirmed by a firman from the Sultan, who in 1489 resided at Cairo.

The revenues of Cyprus amounted at this period to five hundred thousand silver ducats, not including the tax on salt. But as they were converted into the produce of the country, and this was transported to Venice for sale, the real amount was two hundred and eighty thousand gold florins.

The feudal system was abolished by the redemption of all the crown lands and estates belonging to Frenchmen by the Venetian government.

The new system was certainly no improvement on the old, as far as the Cypriots were concerned, Venetian laws were strict, Venetian punishments cruel, nor was the trade of spy unknown to the countrymen of Iago. The next eighty years were years of commercial prosperity, for the almost exclusive benefit of foreigners. A terrible earthquake occurred in 1492, a fearful drought in 1547, and a bad harvest was followed by starvation and riots in 1565. Otherwise Cyprus had the good or the bad fortune of a people about whom history need say nothing. A dependency of Venice, so admirably suited to be a lounge for the wealthy curled darlings of the Rialto, could have been under no very exalted moral influences. The excellence of her own wine was the immediate cause of her subjugation by the Turks. The Sultan Selim II., having tasted it, resolved to become master of the vineyards which produced it, and sent an ambassador to Venice to demand simply and solemnly the evacuation of the island.*

This being refused, war was declared, and in July, 1570, an Ottoman fleet appeared before Limasol, disembarking troops, who took possession of the town, and wasted the country almost unopposed. The Venetians thought only of protecting themselves, caring nothing for the fate of the natives. They reserved their strength for the defence of Leucosia and Famagousta, and actually massacred many of the men of Limasol, carrying the women and children away to the mountains. Leucosia was taken by storm after a siege of forty days, during which its brave garrison suffered all extremities of hunger, cold, and sickness. The commander, Dandolo, was beheaded and chopped to pieces, and all the outrages which Moslems delight to inflict on Christians were perpetrated on the unhappy populace, nearly fifteen thousand of whom were slain in one day. We have already described the bravery of Maria Suncletikê in blowing up and burning the ships which were carrying herself and a thousand other women to Constantinople.

The period of Venetian rule closed with the surrender of Famagousta, whose inhabitants, after a ten months' resistance, suffered a fate similar to that of the Leucosians in August, 1571. The shameful treachery of Mustapha, and the sufferings of Bragadino have been related by us in a former chapter.

The rule of the Turks in Cyprus was such that its

---

* Selim died in 1574. Having drunk freely of Cyprian wine before entering his bath, his foot slipped, he fell, and his skull was fractured.

population decreased until, in the middle of last century, it numbered only forty thousand. There were three formidable insurrections, those of 1764, 1765, and 1833, the two last being suppressed with great brutality. Least of all can the Cypriots forget the execution of their beloved archbishop, George Dragoman, at Constantinople, in 1812. The British and Russian ambassadors, who had interceded for him, found only his headless body when they hastened to the Grand Vizier's palace with the Sultan's pardon. Nor can they forget the still more terrible tragedy of July, 1821, when the Archbishop Cyprian, with six bishops and most of the leading orthodox Christians in the island, were tortured and executed amidst the savage exultation of the Turks. We do not dispute the right of a government to punish rebels, but the peculiarity of the Ottoman one is that it takes no pains to distinguish betwixt the innocent and the guilty. The history of its dominion in Cyprus shows many an equally dark page, which we have no wish to turn over.

It is now a thing of the past. A new chapter has to be written,—what materials shall we supply for it? We have begun with a sincere desire to do the Cypriots good. They have a sure place in the heart of Great Britain. But to err is human, and we must not flatter ourselves into the belief that we can make no mistake. Such an one was that described by Mrs. Scott Stevenson on page 198 of her narrative, when three hundred criminals were made to march from Leucosia to Kyrenia, to be handed over to the Turks. The distance was not great, only sixteen miles, but it was a sultry day in

August, and the wretched creatures had almost lost the power of using their limbs, having been confined within four walls, some of them for more than twenty years. So intense was the heat that some of the Ghoorkas who formed the escort, unable to walk further, made the prisoners carry them, and a detachment of the Black Watch had to be sent up the pass from Kyrenia to bring them down. It was not a case of heartless cruelty, but of red tape and thoughtlessness on the part of some official. Yet in what country, save in our own and in America, could an officer allow his wife to write about such a thing without seriously injuring his own prospects? or making himself liable to what the Germans call *Festungstrafe*, *i.e.*, imprisonment. The fact of the incident being publicly reported is as great a credit to our free institutions as the incident itself is a reproach to the man who caused it.

Cyprus, if wisely treated, will form one of the piers of that bridge which connects the severed parts of our great empire. The Turkish portion of her people will enjoy more rights under our rule than under that of their pashas, and will perhaps teach their co-religionists to admire Christian institutions. The Cypriot Greeks will find that, as British subjects, they can do infinitely more for their own race than they could do by giving their allegiance to Athens. It is good for nations to be autonomous and independent, but it is good too, in the interests of the world at large, that some boughs of a great ethnic tree should be grafted on another stock, and partake of its root and fatness. Thus free peoples may learn to understand one another better; and no Greek can say that this is not necessary as between his country and ours. Our dislike to the Russian advance has, in this instance, made us do less than justice to an enthusiastic and progressive, if somewhat vain, people; and to forget that, until we are prepared for the restoration of the Jews, they are the only Eastern race which is in the least capable of assisting us to check that advance. Our sympathy for the Bulgarians must not blind us to the fact that their country is not fitted by Nature to be the cradle of freedom. It is the ancient Thrace, its coast-line is indented by no gulfs; its people have the stolidity and timidity of a purely agricultural race. The Armenians are not without enterprise, but the nation would be most difficult to reconstitute. Greece, if enlarged by the islands, and by that part of Asia Minor which has a Hellenic population, would be a better ally to us than Turkey. It would be wiser by far were we to hold Cyprus as the pivot on which our friendship to her should rest, than as a pledge of our protection to a barbarous and slippery government like that of the Sultan.

CHAPTER XVIII.

CONCLUSION.

Capabilities of the Island—Products—Caroub-tree—The Olive—Wheat —Cotton—Wine—Grapes—Fruits—Copper—Henna—Salt—Products of Cyprus and Malta Compared—Character of Turks and Greeks—Desire of Greeks for Cyprus—Advantages of Speaking Greek—Greek Aspirations for Political Unity.

THE preceding pages will have been written in vain, if the reader has not gathered from them some clear idea as to what are the capabilities of the lovely island round which we travelled, and of what are likely to be the relations betwixt its native population and ourselves.

The first is easily learnt from guide-books and from official reports; but he who would do justice to the second must have enjoyed some opportunities for observing not only the temper of the Cypriots themselves, but that of the several nationalities to which they are closely related.

First, as to the capabilities of the island. Ancient writers are sometimes at a loss for words in which to praise its exhaustless fertility,* a fertility which won for it the name of Macharia, the Blessed Island. The soil of Cyprus, with the exception of a few

* Opimam Cyprum. *Æneid*, i, 621.
βαθύπλουτον χθόνα καὶ τῆς 'Αφροδίτης πολύπυρον αἶαν
ÆSCHYLUS. *Suppl*, 555.

sandy tracts, never requires manure, an occasional rest and light ploughing, or rather scratching, suffices, if there be no locusts, to put into the farmer's hand five or six times the value of the seed which he has carelessly sown. In the plain of Messaria, after a rainy winter, he has even been known to reap twenty-fold.

The caroub-tree grows spontaneously. Nowhere else does it attain to a larger size, or furnish a more abundant harvest of those husks which served John the Baptist for meat, and are still an approved article of diet amongst the peasants of Russia, to which country they are largely exported. It is supposed that they are the chief ingredients in 'Thorley's Food for Cattle.' The olive, too, grows well, and might form a better source of profit were more care bestowed on the preparation of its oil. The exportation of this is, I understand, limited to the shores of neighbouring countries, its coarseness rendering it unacceptable in the markets of Europe. Cyprian wheat is of very fine quality; that of Paphos being considered the best in the East. It needs only that the peasants be freed from the grasp of the money-lender; that the taxes be equitably collected (as they doubtless are under British rule), and that the capitalist be assured of our permanent hold on the island, to make the plain of Messaria regain its ancient fame as one of the recognised granaries of the world.

The cotton of Cyprus is second only to that of Egypt, and the madder to that of Smyrna. The culture of the mulberry is widely diffused; the silk is spun on handlooms, and takes a peculiarly brilliant dye, which causes it to be used in France as the foundation for gold embroidery. That of the vine forms a sixth part of the whole productions of the island. Pliny says that the Cyprian vine is older than any other tree, that no wood lasts longer; and it attained such a size that the roof of the temple of Diana at Ephesus was approached by a ladder made out of a single Cyprian vine-stock. Aponius compares its grapes to those of Eshcol.

The Cypriot wine most celebrated in modern times is the Commandaria, which received its name from having been grown on the property of the Knights Templars—I suppose, because *commandatore* is the Italian word for knight. Its taste is luscious, something like that of Madeira, and indeed the vine of the Atlantic island is the offspring of that of the Mediterranean one, having been originally transplanted in the fifteenth century, and renewed from the parent stock, after the ravages of vine-disease in Madeira thirty years ago.

Efforts to introduce the Commandaria wine into France were made by Francis I., and were an entire failure, owing to its unsuitability to the soil and the climate. All Cypriot wines improve by keeping, even for an indefinite time, and such is the excellence of the old Commandaria that the enthusiastic Gaudry suggests the possibility of its having been the nectar of the Olympian gods.

The fruit of the palm-tree does not come to maturity in Cyprus. The orange, the lemon, the apricot, and the pomegranate were in old times supposed to have been planted by Aphrodite herself. The island, indeed, was meant to be one of Nature's gardens, and the ruthless foot of the Turk has not succeeded in robbing it of its heritage of verdure and of flowers.

But where are its forests? Where are the oaks and the pines which once enabled its kings to construct a whole fleet without any help from foreign countries? Where are the cedars which surpassed those of Lebanon? The benefits of English rule will soon be felt in other things, but centuries must elapse ere the *trabs Cypria* can wholly regain its ancient fame.

Whether Cyprus received its name from copper, or copper from Cyprus, κύπρος, or both together from the gopher or henna plant, will probably never be known. Copper was once so abundant that a mountain near Soli was composed entirely of it, and was of course quarried away. The mines were long ago exhausted, the scoriæ from them having probably been re-smelted.

Henna is now imported for the use of the Turkish women. One variety of this plant bears a bunch of berries which sometimes looks like grapes; it is the 'cluster of henna-flowers in the vineyards of Engedi,' referred to in the Song of Solomon, the Βότρυς τῆς Κύπρου of the Septuagint.*

The salt-producing lakes near Larnaca are a government monopoly.

The Cypriots are already receiving from us three substantial benefits. The first is that of good roads, which perhaps, with their present habits,

---

* King James's translators were evidently puzzled by this word. They called it camphire, or cypress.—See Authorised Version, *Song of Solomon*, i, 14.

they may be slow to appreciate; the second is elementary education, whose effects will not be at once felt; and the third is the priceless gift of public security. What the lack of this has been and how great the change may be estimated from the experiences of De Cesnola at Neo-Paphos in 1868, and at Kyrenia in 1876. At the one place his diggers had to run for their lives, at the other he and his fellow-countryman, General Crawford, had to be on the *qui vive* all night, a fight having taken place betwixt their men and the inhabitants. The Mussulmans of both places then enjoyed the worst of reputations, yet in 1886 we slept beneath the roof of one without hearing a whisper of danger.

The historian Finlay speaks thus of the conquest of Cyprus by Richard I.:

'Richard remained in possession of the island for several months, and established a domination (that of the Lusignans and the Venetians), which lasted for centuries, and was transferred to various nations of aliens. These have treated the Greeks of Cyprus more as serfs than as subjects until the present hour. Since their conquest by the Turks, the people have been sinking from age to age into an inferior state of society, in consequence of the destruction of capital and of property. The island is now incapable of maintaining in wretchedness one-tenth of the population which it nourished in abundance in the time of Richard I.'

He says also that 'in 1877 Cyprus was the most wretched portion of the Greek nation.'

Few visitors to the Colonial and Indian Exhibition of 1886 can have failed to be struck by the great difference betwixt the products of Cyprus and those of Malta. These speak of wealth, those of penury; these minister to the needs of the luxurious, those certainly include some bright silks and some luscious wines, but the atmosphere around them reeks of homespun. All honour to the Cypriot peasant, with his bullock-cart and his threshing-board; we hope that he may retain his rustic virtues, and that when his island shall have been under British rule for eighty-six years, like Malta, he too may show us some carriages and some upholstery, with plenty of gold and silver jewellery and lace.

The two islands have much in common, yet the difference in material prosperity is very striking. Both were colonized by the Phœnicians, and both were held for about the same period of time by crusading knights. But the smaller island has never been under the Turks, and has enjoyed the advantage of British rule since 1800. The statistics of the two, given in the 'Almanach de Gotha' and 'Whittaker' for 1885, are very suggestive:

Size . . .	Cyprus: 145 miles by 50. Area, 3707 square miles.	
,,	Malta: 17 miles by 9. Area, 95 square miles.	
Population . .	Cyprus (19 to square kilomètre) .	186,084
,,	Malta (464 to square kilomètre) .	149,782
Revenue . . .	Cyprus	£172,072
,,	Malta	£206,000
Expenditure .	Cyprus (exclusive of tribute to Porte)	£112,085
,,	Malta	£206,000
Shipping, 1884.—	Cyprus—vessels entered . (tons)	187,989
,,	Malta	4,517,498

Cyprus was doubtless in ancient times a maritime

power of the first order. The Phœnicians had stations on its coasts, and, after the Hellenization of the island, the alliance of its petty kings was eagerly coveted by the Grecian states and by Persia. The successors of Alexander fought for its possession; and its fortunes were for centuries more or less entangled with those of Egypt. Nature, we may say, has willed that it should be so. The importance of Cyprus to us consists, not in its agricultural nor its mineral resources, but in the position which it occupies in the centre of the Levant. This, and this alone, Lord Beaconsfield had in view when he negotiated its cession.

He meant Cyprus to be a place of arms. Not a mere sanatorium for our troops, though for that purpose it is unequalled. Does the island offer any facilities for the fulfilment of his designs?

We must not be misled by its ancient maritime fame. The sea seems to have retired somewhat from its southern shore, and the inclosed harbour of Citium is now a marsh. And the introduction of steam has enlarged to an astounding degree the scope of our modern requirements.

Larnaca and Limasol, though most useful for mercantile purposes, will never shelter fleets. Both have excellent anchor ground, and vessels furnished with good cables may there safely ride out the worst of storms. But no one would call them natural harbours, they are simply open roadsteads. Kyrenia, the only port on the north coast, will soon rejoice in a new harbour, but the works there will be expensive. The large gulf of Pendaïa, or Morphou, on the west coast, is open to all winds. Famagousta is the only place which at all corresponds with Lord Beaconsfield's intentions. We need hardly inform our readers that these intentions have not yet been carried out; and probably no government will undertake the great expense of restoring the ancient harbours and draining the marshes of the eastern coast until public opinion has definitely settled the question, 'What are we to do with Cyprus?'

No one dreams that it will ever be given back to Turkey. The hands on the clock of Time cannot thus be put back, the islanders, however ungrateful they may eventually prove, can never be consigned to that oppressive rule. To do so would be to tarnish the scutcheon of British honour; it would be a libel on Christianity itself. So much is certain. If we do not keep it ourselves, we must resign it to some other western Power, or to Greece.

We cannot of course do the former; for we can permit no possible rival to plant herself in the path of our march to and from Cathay. Let us examine what chance there is of the latter.

The Greeks have no right to Cyprus, say some. We agree with their verdict, but not at all with their reasons. Greece never had Cyprus, that is true, but it is stretching a point beyond the bounds of truth to say that her population is not in the main Hellenic. For what constitutes nationality? Blood and language, which are strongest in their ties if woven closer by a common religion.

The population of Cyprus is of course mixed. One fourth is avowedly Turkish, and the remainder must undoubtedly have received many contributions from Semitic and European sources. But the main stream of Hellenism has absorbed these; the spoken dialect alone being sufficient to prove that the island has been substantially Greek since the time when history began to be written. The dialect is of course not pure. No academy nor common school has kept it free from corrupting elements. The influence of Venetian and of Turk has been employed to overpower it, but for that very reason its evidence in favour of the nationality of the peasants who speak it is the more unimpeachable and convincing.

Mrs. Scott Stevenson tells us that English officials greatly prefer the Turk to the Greek, especially as a member of the zaptich force; the Turk, she says, is more truthful, sober, honest, brave, simple, and devout, and, above all, more cleanly in his habits and customs.

There must be some truth in this, for all residents in the East agree in praising the Turk for these very qualities, although, they generally add, more stupid. One cannot help respecting a man who, in obedience to the precepts of his religion, practises self-denial in abstaining from wine whilst he sees others enjoying it. At the same time one must never forget that he is virtuous only whilst he remains poor. Let him rise in the world, and take to himself several wives, then the harem system will come into play, and his children will be educated to every kind of self-indulgence, drunkenness perhaps not excepted. Many of the precepts of the Kurân are excellent; but we have to bring against that book the charge not only of degrading women, but of guiding the human mind into a groove out of which it cannot raise itself, and of thus limiting human progress.

The Greek peasant is quite as devout as the Turk, according to his lights, and we maintain that he, being a Christian, is capable of more, because the Book he believes in speaks of a spiritual heaven, not of a paradise of running streams, shady groves, embroidered couches, and houris. Educate him, and he will throw away his idols. We write about what we know; for we are often deeply touched by the moral and religious exhortations which we meet with in Greek periodicals. If Englishmen will not give themselves the trouble to understand the Greeks, they will, of course, prefer the dog-like docility of the Turks. We submit that Captain Scott Stevenson did not act with an Englishman's wonted impartiality when he dismissed his Greek zaptiehs because they objected to wear the turban, lest they should be mistaken for adherents of a faith which their fathers had refused to embrace at the peril of their lives. Did he reflect on what would have been the consequences had he asked the Turkish zaptiehs to wear a cross?

We can believe that the Moslems adopt habits of cleanliness more readily than the Greeks. But those who prefer the former on that account are somewhat inconsistent, if they consider it a mark of degeneracy in the latter. If we may believe the ancient poets, travellers in Greece have at all times been wont to carry about their own beds, and have been obliged to ask in what lodging there were fewest bugs κόρεις ὀλίγιστοι. We suspect that few modern admirers of Socrates would have liked to wear his old cloak, except metaphorically. It was scarcely a mark of his wisdom that he did not buy a new one. Semitic races have always been in advance of the Greeks in this respect, for the Hebrew Pharisees at least made clean the outside of the cup and the platter, and though the Turks are not Semites, they cannot fail to be influenced in favour of cleanliness by the teachings of the Arabian prophet.

We could not help observing that the Cypriot peasants are far less lively than those of Continental Greece. This is not owing altogether to their lack of education, but it is because all spirit has been effectually crushed out of them. The men are less active, and of a slighter build; the women less comely, though they are said to excel in all domestic virtues, and to offer a complete contrast, in point of morals, to their ancestors, the worshippers of Astarte-Aphrodite.

Do the majority of the islanders wish to be annexed to Greece? We cannot answer this question, but we think it probable that they are not yet sufficiently well educated to formulate their wishes. The ancient Cypriot earned through his ignorance the epithet of βοῦς Κύπριος, being equivalent to ὗς Βοιωτία;* and the natives of Lapithus were so superlatively stupid that λαπάθιον meant a fool. The modern Cypriot is not so stupid as

* Bœotian pig. It is worth noticing that in modern times 'Bulgarkephalê' has a similar signification.

he is taken to be by the people of Beyrout, who, when anyone tries to over-reach or to bamboozle them, are wont to ask,

'Do you take me for a Cypriot?'

He has, above all, an eye to the main chance. He is industrious and thrifty, and he will be able to judge as to whose rule will best further his worldly interests. But let us not deceive ourselves. This state of mind will last so long as he cannot read the newspapers. What then?

Some day he will read Greek ones. Whether or not he wishes for incorporation in the kingdom of King George, there is no question as to whether King George's subjects want him. Athenian newspapers, whenever they deign to specify what they mean by the expression: ἡ δούλη Ἑλλάς, 'enslaved Greece,' enumerate Epirus, Macedonia, the islands, and Cyprus. So fervent are their aspirations for its acquisition, that I have heard an Evangelical missionary in Constantinople, though himself an Englishman, when leading the devotions of a Greek congregation, pray for the enfranchisement of this part of his own sovereign's dominions.

I have in my hands a book lately published by a Cypriot, entitled: 'A Manual of the Topography and General History of Cyprus.'* Perhaps my readers would like to hear what he says on this subject:

'Cyprus,' these are his words, 'suffered much, and was very wretched during this last historical period (*i.e.*, under Turkish rule). The only thing that

---

* Ἐγχειρίδιον χωρογραφίας καὶ γενικῆς ἱστορίας τῆς Κύπρου ὑπὸ Εὐρυβιάδου Ν. Φραγκούδη ’Εν ’Αλεξανδρείᾳ. 1886.

has remained unimpaired and unsettled by these terrible afflictions is her national and religious consciousness. Neither under the Franks nor under the Turks was the Cypriot shaken in the principles he held about his faith and his fatherland. The imperfect schools of that epoch recalled to him memories of the great Past; and the poor churches in which he found a momentary consolation introduced him to a horizon of the Christian and the avenging future. He preserved his language uncorrupted; he remained in the faith of his forefathers; he was hung; he was cut to pieces; he was impaled, but he did not abjure it; he was broken, but he was not bent, and, whilst being slaughtered, he did not curse his tormentors. Marcello Cerrutti, a distinguished Italian, formerly an ambassador, now a senator, who had studied the Cypriots closely, characterized them truly when he said to me a few years ago in Rome: " Cyprus is the noblest aspect of Hellenism." (" Cipro è la più nobile fisionomia del grecismo.")

'The tendency of Cyprus towards decline and desolation dates chiefly from the end of the twelfth century, after the Christian era. Then conquerors, who were strangers in race, in religion, and in language, began succeeding each other until the present day. What greater proof can we have that a foreign domination is a veritable gangrene in every respect to peoples, and that, where there exists no connecting link in the identity of interests and of aims, there is no effective mutual guarantee betwixt rulers and ruled? There is no legal, political contract which is just to both; everything is phenomenal; and whatever is really profitable, permanently progressive, and thoroughly salutary, is never begun sincerely, or, if it is begun, it does not take root. Rather, on the contrary, all measures taken by the rulers, either intentionally or through ignorance, contain the germs of some kind of dissolution, material or otherwise. In one word, foreign dominations, even the most tolerable and tolerant of them, the most gentle and the most scrupulous in the fulfilment of their promises, are always step-mothers, never mothers. Let us hope that the period of adopted mothers, at least so far as concerns Cyprus, is now fulfilled. The true nurse, the genuine mother, who has long been thrust aside, who has been considered dead, but whose death was only apparent, has grown strong and has risen from her bed, and gathers round her, one by one, her wandering offspring. First there came to her the venerable group of the Ionian islands, and then followed other renowned seats of primordial Hellenism. Cyprus to-day, to-morrow, at some hour by no means distant, will also come skipping and leaping, like a fawn, to the national flock, in order that she may be cleansed from the stain of servitude, and then clothed in her festive raiment, with those of her own blood who have been already redeemed, and those who shall be redeemed in the future, she will enter on the laborious struggle for civilization; the struggle bequeathed to her by her forefathers, those incomparable pioneers of humanity under its manifold phases.'

The same writer says, in another place:

'Massimo D'Azeglio, the distinguished Italian

politician, said, a few years before the war of 1859 against Austria, when he was a prey to incurable and sinister apprehensions :

'"Italian unity is the first of my wishes, and the best of my hopes." We, who are the interpreters of our own sentiments no less than of those of our compatriots, have not the least hesitation in expressing this optimist opinion : "The annexation of Cyprus to Greece constitutes the first wish of the Cypriots and the first of their hopes."'

On another page he tells us of the delightful excitement which was produced in the island by the news of the cession, how the price of horses and of land rose threefold, and how unaffected joy took possession of every heart, 'because that day marked the setting of a three-centuries' tyranny, and the rise of a new life ; the bait of the unknown had ensnared everyone ; they did not shut their eyes to the fact that it was a simple shifting of their yoke, but they, nevertheless, made a distinction between a Christian xenocracy and an anti-Christian one. In short, notwithstanding some stings of national pride, public opinion was in a state of high expectation. But, ere many days had elapsed, a distinguished Maltese merchant, who had landed some goods beyond the space assigned for disembarkments, was condemned to be beaten with forty strokes. Thus was given, at the very first blush, the measure of the liberties brought by the new foreign government, and the circumstance awakened the most painful reflections. "How is this?" asked the Cypriots. Corporal punishment, the cherished system of the Ottoman despotism, the system which recalls to us the saddest days of slavery, the system of which such a harsh use and abuse was made in Cyprus until the year 1850, is it to be again disinterred and placed in the orders of the day by the sworn champions and standard-bearers of human civilization and political liberty?" So the error was but for a moment, and, ever since, the feeling of the place, unanimous and unshaken, has been more national than ever, and the mind of every Cypriot who is in the slightest degree freed from the feeling of servitude, turns eagerly, not towards deceitful appearances, but towards the far-shining and ever-brilliant light of a national guidance.'

Again, he says:

'The nominal and mouldering titles of the Caliph disturb very little the golden dreams in which the joyful Cypriots indulge. They, if they love the dominion of the English, a dominion which is defective in many things and sometimes devoid of love, do so in consequence of the idea which is firmly rooted in our consciousness, that it is necessarily transient, and will turn out to be the bridge designed by Destiny for our transfer to the beloved and classic land, which has fostered us, cradled us by never-to-be-forgotten lullabys, and held a torch to us when we wandered in darkness and in the shadow of death; to her from whose simple name there flowed strength in unceasing danger, consolation in times of calamity, promises about a common future, about a day of restoration, of which the dawn appears already on the horizon, cloudless and rosy, darting its first beams over the summit of the Cyprian Olympus. No, these are not winged words;

it is sufficient that we show clearly the undoubted right which we possess of protesting by every lawful method against those who consider us as merchandise or as a flock of sheep, always ready to be sold, without strength or will, forgetful of all the past and of the teachings of history, insensible to national disgrace, blind to the obvious and humiliating reality, to the signs of the times, to the manly attitude of other peoples, and culpably irreverent towards the holiest and noblest traditions.'

This, some of my readers will say, is simple rhodomontade. But, nevertheless, we shall be judicially blind if we do not take some account of the feeling it expresses. Sentiment governs the world more powerfully than some people suppose.

We need not fear that the Greeks will ever be able to wrest Cyprus from us. But they have before them the precedent of the Ionian islands, and they may succeed in making our rule unpopular, and in getting up an agitation which would be disagreeable to us and injurious to their own best interests. How are we to prevent this?

By ceasing to encourage education? Such a course would be most unworthy of us, and impossible in the light of nineteenth-century progress. By encouraging an immigration of Arabs? I blush to say that I have heard this seriously proposed; but, in justice to my fellow-countrymen, I must add that it was by a man who knew nothing whatever of the island. Only two methods commend themselves to me, and there is no reason why they should not go hand in hand. The first is, to encourage the settlement of English families, and the second, to place ourselves in sympathy with the islanders by endeavouring at least to understand Hellenic aspirations.

Sir Samuel Baker says that 'one of the most urgent necessities is the instruction of the people of Cyprus in English, because it is not to be expected that any close affinity can exist between the governing class and the governed in the darkness of two foreign tongues that require a third person for their enlightenment. The natives dread the interpreter; they know full well that one word misunderstood may alter the bearing of their case, and they believe that a little gold judicially applied may exert a peculiar grammatical influence upon the parts of speech of the dragoman which directly affects their interests. It cannot be expected that the English officials are to receive a miraculous gift of fiery tongues, and to address their temporary subjects in Turkish and in Greek; but it is highly important that without delay schools should be established throughout the island for the instruction of the young, who in two or three years will obtain a knowledge of English. Whenever the people shall understand our language, they will assimilate with our customs and ideas, and they will feel themselves a portion of our empire; but until then a void will exclude them from social intercourse with their English rulers, and they will naturally gravitate towards Greece through the simple medium of a mother tongue.'—pp. 409, 410.

Some of these words are golden, and we have Mrs. Scott Stevenson's evidence for the fact that the natives were in 1880 cruelly defrauded by a lying interpreter.

We would ask respectfully, Are a handful of English officials to do in a few years what the sociable Frenchman and the super-subtle Venetian, during a domination of three centuries, failed to accomplish? Are they to change the spoken tongue of a people? The English in Cyprus are the sons of gentlemen, whose ancestors have for many generations enjoyed the advantages of culture. Is it reasonable to suppose that they are inferior in intellectual power or in capacity for acquisition to the sons of men whose minds have for ages and ages been all but dormant? We may indeed wonder that the Cypriot is not quite brutalised, considering the kind of masters he has had. Is it quite impossible for Englishmen to speak Greek?

We fear the fault must be sought for in our public schools. Our conjecture may be rash, for we have had no experience of these, and are quite ignorant of the systems pursued there. But we judge by the results. Why are English boys, who can construe the prose of ancient authors and imitate their poetry, so totally at a loss when they need to employ a foreign tongue for the common necessities of life?

We have an old-fashioned belief that languages were meant, in the first place, to be spoken. Had writing been the chief consideration, they would assuredly have been called *calamus* and γραφίς, not *lingua* and γλῶσσα. The ear never forgets sounds or phrases with which it has become familiar, the eye often does. A girl may not open a French book for years after she has left school, but she will not forget it as her brother will Latin. And it seems to me that a thorough reform in our teaching is needed, especially in our teaching of Greek.

But how can this reform be brought about? How can Greek become to us what it is to our Cypriot fellow-subjects, a living language, whilst our university professors persist in their present pronunciation of it? That pronunciation was first introduced by Erasmus, but we cannot believe that it would have been adopted had not the true Greek sounds and the true Greek accent been forgotten, owing to the slightness of our intercourse with the natives. We can more readily conceive how this took place with Greek than with Latin, because, so long as the English Church remained in communion with that of Rome, Greek priests cannot have been welcome guests on our shores. Modern Greek may in a few instances, notably in those of η and of the aspirates, come short of what it was in ancient days, but we submit that no other pronunciation places the language in full harmony with those tongues which have been more or less developed from it, or explains so clearly the changes which human speech has undergone.

Take, as an instance, the diphthongs, and see what they become in Latin,—in Latin, I mean, which is pronounced as the Italians, and all nations of the world, except ourselves, believe that it should be pronounced. How naturally, then, do the sounds of the one tongue slip into those of the other! Οἶνος, once spelt Ϝοῖνος with the digamma, becomes vinum, λείβω and λοιβή pass into libo, whilst lito is apparently related to λειτουργία, and νείφω and νίφω

CONCLUSION. 333

to nivus. Νεῖλος becomes Nilus, and πειρατής, pirata.

But the case is stronger when we turn to the transliteration of proper names. Naturally, if a Roman author wished to make his countrymen understand how the Greeks pronounced these, he employed those letters which represented the same sounds in Latin. How comes it then that the Greek diphthong οι always becomes in Latin œ, and that αι becomes æ. Βοιωτία becomes Bœotia, Μαίανδρος Mæander, Μαιῶτις Mæotis. And as a further defence of itticism, we would mention two instances in which Homer writes δοίω, instead of δύο, viz., in *Iliad* iii., 236, and xxiv. 648. Ου, pronounced *oo* in modern Greek, becomes *u* in Latin. Thus Θουκυδίδης Thucydides.

Ευ was undoubtedly *ef*, if we may trust the ΒασιλεϜς of the inscriptions. But we do not intend to go deeply into this question. We only wish to indicate that those teachers who adhere to an erroneous pronunciation are doing much to unfit their pupils from becoming good linguists.

I am more and more convinced, for my own part, that no language helps its possessor in the acquirement of other tongues as Greek does. Those whose mother-tongue it is are more likely to be polyglots than are Englishmen or Frenchmen, and the light it casts on other European languages is simply wonderful. When pronounced properly, the βούλεσθε (voolesthe) of the Greek passes readily into the *voulez-vous* of the French, and so on in a thousand other instances. Its grammar is as methodical and offers as good a training to the mind as the Latin one, and its unrivalled flexibility gives to the mind (and perhaps to the organs of speech) a versatility which could not be acquired by years of poring over the written page; and which makes the acquisition of other tongues, even of Semitic ones, comparatively easy. It is commonly said that Greek has no affinity with Arabic. Nor has it, so far as mere words are concerned. To say that there is any resemblance in the two grammars would be to make the hair of a philologist stand on end. Yet, if we accustom ourselves to talk both languages, we will find subtle analogies between the two which point to a similarity in the modes of thought of the peoples who use them, and which greatly facilitate our speech in either.

The plan of learning a language by trying to speak it from the very beginning of our study, has such advantages that one wonders why any other is ever pursued. It obviously excludes cram, because the pupil's mind at once assimilates or digests its daily lesson. And, if we may judge from our own experience, a student will make more rapid progress in conversation if he will do his best to talk with one of his fellows who is on the same level as himself, and who also wishes to master the art of speaking, than with a native of the country whose patience is put to a severe trial, and who is probably more anxious to learn English than to impart a knowledge of his own tongue. When the student has already acquired some facility in the language, intercourse with natives will be found more advantageous than at the beginning.

It ought not to be difficult for Englishmen to speak Greek. Turkish and Arabic we may excuse them, but the tongue in which the New Testament was written, the tongue which lends of its treasures for the formation of all new scientific and technical words, and which enters so much into the structure of our own language, is surely attractive enough to make its cultivation a labour of love. But if we cram boys with it before they have entered on their teens, before they are capable of appreciating the beauties of English literature, and burden their memories with a host of other things at the same time, what wonder if it appear to most of them as a heap of dry bones?

Far better would it be if we could teach children first the rudiments of Latin, then some modern language, such as French or German, conversationally, and leave the study of Greek till an age when its value would be appreciated. One of the greatest charms of Homer is his *naïveté*, and can this quality be discerned by a boy who is as yet ignorant of the more laboured masterpieces of literature?

So much for the Greek language. I have said that we should seek also to understand our Cypriot fellow-subjects, by placing ourselves in sympathy with modern Greek aspirations. It has become too much the fashion with a certain section of our fellow-countrymen to sneer at these. True, we sometimes meet with boasting and bombast which are in ludicrous contradiction to the realities. True, the direction of affairs at Athens may again fall into the hands of an incompetent politician, who cares not how he wounds the just susceptibilities of the Great Powers, and relies too much on the fact that these Powers are the virtual protectors of his country. We cannot undertake to say that our government was wrong when it joined in the blockade of the Greek ports; although, possibly, it was simply playing the game of Austria. The time for war was then inopportune. But we do say that Englishmen ought to realize a little better the position in which the Greeks find themselves. The greater part of the nation is not yet free. The age of massacres and of fierce oppression may be past, but still the Christians of Turkey are condemned to pay heavy taxes, for which they get no corresponding benefit in the way of protection, or in the supply of many things which are now absolute necessities in civilized life. Foreigners may talk of Turkish enlightenment and of Turkish tolerance, when they have themselves got some valuable concession for making a railway; but the very fact of their having to place themselves under the protection of their own government proves that they cannot trust to Turkish justice.

How long is this state of things to last? How long are four millions of Turks to rule over thirty-two millions of other people? most of whom are their superiors in all those qualities which constitute man superior to the brutes. How long are they to clog the wheels of progress by their *vis inertiæ*?

And the rulers of Turkey are now hardly Turks. They are, with few exceptions, the sons of Greek and Armenian mothers; or, worse still, they are members of the subject races who have embraced Islam. They are mostly adventurers, who have attained to high position by the exercise of their wits. Turkish rule, in our eyes, is now a vast system of legalised iniquity. The way in which it degrades women is simply intolerable.

No one doubts that it would not last were it not for the greed of some European powers, and for the jealousy of others. In the natural course of things, it would long since have been swept away. Can we wonder at the Greeks being restless? Englishmen would be equally so, if placed in similar circumstances.

Let us consider the spectacle. We see the little Greek kingdom, not always conducting itself with discretion as regards foreign affairs, with a parliament which too often exhibits the vices inherent in ultra-democracy. But its internal affairs are well managed. Within its bounds there is perfect security for life and property. Schools, posts, telegraphs are everywhere under government management. Then let us turn to Turkey. Her people are heavily and unjustly taxed, yet they have no roads, no security, no native post-office. Stand on the outskirts of Constantinople, and, far as the eye can reach, you will not see an inhabited house, for none outside the city would be safe from robbers. The shopkeepers of Pera, despairing of protection from the police, have engaged a number of 'hammals,' or porters, to walk about the streets all night, and show that they are awake and watchful by rapping on the pavement. These men have been known to club together and rob their employers. If you wish to ride for a few miles inland, on either side of the Bosphorus, no consul will guarantee your safety without a doubtfully trustworthy escort

And you can hardly do so in spring-time without sinking knee-deep in mud. The civil servants of the Ottoman empire are sometimes prevented from going to their offices, because they cannot pay the cost of transit. The soldiers are supposed, in time of war, to live by rapine. I wish those who extol the Turk at the expense of the Greek, would ask themselves a few questions. Why does not a foreigner resident in Athens ask the government of his own country to protect him by capitulations? Why does he try to create no consular court? and why, in every part of Greece is he contented to receive his letters through a native post-office? Surely the Greeks must be a little more trustworthy as a nation than the much-lauded Turks.

A case in point occurs to us. We happened, on our homeward voyage, to meet with a young Jewish merchant from Salonica.

'What is your nationality?' we asked him.

'I am a Turk, but my eldest brother is an Englishman, and my youngest an Italian.'

'How is that? Are they your half-brothers?'

'No; it is for our business. If we have a lawsuit, the native courts favour our firm for my sake. If the law-suit is with an Italian, my youngest brother seeks the help of the Italian consul, and if it is with an Englishman my eldest brother represents us.'

'Are you contented under Turkish rule?'

'The present system is favourable to us. We have got accustomed to it, and we wish for no change. If the Greeks come, we shall not like it, but we shall remain. If the Austrians come' (with a shrug of his shoulders), 'we must seek a home elsewhere; the world is wide enough. The Austrians are very harsh. Les Autrichiens sont durs, bien durs. I cannot see what advantage would accrue to Great Britain through Austria getting Salonica.'

Greeks and Moslems get on pleasantly enough when they live together in the same community. But in the cities the Greeks and the Jews must be like new wine seeking to burst through old bottles. Their intercourse with Europe makes them keenly alive to what civilization is, and they feel it hard to be debarred from its blessings. In the more remote districts they suffer in their feelings, if not in their purses, from the undisguised contempt of their Moslem fellow-citizens.

The sight of Greek women in Turkish harems must be peculiarly galling to their fellow-countrymen. Many of these are the daughters of mothers taken captive after the massacres of Chios. They may have been educated to Moslem habits of thought, but that is of itself a degradation.

The whole current of forces, moral and intellectual, is now strongly set against this state of things. And why should ours be the ungrateful task to stem it?

But the Eastern Christians, say some, are no better than the Turks. This may be so in individual cases, and there is no hiding the fact that the former still persist in the image or idol worship which brought the scourge of the False Prophet on the backs of their forefathers. But the Greek Church has life in it, for it still looks to the sacred Scriptures as an infallible guide. Without freedom there can be no thorough education. Education, in its turn, awakens the desire for freedom. Some day it will induce both people and priests to rise and resolutely to sweep away whatever cannot be justified by a reference to the sacred canon.

And we believe in the Holy Ghost. He is the Lord and giver of life. No Christian church is so dead nor so sunk in superstition that He may not breathe upon it. We do not suppose that He can be expected to breathe upon Islam.

Cyprus, I think, we ought to keep. Our material, our imperial interests seem to require it, and, should we purchase the Sultan's rights over it, we shall have as good a title to show as anyone to whom it ever belonged. But let us try to cement our rule there in the hearts of the people, and then we shall not, like the Venetians, have a hostile garrison within our ramparts. Let us acknowledge that three-fourths of the Cypriots are Greeks, and take a deeper interest in the Greeks for their sakes.

APPENDIX.

CLIMATE OF CYPRUS.

The extreme beauty of the scenery around Kyrenia, and the balminess of its air, made so favourable an impression on us that, as I have already mentioned, I wrote to Mr. Maurogordato in order to ascertain what was the opinion of the island physicians as to the suitability of the place as a winter residence for English invalids. Mr. Maurogordato courteously supplied me with an extract from Dr. Barry's report on Cyprus dated 1881, and also with statistics of the rainfall; which I subjoin.

'All doctors in Cyprus,' said Mr. Maurogordato, 'are of opinion that this is a capital climate for consumptive patients. Kyrenia is not at all damp, and the nights are delicious in autumn and spring. Although the rainfall may appear great in February, it does not render the atmosphere damp for any length of time, because the showers are very heavy, but of short duration, and you will frequently find splendid weather half-an-hour after several inches of rain have fallen. The sudden change of the weather is marvellous at times.

'Accommodation, although not perfect now, could easily be got on short notice, and, if only Kyrenia had the chance of becoming a health resort, I have no doubt that the very best of everything would be easy to procure.

Dr. Barry, who was Sanitary Commissioner in Cyprus in 1881, says:

'From a careful observation of the country and climate, I have no hesitation in saying that, with proper precautions as to dwellings, food, and sanitary arrangements, it is well-fitted for the residence of English people. From its physical features, the island possesses the advantage of offering the choice of a variety of climates.

'Persons preferring a damp atmosphere can have it by remaining at the coast, whilst those to whom a drier air is more suitable can reside near Nicosia; and both may retire from the heats of summer to the breezy heights of Troados. For phthisical cases, Cyprus is a station second to none in the Mediterranean, and there can be no doubt that, when the reformed municipalities have thoroughly attended to the wants of their respective towns, Cyprus may look forward to becoming one of the favourite health resorts of the Mediterranean.'

Dr. Barry's suggestion that Cyprus offers the choice of a variety of climates is a valuable one, and is certainly founded on fact. Kyrenia, Nicosia, and part of the Troados are hardly twenty miles from each other; so that an invalid could change his climate by an easy carriage drive the moment he felt that a place did not suit him. If some enterprising hotel proprietor would establish three simply-furnished little mutually-connected sanatoria on well-chosen sites in these three places, we think it might prove the nucleus of something greater. As for the cost of living, is it not a fact that the owners of passenger ships in the Mediterranean consider Cyprus the cheapest place to take in provisions?

Mrs. Scott Stevenson, in her book, 'Our Home in Cyprus,' speaks to the same effect.

'Kyrenia,' she says, 'is not only one of the loveliest, but

I may also say one of the healthiest spots in Europe. It is almost unexplored ground, and only waiting to be known to become one of the favourite winter resorts of the Mediterranean.

'In the winter the climate was *perfect;* the storms of rain we read of in the papers were perfect inventions. There was only one hurricane here last year, and that was in September, before I came out. The Cyprus rains, as far as my experience goes, are delicious, refreshing showers, like those of April and May in England, making the grass sprout, and the trees and flowers glisten with drops, and leaving a delightful freshness and sweetness over the land. In winter, the climate (of Kyrenia) was most remarkable for the evenness of the temperature; no sudden changes from heat to cold, or wind to rain; always the sun shining brightly; slight frost *sometimes* in the morning; gentle, soft winds and refreshing showers, though occasionally, during the *night*, a real downpour would sometimes set in, only to cease with the appearance of the sun, and forcing one, as it were, to go out and enjoy the freshness and fragrance around. In spring we had the loveliest flowers, in summer the sea-bathing, and now are revelling in the finest fruits of the earth.

'I have never felt so strong, or in such buoyant health, in my life. Fever is *unknown* in this district this year.'

She thus describes how the 42nd Regiment were attacked with fever:

'They landed in Cyprus about the end of July, during the hottest season of the year. On the day of their arrival the commissariat arrangements were so bad that no food was to be had for the troops till many hours afterwards. Even water was not to be procured. The 42nd were encamped at a place called "Chifflick Pasha," the very hottest spot that could possibly have been selected. For miles around there was not a tree or a shrub, and the blazing sun penetrated through the thin canvas of the single bell-tents. These wretched tents are only fitted for sham fights in England, or for the volunteers at Wimbledon. Though giving every encouragement to the sun, they carefully exclude all passage of air to lessen the torture of the poor men, who lay all day gasping in the intolerable heat.

'The nights were cold and chilly in comparison to the day-heat; and for three months the soldiers, having no mattresses, were forced to sleep on the bare ground, with only a blanket to cover them. Thus, on the very hour of their arrival, their constitutions received a shock which rendered them unable later to cope with the fever; the result entirely, in my mind, of solar exposure. Near Chifflick Pasha is the Salt Lake of Larnaca, and the various vapours that always arise from these stagnant pools cannot have helped to render the air more salubrious.

'It should be noted that the fever was seldom fatal; for, although one-fourth of the men (in Captain Scott Stevenson's regiment) were in hospital at one time, only three deaths occurred.'

In another place she says:

'Nothing will induce me to believe that Kyrenia is unhealthy, if the troops be properly treated. The 20th Regiment, which arrived in the autumn, and was at once properly housed and cared for, had *no* cases of fever in its ranks. As I have said before, there is no comparison between this climate and that of Malta, an opinion in which my husband quite agrees.'

Monsieur de la Mas Latrie expresses a similar opinion:

'It is true,' he says, 'that Cyprus comprises three *foci* of pestilence, and it is remarkable that these are found exactly near the gates of three important towns, Larnaca,

Famagousta, and Limasol. Some stagnant marshes, which the lack of flow in the rivers has developed close to these towns, exhale deleterious miasmata. A state of things like this cannot last long under the new administration of the island. We have observed, with pleasure and confidence, that Colonel Stanley, the Minister of War, in his recent speech at Blackpool, affirmed that the insalubrity of Cyprus would soon disappear, like that of the Ionian islands.

'Already at Larnaca, thanks to the initiative of labour and of private interest, the mortality has become much less since a few sensible drains have been made near the pools, and a great part of the ground, which was overflowed by the shallow water, has been restored to culture.

'In ordinary times, the fevers of the island are due to other causes than local ones. These are, amongst the lower classes, insufficient nourishment, and the custom of sleeping in the open air. Amongst the rich and amongst strangers, there are excesses of all kinds, the abuse of watery fruits, and, above all, catching cold. These causes, accidental but, unfortunately, very frequent, probably occasioned the deplorable losses which the British army sustained at Nicosia, one of the most healthy places in the island, and the maladies, likewise, which ravaged the army of St. Louis, in the campaign of Limasol in 1248.

'One can form no idea of the stunning effects produced by catching cold in Cyprus. Fever and death are the almost inevitable consequences.

'I ought to add that, in the neighbourhood of Paphos, there are some pernicious fevers, of a more persistent character, but which present nothing serious or infectious.

'The plague has not been mentioned in Cyprus for many a long year. Ophthalmia and dysentery, so terrible and so common in Egypt, are there almost unknown.'

Mr. Hamilton Lang says:

'The island is commonly called unhealthy, but I object to the expression until I know what is meant. If it is meant that Englishmen cannot go out there without considerable risk, during the summer months, of catching fever and ague, I admit its correctness. But to what country, with the thermometer generally about ninety degrees in the shade, can Englishmen, with their national love of heavy eating and alcoholic liquors, be sent without incurring a considerable risk of sickness of some kind? A large portion of those who go to Cyprus will enjoy as good health as they can hope for in any country. Further, I object to blaming the climate for evils which result from defective sanitary regulations, and especially from the overcrowding, without previous preparation, of towns without sewers, without street-cleansers, surrounded by stagnant pools, and all that the laziness or indifference of man can accomplish to infect the air. I must judge of the healthiness or unhealthiness of the climate from its effects upon those who, from long usage, live in accordance with its requirements, and who inhabit places free from exceptional and removable disadvantages. Judged by this standard, Cyprus cannot be declared unhealthy. It is inhabited, as it has been from time immemorial, by a perfectly healthy and robust native population, free from all serious sickness, and living to a hale old age. The climate of which this can be said cannot be called unhealthy. It is a fact that I lived in Larnaca, and went about the island summer and winter during nine years, and never enjoyed better health anywhere. Of the pernicious fevers recounted by Dr. Clark, who spent ten days in the island, I can only say that I never heard of them during my residence, although they may have existed before my arrival.

'Watchfulness and proper precaution is the best preventative against intermittent fever and sunstroke. Excessive exertion is imprudent. All ices are to be avoided. My experience was that all cold drinks and too cool clothing are unsuitable to the climate of Cyprus. I had to avoid linen clothing from a tendency to catch a chill, producing dysentery. I found light flannel or tweed clothing the safest. He will suffer least in the long run who bears patiently with the heat, and neither increases it unnecessarily, nor tries to drive it out of him unnaturally.

'Life under canvas, and sleeping on the ground, or without good cover from the dews, are both to be avoided. Inactivity and a dull life predispose to fever. I never had a thorough attack, but, when I felt the least premonitory symptoms, a free perspiration after a good gallop, and a pill of quinine, sufficed to put me all right.'

Let us also hear Sir Samuel Baker.

'At some future time,' he says, 'Cyprus will become the resort of delicate persons to escape the winter and spring of England, as the southern portion of the island is most enjoyable during the cool season. English people are somewhat like sheep in following each other, and a quiet beginning (of a hotel) would quickly develop, and Cyprus would be linked with the beaten paths of tourists.

'So much has been written and spoken against the climate of Cyprus, that an unprejudiced account may be acceptable. There are serious disadvantages to those who by their official positions are obliged to remain in the low country during the summer months, where the extreme heat must always be prejudicial to the health of Europeans. From the middle of October to May the climate is most agreeable, but the five intervening months should be passed at higher altitudes (such as the Troados) which, as I have already described, afford a variety of climates.

'My own people never required a dose of medicine,

although we were living in tents through winter and summer.

'The water is generally wholesome, therefore dysentery and bowel complaints are rare; *consumption is unknown,** and pulmonary affections are uncommon. Fevers, including those of a typhoid character, and ague from malaria, are the usual types; outbreaks of small-pox have been reduced by general vaccination. The improvement in sanitary regulations will no doubt diminish the occurrence of typhoid fevers, which even now are rare, considering the filth of the villages and the generally dirty habits of the population. Hydrophobia among dogs is very rare, and distemper among puppies is unknown.'

We have quoted largely from these various writers, not only because of the extreme interest which the subject possesses for our suffering fellow-countrymen, but because of its political importance. Nothing would so effectually weld the island to our empire as its occupation during nearly three-fourths of the year by a number of moderately wealthy English families. Three things are required to effect this: first, there must be a thorough uprooting from the public mind of all mistaken ideas about the climate, ideas which are eagerly fostered by foreigners, jealous of our hold on this gem of the Mediterranean. Secondly, there must be a direct line of passenger steamers established betwixt Marseilles and Kyrenia or Larnaca, with a weekly or bi-weekly post; and thirdly, three little hotels must spring up, one at Leucosia, one at Kyrenia, and one on the Troados. The third item is by no means the most pressing one. Our countrymen in Cyprus are most hospitable, and would, I am sure, do everything in their power to find good accommodation for those who were willing to

---

* Consumption, it must be noticed, is very prevalent among the natives of Mentone.

APPENDIX. 349

pay a reasonable price for it. The want of a hotel on the Troados might be supplied for a short time, as it now is, by the monasteries, and by summer tents.

KYRENIA, 1881.						
MEAN TEMPERATURE OF THE AIR IN THE SHADE.				RAINFALL.		
Months.	9 hours.	Mean of Minima.	Minimum.	No. of days Rain.	Total Fall	Greatest Fall in 24 hours.
January .	58·4	44·1	34·5	9	1·845	0·530
February	55·4	45·1	35·5	14	5·519	1·890
March . .	61·0	52·6	40·5	6	0·905	0·300
April. . .	65·5	58·5	49·7	6	1·645	1·247
May . . .	71·3	61·9	55·7	6	2·155	0·800
June. . .	76·2	68·1	61·8	0	0	0
July . . .	85·2	72·4	66·5	0	0	0
August .	89·4	72·7	70·5	0	0	0
September	84·5	70·6	63·5	0	0	0
October .	76·0	64·8	60·5	2	0·640	0·620
November	64·9	56·1	50·5	15	3·333	1·120
December	58·6	51·1	39·7	11	2·271	0·841
Year. . .	70·5	59·8	34·5	69	18·313	1·247

KYRENIA, 1882.

Highest Temperature not recorded.

Lowest, 32 deg. 5 min. Fahr. on 12th February.

Births 38, Deaths 13, throughout year, out of a population of 1159.

RAINFALL.

MONTHS.	No. of days of Rain.	Total fall.	Greatest fall in 24 hours
January . . .	8	2·520	1·380
February. . .	12	1·788	0·510
March	4	0·680	0·370
April	7	3·570	1·630
May	4	0·940	0·340
June	1	0·350	0·350
July	0	0	0
August	0	0	0
September . .	0	0	0
October . . .	4	1·330	1·000
November . .	3	1·520	0·900
December . .	8	1·840	0·800
Year	51	14·538	1·630

KYRENIA, 1883.

TEMPERATURE AND RAINFALL.

January	... varying from	40 deg. to 50 deg.	Fahr.,	minimum.
,,	,,	55 deg. to 69 deg.	,,	maximum.
February	,,	50 deg. to 60 deg.	,,	minimum.
,,	,,	60 deg. to 71 deg.	,,	maximum.

RAINFALL.

January ..... 7·8.
February .... 2·4.

KYRENIA, 1884.

TEMPERATURE READINGS.

Maximum .... 108·0 Fahr. on 6th August.
Minimum .... 40·0 ,, 6th January.

RAINFALL.

50 days rain.—Total, 23 inches.

THE END.

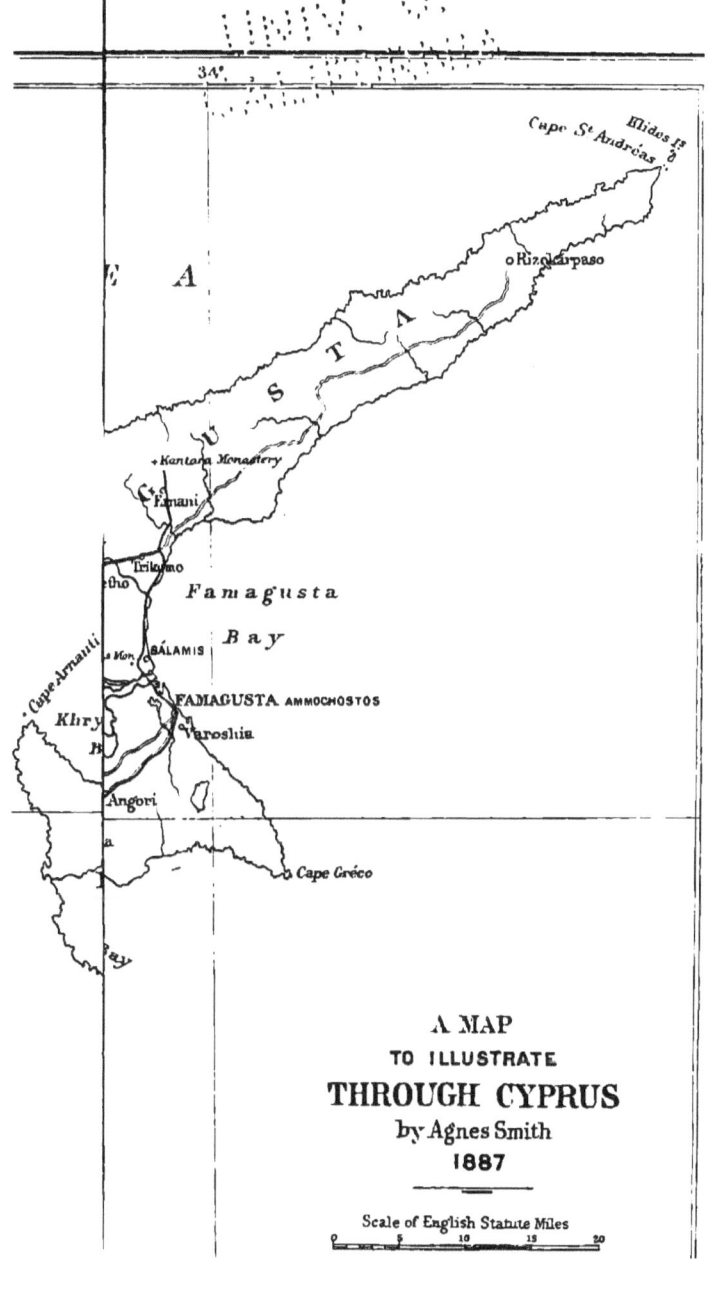

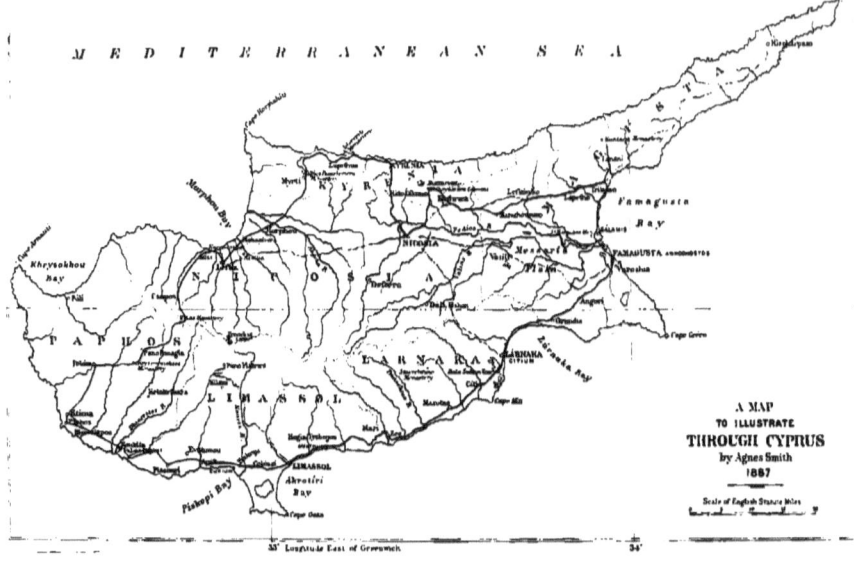

www.ingramcontent.com/pod-product-compliance
Lightning Source LLC
Chambersburg PA
CBHW020314240426
43673CB00039B/804